Your Early Childhood Practicum and Student Teaching Experience

Guidelines for Success

Second Edition

Carroll Tyminski
Elizabethtown College

Merrill

Boston   Columbus   Indianapolis   New York   San Francisco   Upper Saddle River
Amsterdam   Cape Town   Dubai   London   Madrid   Milan   Munich   Paris
Montreal   Toronto   Delhi   Mexico City   Sao Paulo   Sydney
Hong Kong   Seoul   Singapore   Taipei   Tokyo

Vice President and Executive Publisher:
   Jeffery W. Johnston
Acquisitions Editor: Julie Peters
Editorial Assistant: Tiffany Bitzel
Director of Marketing: Quinn Perkson
Marketing Manager: Erica DeLuca
Marketing Coordinator: Brian Mounts
Project Manager: Renata Butera
Operations Specialist: Renata Butera
Creative Art Director: Jayne Conte
Cover Designer: Lisbeth Axell

Manager, Visual Research: Beth Brenzel
Manager, Rights and Permissions: Zina Arabia
Manager, Cover Visual Research & Permissions:
   Karen Sanatar
Cover Art: Jose Luis Pelaez/Iconica/Getty Images
Full-Service Project Management: Mohinder Singh/
   Aptara®, Inc.
Composition: Aptara®, Inc.
Printer/Binder: R.R. Donnelley/Harrisonburg
Cover Printer: R.R. Donnelley/Harrisonburg
Text Font: Palatino Light

Photo credits: Anne Vega/Merrill, pp. 1, 8, 61, 99, 119, 181; Anthony Magnacca/Merrill, pp. 12, 26, 45, 111, 132, 157; Valerie Schultz/Merrill, p. 21; Laura Bolesta/Merrill, p. 33; Kathy Kirtland/Merrill, p. 43; Barbara Schwartz/Merrill, p. 57; Scott Cunningham/Merrill, pp. 79, 83, 87, 127, 141, 164, 191; David Mager/Pearson Learning Photo Studio, pp. 167, 189; Tim Cairns/Merrill, p. 184; Jay Penni/Prentice Hall School Division, p. 199

Library of Congress Cataloging-in-Publication Data

Tyminski, Carroll.
   Your early childhood practicum and student teaching experience : guidelines
for success / Carroll Tyminski.—2nd ed.
      p. cm.
   Includes bibliographical references and index.
   ISBN-13: 978-0-13-715290-2 (alk. paper)
   ISBN-10: 0-13-715290-6 (alk. paper)
   1. Student teaching—United States. 2. Preschool teachers—Training of—United
States. 3. Primary school teachers—Training of—United States. I. Title.
   LB2157.U5T96 2010
   370.71′1—dc22

2009002976

Merrill
is an imprint of

10 9 8 7 6 5 4 3 2 1
ISBN-13: 978-0-13-715290-2
ISBN-10:   0-13-715290-6

www.pearsonhighered.com

Your Early Childhood Practicum and Student Teaching Experience: Guidelines for Success is designed for students who are assuming the responsibilities of teaching young children while receiving guidance and supervision. Students may be taking part in a variety of student teaching experiences. These may include capstone courses for 1-year certificate programs and for associate degree programs, practicum experiences in a community college setting, as well as traditional early childhood programs in a 4-year university setting. This text offers both theory and practical application to guide each student to a successful conclusion of the practicum and student teaching experience.

I have mentored and supervised countless preservice teachers over the years. Students' recurring questions and comments became the impetus for this book. Thus, it became readily apparent that there was a need for a reality-based guide to shepherd students through this important experience.

FEATURES OF THE BOOK

This book provides an opportunity for present and future early childhood preservice teachers to benefit from the experiences of those who have recently gone before them. Each chapter contains "Voices of Reality: Student Teachers Speak,"* quotes from recent early childhood student teachers. I believe it is important for students to reflect on their experiences and to share their stories with others. Relatively little research has been reported concerning the student teaching experience itself. Therefore, the anecdotal comments, quotes, and electric wisdom of early childhood student teachers and teacher educators have been included as valuable teaching and learning tools.

In addition, this book is a reference containing research-based practical advice on such topics as developmentally appropriate practices and teacher competencies. Great care has been taken to include a broad range of early childhood experiences from birth through age 8. The book places special emphasis on being a professional as well as the importance of ethics.

*Extracts reprinted by permission of Odessa Armstrong.

The book guides students from the early days of preparing to begin the practicum through the final days of leaving, as well as everything in between. The author provides real-life examples in each chapter as an effective way to help students understand how to apply the suggestions given. Activities are suggested at the end of each chapter to encourage student reflection and application of the information.

Several areas receive particular attention. For example, communication is emphasized as an important skill for teachers. There is also an overview of strategies and key questions to improve communication with both children and adults.

NEW TO THIS EDITION

Special care in this edition has been taken to focus on professional behavior, lesson planning, portfolio development, diverse family structures, cultural diversity, inclusion, and working with children who have special needs. Current information on national and state standards, reauthorization of the No Child Left Behind act, and assessment has been included.

This edition includes the following new features:

- Current information on national and state standards
- Reauthorization of No Child Left Behind
- Assessment of *all* children
- Diverse family structures and family systems such as grandparent-headed families, families with one or more lesbian, gay, bisexual, or transsexual (LGBT) parents, military families, single-parent families, and families experiencing poverty
- Expanded focus on inclusion, and on working with children who have special needs and with their families
- Expanded focus on professional behavior
- Lesson planning with sample formats
- Electronic portfolio development and expanded portfolio activities
- Helpful Web sites on each topic

Diversity Coverage

The education of children with special needs is also an essential component of this book because of the increasing demand for inclusionary practices in early childhood programs. Another recurring theme throughout the book is the importance of culture and human diversity. There is a focus on examining cultural assumptions. Students are asked to think about those aspects of their cultural experience that might influence their interactions with children and

adults. Important issues related to family diversity are included, and there are questions for reflection in order to help students develop cultural competency.

FORMAT AND CHAPTER SEQUENCE

Chapter 1, "Preparing to Begin Student Teaching," includes making a good first impression, examination of personal assumptions and beliefs, initial meetings, personal preparations, and development of a support system. Real-life examples are provided to help students understand how to apply the suggestions given.

Chapter 2, "Becoming a Professional," discusses what it means to become a professional, ethical guidelines and professional standards, confidentiality, sources for professional decision making, and professional growth as a team member. This chapter focuses on ethics as a foundation for being a professional.

Chapter 3, "Establishing Effective Professional Relationships," focuses on establishing positive relationships with your cooperating teacher and college supervisor, developing effective communication skills, and stages of student teaching. Practical suggestions are provided to encourage dialogue.

Chapter 4, "Guiding Young Children in the Classroom," considers discipline and guidance, guidance strategies, class meetings, additional behavior management techniques, and real-life ethical dilemmas. This chapter provides an in-depth look at the guidance function as essential to the student teacher's success in the classroom.

Chapter 5, "Classroom Management: Environments and Routines," includes topics related to physical space, emotional climate, safety, classroom routines, time management, and transitions. This chapter addresses the concept of meeting children's needs through the physical environment.

Chapter 6, "Observations and Evaluations of Student Teaching," includes topics related to making the most of the observation/evaluation process. It considers the purposes and format of observations, receiving criticism, reflective journaling, portfolios, state standards, certification, and Praxis tests.

Chapter 7, "Assessment of Young Children," discusses the purposes of assessment, standards, examples of formal and informal assessment, types of authentic assessments, and alternative assessment. Examples and formats for data collection are included as well as the linkage between assessment and teaching practice.

Chapter 8, "Supportive Instruction," deals with relating instruction to young children's ways of knowing, multiple intelligences, applied concepts of developmentally appropriate practice, integrated curriculum, the project

approach, and technology. Important concepts related to curriculum and how children learn are included.

Chapter 9, "Understanding Diverse Communities and Interacting with Children's Families," begins with a discussion of changing cultural demographics. It includes topics such as breaking down cultural barriers, developing positive home–school relationships, creating culture-friendly classrooms, parent conferences, and nonverbal cultural codes. Practical suggestions are provided as well as questions for students' reflection on their own culture and their experience with diversity. Additional topics include diverse family structures and family systems such as grandparent-headed families, families with one or more LGBT parents, military families, single-parent families, and families experiencing poverty.

Chapter 10, "Completion of Student Teaching: Looking Ahead," gives practical suggestions for leaving your student teaching practicum, the final evaluation of the student teaching experience, and tips for planning ahead in the areas of networking, resume writing, applications, and interviews.

USING THE BOOK

Instructors are encouraged to select the chapters most relevant to the needs of their particular students. For example, if students are already familiar with their practicum site, then portions of Chapter 1 may be omitted or skimmed. If students already have employment in childcare settings, then portions of Chapter 10 may be omitted.

SUPPLEMENTARY MATERIALS

Supplementary products have been created to support this text. The *Online Instructor's Manual* and the *Online Test Bank* include instructional tips and assessment items. Contact your Pearson representative to learn how to download this resource from a secure online site.

ACKNOWLEDGMENTS

I would like to acknowledge the contribution of my late mother, Erdene B. Rountree. Without her love, her support, and her regular phone calls to ask, "How is that book coming along?" the first edition might not have been completed. I would like to give special acknowledgment to my youngest daughter, Katie Tyminski. Without her frequent phone calls, visits, and supportive hugs, the second edition might not have been completed. Katie is

definitely a full member of the "steel magnolia club." We have kept each other strong as we accomplish our individual goals. What a blessing to have such love and support!

I also wish to express appreciation to the many students and cooperating teachers who offered their support and contributed in one way or another to this book. Special recognition goes to the following: Odessa Armstrong, Jamie Brandt, Lauren Crane, Angie DePauli, Adam Dively, Jennifer Dotson, Amanda Fisher, Megan Hilperts, Elisabeth Kimmel, Diane LaMonica, Melissa Elliott, Amanda Myers, Beth Nickle, Susan Pitcher, Megan Tyson, and Krista Unger.

Many thanks go to Helen Greenberg, the copy editor of this book, whose careful editing and tactful suggestions greatly improved the quality of the manuscript. Additionally, I am grateful to Julie Peters, the acquisitions editor of Merrill/Pearson, who has provided invaluable support and advice.

Thank you, also, to those who reviewed this book and provided valuable comments: Ginny A. Buckner, *Duke University;* Kathy Campbell, *Ivy Tech Community College;* Carolyn Perry, *Citrus College;* Susan VanNess, *Manchester Community College;* and Sandra C. Williamson, *Wilmington College.*

BRIEF CONTENTS

CONTENTS

Note: Every effort has been made to provide accurate and current Internet information in this book. However, the Internet and information posted on it are constantly changing, and it is inevitable that some of the Internet addresses listed in this book will change.

CHAPTER 1

Preparing to Begin Student Teaching

Only the brave should teach. Only those who love the young should teach. Teaching is a vocation. It is as sacred as priesthood, as innate as desire, as inescapable as the genius which compels a great artist. If he has not the concern for humanity, the love of living creatures, the vision of the priest and the artist, he must not teach.

Pearl S. Buck

Pearl S. Buck's characterization of teaching as a sacred vocation may sound somewhat dramatic. It contains, however, basic elements central to successful preservice teaching. Many veteran teachers agree that the best teachers have a passion for teaching that may be compared to a sacred calling. They have an intense desire to teach. They may describe it as a wish to make the world a better place or to make a difference in human lives—one child at a time. They have the courage to believe that *all* children can learn, regardless of their diverse cultural backgrounds and abilities. They also have a sincere love of the young, as indicated by the respect, dignity, and concern that they show each child.

Successful students find that they are embarking upon a career that is a life choice, not a nine-to-five job. They think about "their" children after they leave school; they become consumed with the desire to improve each child's well-being in a holistic sense. They focus on social, emotional, and physical concerns as well as academic improvement. In other words, they exhibit what Pearl Buck describes as a passionate, visionary concern and love for living creatures.

❖ FINAL PREPARATIONS FOR DAY 1

Now that your passion, vision, and love for children have been acknowledged, how do you prepare to begin this all-important student teaching experience? What are your concerns? What excites you as you anticipate your first days and weeks?

Voices of Reality: Student Teachers Speak

I am bubbling with excitement. The possibilities for touching and helping to shape these lives are endless; and to think that I may have a hand in this impact fills me with warmth from head to toe.

Karla S.

I'm terrified of failure. I'm afraid that I won't be able to balance being friendly and firm, and the students won't like me. What if my lessons are all a flop? What if I can't get the kids to understand and make the connection?

Luke B.

I am mostly afraid that I will not be adequately prepared for the job that lays [sic] ahead of me. That I will not be able to be a successful student teacher. That I will fail.

Meisha T.

I'm excited to get started. Concerned about not having control of the class, fitting in at the school, working with my coop. I'm just a bit nervous (but again excited).

Jamal D.

I met my coop. She gave me a building tour and introduced me to the principal, and I called today to remind her I'm starting tomorrow. . . . I know it will be successful.

Keeley N.

After an informational meeting for the early childhood student teachers who were beginning their practicum or their student teaching the next day, the students voluntarily shared their feelings in a small-group setting. You may be a little surprised by their candor. Some expressed strong self-doubt, whereas others exuded confidence. You may find yourself somewhere between these two extremes.

Most students approach a practicum or a student teaching experience with a mixture of nervousness and excitement. This is normal. Sometimes it is helpful to realize that you are not alone as your emotions swing among enthusiasm, excitement, frustration, and anxiety. You may recognize the feeling of butterflies in your stomach, periods of restless sleep, loss of appetite, or any combination of these reactions. Any time you begin a new experience with uncertain outcomes, you may have mixed feelings. However, there are several steps you can take to lessen your uneasiness and increase your chances of success before you begin. Generally speaking, the student teaching practicum is a rewarding, positive experience for everyone involved.

❖ TERMINOLOGY OF STUDENT TEACHING

Depending on the geographical area, the customs, and/or the characteristics of a particular educational program, the terms used to describe student teaching and the key people involved may vary greatly. Student teaching may be referred to as a *practicum*, a *professional internship*, or a *field experience*. You may have chosen the setting of your student teaching practicum or you may have been assigned a location unfamiliar to you. Regardless of these differences, there are generally three key people involved in the experience.

[**Note:** For the sake of simplicity and consistency, gender references, when used at all, will be female. This choice of gender in no way implies bias related to role or position of authority.]

- **Cooperating teacher:** This person is sometimes referred to as the *coop*, the *lead teacher*, the *supervising teacher*, the *master teacher*, or the *clinical teacher*. She will supervise work, model good teaching practices, and mentor your professional growth on a daily basis.
- **Supervisor:** You may be assigned to a supervisor. This person is sometimes referred to as the *college/university supervisor*, the *teacher trainer*, the *off-campus supervisor*, the *practicum instructor*, or the *clinical supervisor*. She will make regular visits and serve as a mentor and resource to both you and your cooperating teacher.
- **Student teacher:** As a student teacher, you may sometimes be referred to as an *intern* or an *apprentice*. You will experience a consecutive period of supervised planning and teaching during which you assume increasing responsibilities. This experience may be part of a course in which you are currently enrolled or it may be the culminating experience undertaken after the completion of your education coursework.

Regardless of these differences, you have a wonderful opportunity to influence the lives of children and to embark upon a personal journey of growth.

❖ MAKING A GOOD FIRST IMPRESSION

You have completed all your prerequisites, and now you have the opportunity to shine as you polish your professional skills. You want to get off on the right foot by making a good first impression.

Develop a Knowledge Base

You have been assigned to a child development center or a school for your student teaching experience. Unless you are already quite familiar with the

Demographics
refers to vital and
social data such as
racial and ethnic
populations and
the number of
students receiving
special education
services. It may
also include
characteristics that
classify people by
age, gender, and
income.

setting for your practicum, consider doing some homework before you begin your student teaching. Go on the Internet and try to locate information about your center or school. Many child development centers and public or private schools have their own Web sites. If your assigned location is part of a public school system, you can go directly to your state's Department of Education site and locate your district and specific school. State Web sites include such information as enrollment, enrollment stability, class size, programs available, teacher absenteeism, and assessment results. If your school is either a private facility or a center specifically for infants and preschoolers, you may be able to obtain informational booklets printed for prospective students and their families. You will make a better first impression on your cooperating teacher and school administration if you are knowledgeable about the school itself, its mission, and its **demographics.**

❖ EXAMINATION OF PERSONAL ASSUMPTIONS AND BELIEFS

**Pluralistic
societies** may be
described as those
in which diverse
cultural groups
maintain their
unique identities
as they coexist.

Be aware of your own reactions to the diversity or apparent lack of diversity you encounter in your placement. We may assume that everyone's teacher education curriculum has included elements of multiculturalism and diversity training. As students in a **pluralistic society,** you have been taught to avoid stereotypes of particular socioeconomic, racial, or ethnic groups.

Nevertheless, it may be helpful to reflect once again on your personal expectations. You pass through the local neighborhoods on your way to your practicum each day. Do you have preconceptions based on your impressions that the neighborhoods apparently contain children of high-income families or children of impoverished families or children of a particular racial or ethnic background? Our own culture is so entwined in every aspect of our existence that "it becomes the invisible script that directs our personal lives" (Hollins, 1995, p. 72). You may strongly believe that you harbor no stereotypes, but "most teachers, though unknowingly, discriminate against culturally different students by lacking the sensitivity, knowledge, and skills necessary to teach them properly" (Diller & Moule, 2005, p. 2). Whether you are a member of a minority culture or a member of the White middle-class majority, you may be unaware of your own biases that can be inadvertently communicated to children and coworkers.

Reflective Inquiry to Raise Awareness and Reduce Harmful Assumptions

Accordingly, as you begin your early childhood practicum, you may consider several topics for ongoing reflective inquiry. These reflections may become particularly significant if your own cultural heritage differs from that

1.1 Questions for Self-Reflection

1. What are my own beliefs about young children from particular cultural groups?
2. What are my assumptions about young children from particular socioeconomic groups?
3. What beliefs do I have about instruction that may reflect my own biases concerning cultural values?
4. What similarities and differences do I believe exist between social interaction in the classroom and social interaction in the children's home environments?
5. What significant experiences do I believe young children may bring to the classroom?
6. How much do I know about the cultural values, beliefs, and practices in the homes of my young children?
7. How much do I know about political and/or social influences within the local community that may affect interactions with the families of my young children?

(Hollins, 1995)

of your children. The likelihood of this cultural diversity increases as our nation continues to experience demographic changes.

Part of your lifelong professional growth as a teacher involves developing the ability to be objective, empathetic, and sensitive in your responses to the needs of young children and their families. Few, if any, of your children will have your exact family background. You will strive for shared understanding. This is not an easy task. At one time or another, you may be communicating with children and families of widely diverse backgrounds including but not limited to the following: African American families, Asian American families, Native American families, single teenage parent families, stepfamilies, grandparents as substitute parents, families with children who have special needs, and gay and lesbian families. No one expects you to have perfected your communication skills by the time you become a certified teacher. You may feel uncertain at times. Nevertheless, your humility, honesty, flexibility, energy, and dedicated advocacy for young children and their families will enable you to be perceived as a caring teacher. As the famous quote by an unknown author says, "No one cares how much you know until they know how much you care."

Potential for Cultural Misconceptions

You may or may not be surprised to learn that data collected by the National Education Association (NEA) indicate that over 90% of teachers in the United States are White, and the majority of these come from middle-class backgrounds (Fuller, 2001). At the same time, the number of children from minority backgrounds is increasing rapidly. In some states, California for example, the majority of the children in school programs are from cultural minority groups (Fuller, 2001). The population of immigrant children in our schools is also increasing rapidly; reports indicate that over 3 million children are considered English-language learners. Many of these children and their families experience "struggles with [both] a new culture and a new language" (Miller & Endo, 2004, p. 786).

With so many differences between the culture of the teachers and the culture of the children, the potential exists for misconceptions to develop between schools and families. In fact, "the student's culture is often in conflict with the culture in the school" (Ducette, Sewell, & Shapiro, 1996, p. 363). This cultural mismatch may have a negative impact on children from particular cultural groups that are historically underserved in our public school systems (Hollins, 1995). Therefore, curricular and instructional interventions may be necessary in order to legitimize the connections between traditional learning in the schools and learning in the children's home and community environments (McCarty, Lynch, Wallace, & Benally, 1991; Moll, 1986). We know that "children learn and grow best in schools where parents and teachers understand one another, share similar, visions, and collaborate on guiding children" (Grant & Gomez, 2001, p. 130). Therefore, suggestions for preventing misconceptions and increasing understanding will be discussed later in the text.

❖ INITIAL MEETINGS

Being the conscientious student that you are, you have done your homework concerning the demographics of your practicum or student teaching site. You have addressed your own cultural assumptions and beliefs regarding your children and their families. Now, have you considered how you will communicate effectively with professional colleagues whose experiences, beliefs, and assumptions may be different from your own?

Communicate with the Cooperating Teacher

Your first few conversations with your cooperating teacher are crucial in getting off to a good start. They communicate your interest and initiative. They also give you the opportunity to discuss expectations (yours and hers) and to ask questions.

Accordingly, plan your part in those conversations. You may want to develop a few questions to ask your cooperating teacher. In order to formulate these questions, think about what specific skills you wish to develop or strengthen, what content area thematic units you may wish to develop,

Figure 1.1 **Sample Conversation Starters**

- Do you have any suggestions about what I can do to prepare for student teaching with you?
- What are you looking for in a student teacher? What are your expectations of a student teacher?
- Where did you complete your student teaching? What was the experience like for you?
- What can you tell me about the children in your class—the ratio of boys to girls, minorities, socioeconomic status, ability levels, children with special needs?
- Are there any handbooks for parents describing policies such as those for attendance, illness, guidance, and parental responsibilities that would be helpful for me to read?
- Are there curriculum guides or written descriptions of developmentally appropriate practices or best practices that I will be expected to follow?
- If there are any children with identified special needs in the center or school, are there any individualized written guidelines that I should be aware of in order to help each child?
- Are there any written or unwritten policies regarding the day-to-day functioning of the center or school that I should be aware of before I begin student teaching? Is there a dress code for children and for teachers? Are there rules about the use of copy machines, the faculty room, or the telephone?
- What is the career ladder or hierarchy by which this child development center or school operates (program director, program manager, principal, etc.)?

(Adams, Shea, Liston, & Deever, 1998; Blair & Jones, 1998; Kostelnik, Onaga, Rohde, & Whiren, 2002; McEwan, 2001).

what discipline approaches you favor, and what concerns you have regarding children diagnosed with special needs. Several examples of questions to initiate conversations are listed in Figure 1.1.

In addition to thinking of questions to ask, consider what you want to communicate about yourself to your cooperating teacher. One way of doing this is to imagine yourself in the role of cooperating teacher. What qualities would you want your student teacher to display? Are you looking for a person who demonstrates enthusiasm and excitement? Are you hoping for a student teacher who takes the initiative to jump right in and be an active participant with the children rather than one who remains a passive observer? If you believe you have these characteristics, how will you communicate them to your cooperating teacher in those initial conversations? Remember also that your cooperating teacher may feel a little nervous about beginning this important mentoring relationship with you, particularly if she has not had many practicum students.

Communicate with the Children

You will find that all children, even the youngest ones, are quick to notice the presence of a new face in the room. Your cooperating teacher may suggest an appropriate time for introductions, such as during a morning group time. Notice how the children address the adults in your placement; you will want to follow the customary practice when you introduce yourself. Some schools allow children to call teachers by their first name; others prefer a title followed by their first name; still others require a title followed by their last name.

You may want to plan an age-appropriate name game to introduce yourself and to help you learn the children's names. You may want to bring one of your favorite children's books to share. You might suggest to your cooperating teacher that you create a bulletin board display with pictures and/or objects that reveal interesting information about yourself that you can share with your children. The children will have a natural curiosity about who you are, so expect them to ask questions of all kinds. Do not be surprised if young children ask personal questions, so think about ways (such as using humor) to deflect questions you do not wish to answer. Remember

You may want to get off to a good start with your children by preparing an activity to help you learn their names. You may also want to prepare a collage or poster that you can use to introduce yourself to the children.

also that anything you say about your activities away from school will probably be repeated at home, so use your discretion.

Sample activities that student teachers enjoy using as icebreakers or get-acquainted activities include the following:

- **"All About Me Bag" Activity.**   Put items in a paper bag that tell something about you, such as your favorite children's book, your baby picture, a picture of your family, or objects related to your hobby or special collections. Take each item out of the bag, one at a time, and tell a story about it. As a follow-up, you may give your children the opportunity to prepare their own "All About Me Bags" to share.
- **"Classroom Quilt" Activity.**   Cut a sheet of construction paper to make a quilt square. Decorate it with pictures or drawings that tell something about you. Put your name on it and say what you think your square says about you. Give your children an opportunity to make their own squares to share. Then you can tape these squares together to make a classroom quilt for display in the room.

You may create your own variations of these get-acquainted activities. Many teacher Web sites are available to help you find ideas as you are thinking about activities to try. For example, take a look at *http://www.education-world. com* and *http://olc.sped.sk.ca/de/resources/firstweeklinks/index.htm*.

Communicate with Families

Parents and other family members will be curious about who the student teacher is, so you may want to write a brief letter of introduction to send home with each child. Share your letter with your cooperating teacher. She may have some suggestions and/or she may want to add her own note to your letter. Information that students frequently put in their letters includes the following:

1. Length of time you will spend in your practicum or student teaching placement
2. Your role (e.g., observer, teachers' assistant, student teacher)
3. College or university affiliation and degree and/or certification being pursued
4. Prior teaching or relevant volunteer experience
5. Hobbies
6. Contact information

Remember that your letter to parents and families is often their first introduction to you as an early childhood educator. Be careful to check its spelling, punctuation, and professional appearance so that you present yourself in a professional manner. A sample letter is presented in Figure 1.2.

(Date)

Dear Parents and Families,

I would like to introduce myself to you. My name is _____, and I will be spending the next twelve weeks with your child as a student teacher in _____'s room. I am completing my _____ degree at _____ in Early Childhood Education. While in your child's classroom, I will be working under the close supervision of _____ as I complete planning and teaching activities.

My previous teaching experience includes a practicum in Early Childhood Education at _____. I also have volunteer childcare experience at _____. Over the next few weeks, I hope to teach many lessons that will include music and movement because my college minor is in performing arts.

Please feel free to contact me if you have questions or if you would like to participate in class activities during my student teaching. You may reach me by phone at _____. I look forward to meeting you and working with your child.

Sincerely,

FIGURE 1.2   Sample Letter of Introduction

Maintain Confidentiality

As you begin your student teaching practicum, you must have heightened sensitivity to the importance of maintaining confidentiality. You will have access to personal family information, school records, and medical information concerning each child in your care. You will observe behaviors that trouble you and others that delight or amuse you. You need to discuss this confidential information and your observations with your cooperating teacher.

Remember that some view your role as a teacher to be as sacred as that of a priest. It is understandable that you may feel uncomfortable with that comparison. However, you may find that children and parents confide in you about personal matters. If you find yourself being drawn into conversations that make you feel uncomfortable, then tactfully pass the matter on to your cooperating teacher. For example, some parents may view you as an expert in child rearing. They may ask your advice concerning their child's bed-wetting problem or how to prepare their child for the arrival of a new baby. You should direct these parents to your cooperating teacher, who may guide them herself or direct them to a supervisor who may, in turn, direct them to professionally trained community resources.

Another aspect of confidentiality relates to professional discretion. Remember not to discuss events using the real names or descriptions of children, parents, or teachers. Remaining silent is preferable to being considered a gossip. Comments and discussion should be held with your cooperating teacher or your college supervisor in private, not shared with family and friends. Be careful not to discuss specific people or events in the hallway or the teacher's lounge. A comment that is overheard can have extremely detrimental effects.

Communicate with Your Supervisor

If you have been assigned a college supervisor, she will play a vital role in your development. She will be available to offer support not only to you but also to your cooperating teacher. You may wish to talk with her at the beginning of your practicum. A checklist of topics to cover in that initial meeting may be helpful. Figure 1.3 provides some example topics.

Remember that your supervisor can be an invaluable source of information, someone with whom you can share your frustrations as well as your joys, your advocate and your supporter. Three-way communication among you, your supervisor, and your cooperating teacher may encourage the sharing of ideas and perspectives.

In addition, your supervisor plays a vital role in your success. She is often your best source of information about campus news of deadlines for graduation and deadlines related to program opportunities. If you live off

---

Figure 1.3 Sample Topics for Meeting with the Supervisor

- Exchange of e-mail addresses, home phone numbers, and cell phone numbers
- Requirements such as creation of a student teaching journal, notebook, or dialogue journal
- Frequency of observations
- Format of written feedback and discussion related to observations
- Policies regarding illness or personal emergencies
- Expectations regarding attendance at professional development workshops, inservice days, or faculty meetings
- Expectations regarding participation in parent conferences or home visits
- Policies regarding student teaching during the college's scheduled holidays
- Procedures regarding final evaluations, recommendations, and certification requirements

campus and/or commute from home to your placement, your supervisor may be your only link to this important campus information.

Communicate with the Administration

In your early days at the facility, you may be able to meet the director of the child development center or the building principal. This administrator will be a helpful source of information regarding the history and mission of the school. In addition, she can describe the teaching and learning philosophy that guides educational practice. In many child development centers and schools, the administrator may function as a hands-on learning leader rather than as an inaccessible paper pusher.

The administrator provides the support necessary to ensure that children achieve the intended outcomes (Dufour, 2002). In fact, preservice teachers often declare that "it is the school, not the university [or college], that is the real center of [their] teacher education" (Eisner, 2002, p. 577). Therefore, keep in mind that the administrator, as the school leader, can also add a new dimension to your teacher education.

Communicate with the Support Staff

You must make yourself known to the support staff as well. The **paraprofessionals,** the secretarial personnel, the custodial staff, and others can

Getting to know your administrator is an important way to get your student teaching off to a good start. Make sure to have a friendly smile and a greeting whenever you see her.

make your teaching experience even more pleasant. They play a vital role in the day-to-day operations of the facility. When you need to know the most efficient process for accomplishing routine tasks, the support staff will provide that assistance.

Communicate with Friends and Family

One important area frequently overlooked by students is communication with family and friends, particularly in the early days of the student teaching practicum. Communication is crucial to having a positive experience, whether you are a nontraditional-age student or a more typical-age student commuting or living on campus. In addition, you may be dependent on the income from a job to meet living expenses while you are attending college. These and other personal topics need to be considered. Figure 1.4 lists several reflection questions about your expectations.

Whether you are a college student of typical age living on campus or a nontraditional student with multiple off-campus responsibilities, you may want to consider discussing some ground rules to help you and those with whom you live. For example, you may find that you need to develop new routines regarding bedtimes, early morning preparations for the day, and social activities. Your changes in behavior may affect other people in your life, so you need to communicate your anticipated needs and expectations if you have not already done so. Some preservice teachers express surprise at the fact that their nonteaching friends and family members have little

Paraprofessionals provide direct assistance to children and families; they are supervised by teachers or other trained professionals (Pickett, 1999).

Figure 1.4 **Questions Concerning Expectations**

- Who are the people I will come in contact with regularly outside of my teaching hours (family, friends, employers, etc.)?
- What demands do I expect these people to make on my time and energy during my practicum?
- How much time and energy do I believe I will be able to give to these people during my practicum?
- What difficulties, if any, can I anticipate? How can I prevent potential difficulties?
- What support system is in place to help me if I have questions or need to brainstorm ideas related to student teaching?
- Does my college have any policies concerning my employment or participation in extracurricular activities while I am completing my practicum?
- Do I have adequate transportation? Do I have a backup plan in case of transportation difficulties?

understanding of how much mental and physical energy they direct to teaching even when the work day is over.

Unless you are used to working in an early childhood setting, you may find that you must adjust your daily schedule. Some preschool programs require your attendance before 7:00 A.M. because working parents have to drop their children off quite early. Many primary school programs expect teachers to be on duty well before 8:30 A.M. You should get used to arriving no later than your cooperating teacher. Many successful student teachers make a point of arriving well before their cooperating teachers in order to open up the room and have everything ready for the day to begin.

❖ PERSONAL PREPARATIONS

Generally speaking, your college or university will be carefully monitoring the legal and health paperwork necessary for you to participate in your early childhood practicum. You may want to double-check to make sure that all necessary forms are in order. Some private facilities have additional requirements. Finding this out early can save you unnecessary last-minute stress.

Legal Considerations

Your college or university will be keeping a file containing copies of your criminal background clearance, child abuse clearance, and tuberculin (TB) clearance. Regulations vary from state to state. Public schools and private early childhood centers may also have different requirements. For example, some facilities require that all clearances be current, within the last 12 months. Others accept clearances no more than 3 months prior to contact with children. Check the regulations for the facility in which you are preparing to student teach (Machado & Botnarescue, 2001).

Health Considerations

You would be wise to take care of all personal health concerns prior to beginning your student teaching. For example, if you have been putting off an eye exam or a health exam for a chronic problem, then do it right away. You do not want a recurring problem to become an impediment during this important semester.

Some early childhood centers may even require a physician's report assessing your general health. You may not have had a complete physical exam since enrolling in college. Therefore, a vision and health screening and an assessment of your need for immunizations, such as vaccines against influenza or hepatitis B, may be beneficial.

In addition, you may be asked for a physician's assessment of your orthopedic, psychological, and neurological functioning. In other words, is there any impediment that may interfere with your ability to work effectively with young children? After all, you may be expected to lift children and supplies, sit on the floor or on small-sized furniture, and move quickly to supervise young children.

Stress Management

Even before you get into the daily rhythm of student teaching, you may want to consider a plan for managing stress. Your anxiety will decrease if you follow the suggestions of effective communication previously discussed. Recognize that some stress can be a positive, energizing response to a new situation. Your attitude is the key to managing stress. You may occasionally have some anxiety. You may occasionally feel overwhelmed with responsibilities for planning and teaching. This is normal. You can manage your stress by breaking large tasks into small segments, by thorough lesson preparation, and by using positive self-talk.

The key is how you respond to stress. It may seem obvious, but try to find a way to relax each day, even for 10 minutes. Some students write in their journals daily; others exercise; still others meditate. You will find what works for you. In Figure 1.5, there are suggested stress-related questions you may want to ask yourself in order to assess your stress management.

Figure 1.5 **Stress-Related Questions**

- Am I getting daily exercise, even for 10 or 15 minutes?
- Am I getting enough sleep?
- Am I eating regular meals?
- Do I engage in a brief, relaxing mental activity unrelated to school, such as doing a crossword puzzle or easy reading?
- Am I able to maintain my sense of humor?
- Do I strive for excellence, not perfection?
- Do I communicate with other student teachers to discover what works for them?
- Would I consider counseling if necessary?

(Machado & Botnarescue, 2001; Roe & Ross, 2002)

❖ DEVELOPMENT OF A SUPPORT SYSTEM

A certain ambiguity is inherent in all teaching. There is no defined prescription to ensure feelings of calm and confidence. Therefore, the development of a support system is crucial to a successful student teaching experience.

Need for a Support System

As a preservice teacher, you find yourself split between two quite different worlds. For 8 or more hours per day, you function in the role of teacher, surrounded by professional colleagues. You must meet performance-based standards that describe what teachers must know and do. At the same time, you are expected to enjoy yourself so that your enthusiasm for teaching helps foster a love of learning in each child. These are the daily challenges of the professional community you are joining.

Then, each evening, you return to your other life surrounded by friends and/or family. This split existence can be somewhat unsettling. There will be times when you are bursting with excitement to share a highlight from your day. You may find that your nonteaching friends and/or family do not share your enthusiasm for the stories of your successes in the classroom. Similarly, they may not empathize with your anxieties and self-doubts as you confront new challenges. A sense of isolation can become overwhelming. That is why it is important to create a support system of one or more peers who are sharing similar experiences. Lack of time and exhaustion are common complaints during student teaching. Nevertheless, you may find that phone calls, short dinner breaks, or exercise breaks with fellow student teachers are invaluable opportunities to share experiences and feelings.

Creating a Peer Group Support System

Educators who are dedicated to the concepts of lifelong learning and mutual self-improvement often express a need to talk with colleagues about matters of professional practice. The formation of teacher study groups is one way to create opportunities for dialogue within a community of educators. Birchak and colleagues (1998) promote the formation of voluntary study groups as one way for teachers to eliminate a sense of isolation and competitiveness and to create instead "an investigative environment that supports individually directed growth and influences the school community at large" (p. 143). This concept of study groups may be adapted to meet your needs as an early childhood student teacher.

Accordingly, you and your fellow student teachers may benefit from the formation of supportive groups in order to maintain a sense of community.

Students in a group should have a common interest and focus—for example, the early childhood student teaching experience. As with the teacher study groups described by Birchak and colleagues, participation by student teachers should be voluntary. It is important to define the support group by what it is not. It is not a required course; it is neither a workshop nor a seminar. It is a voluntary group of students who are sharing a common experience. They make the group into whatever they want it to be.

Accordingly, the important issue here is that students have a regular opportunity to share important events in their daily lives. They quickly learn that they are not the only ones who sometimes feel fearful, foolish, or frustrated. They share resources and suggestions. At the same time, they take pleasure in each other's accomplishments, whether it is the excitement of helping a child learn a new skill or the pride of receiving a compliment from a cooperating teacher.

As an illustration, one support group of six early childhood student teachers chose to meet every 2 to 3 weeks. The general consensus was that although time was severely limited, everyone would take a dinner break at some point. They might as well take that break together. These students were teaching at six different schools or child development centers, so they did not come in contact with each other on a regular basis. One student was placed in a large inner-city charter school. Another student was in a small urban setting. Four students were placed in suburban settings. They had different supervisors and were teaching children of different ages. The only commonality was that they were all experiencing early childhood student teaching.

In addition, this particular group held its meetings with an education professor who was a participant/observer. Nevertheless, the success of the group was not dependent on the presence of an authority figure or a mentor. The students guided the meetings, whereas the professor took a nondirective role. Comments and reactions from members of this student support group will be interspersed throughout this text as appropriate.

The Process of Group Support

Each support group gathering began with a brief period of informal conversations and sharing of recent experiences. Conversations were lively and interspersed with comments like "That happened to me too; let me tell you about . . ." Next, students raised questions or concerns for discussion. The group tried to focus the discussion for each session. Topics varied greatly, depending on the needs of the group. Some concerns included how to improve communication with the cooperating teacher and how to meet the needs of *all* children. A timekeeper was appointed at each meeting so that the gatherings could be limited to 1 hour. About 10 minutes before the time was up, the students set a date for the next get-together and agreed on a tentative focus for future discussion.

Benefits of the Support Group

For many of the students, sharing was the primary reason for attending. Hearing about each other's experiences reduced the stress and the sense of isolation that can build up during a lengthy student teaching practicum. For others, the focused discussion was the heart of the meeting. The quality of the information discussed determined whether students felt that their time was spent productively. All students reported that they enjoyed the meetings. Some commented on the developing sense of trust among group members. This trust allowed collaboration to become the group's strength; it created a pathway for mutual improvement during the journey of student teaching.

An added benefit was that the students experienced the social nature of learning. They created a community in which communication flowed freely. They made sense of their experiences personally and collectively in a safe environment of their own choosing (Wink & Putney, 2002). In other words, they were experiencing the Vygotskian principles of scaffolding and social interaction that they had been taught in their child development classes and methods classes. An unintended benefit, therefore, was the personalization of this pedagogical process.

Keeping a Human Connection

You may find that a peer support group is neither possible nor desirable for you because of your particular personal commitments and responsibilities. You may not need such a group because your college already has a class or a required seminar that serves this purpose. If this is not the case, you may be able to maintain a connection with others by e-mail or by phone. However you do it, the human connection and the sense of community will help you maintain a positive outlook as you discover the joys and challenges of teaching.

❖ FINAL THOUGHTS

You have completed all of your preparations. You have already made a good first impression by developing your knowledge base about the child development center or school and its demographics. You are communicating with your cooperating teacher. You have discussed your needs and expectations with family and friends. You even have a peer support system available. You feel ready and excited as you begin the early days of your early childhood practicum.

Even so, you may relate to the thoughts of another student teacher written a few hours before dawn of the first day.

Voices of Reality: Student Teacher Speaks

The reality is beginning to hit me. Wow. To say that my feelings are completely jumbled and scrambled and topsy-turvy would be an understatement. On the one hand, I am bubbling with excitement. Fourteen weeks in which to enter the young lives of 20-plus precious individuals and to welcome these children into my own life. The possibilities for touching and helping to shape these lives are endless, and to think that I may have a hand in this impact fills me with warmth from head to toe. On the other hand, I know the awesome responsibility that this entails fills me with more than a little bit of anxiety. Okay, I'll admit it, I'm really, really scared. I wonder if it's normal to feel this unprepared. Classes in teaching and the handful of lessons developed and carried out during Junior Block are one thing, but student teaching . . . . that feels like an entirely different ball game—like jumping from the dugout, with an occasional inning of play here and there, to a regular spot in the starting line-up. WOW. Am I up to this challenge? Do I truly have what it takes to be one of those special people who "CAN"? When these questions cause me to doubt my own competency, I reassure myself with the reminder that I already possess two of the most essential tools of an educator: an intense love of children and a great desire to become a lasting influence upon young minds and hearts.

Karla S.

ACTIVITIES FOR REFLECTION AND ACTION

1. List the questions and/or concerns you have about starting your teaching experience. Then identify one or more resources you can use to answer your questions and to deal with your concerns.
2. Does your practicum site have the following personnel?

Position	Yes	Name(s)	Location	Contact Information
Director/Principal				
Clerical Staff				
Maintenance Staff				
Health Services				
Paraprofessionals				
Special Needs Support Staff				
Community Liaison Staff				
Others				

3. What do you know about cultural character of the children at your practicum site? Make a list of each cultural group represented. Make a chart that includes the answers you find to the following questions (Fuller, 2001):
   - What famous people and events have shaped the history of each cultural group?
   - What famous people in each cultural group may serve as positive role models?
   - What are the major religious and political beliefs of each cultural group?
   - What are the celebration days of each cultural group?
   - What is the native language of each cultural group?
   - What are the current economic, political, and social issues that concern each cultural group?

4. Ask your cooperating teacher if there are any children at your practicum site who have been identified as having a disability. What do you know about the nature of their special needs? Make a chart that addresses the following issues (Kostelnik et al., 2002; Salend, 2005):
   - List the identified disabilities of the children who have special needs. What do you know about the nature of each disability?
   - Ask your cooperating teacher for information regarding children's early intervention services or individualized written guidelines for educational services. More information about these services and guidelines can be found in Chapter 8.
   - Observe the children who have special needs. You may want to focus on a few areas such as the following: (1) how each child communicates with others, (2) how each child interacts with others, and (3) how each child reacts to sensory stimulation such as touch or sounds in the room.

5. In order to help you get off to a good start, prepare an icebreaker activity that you can use to introduce yourself and to get to know the children. Share this activity with your instructor and the students in your class. You may start a collection of get-acquainted or icebreaker activities that will be useful with young children at a variety of age levels.

6. Write a brief letter of introduction that you can send home with each child in your practicum or student teaching placement. Then share your letter with a partner in order to receive feedback.

7. *Portfolio:* A copy of your letter of introduction may be included in your portfolio as an example of your effective communication with parents and families. See Chapter 6 for a discussion of portfolios.

CHAPTER 2

Becoming a Professional

Teaching is a process of becoming that continues throughout life, never completely achieved, never completely denied. This is the challenge and the fun of being a teacher—there is no ultimate end to the process.

Frances Mayforth

As a student teacher, you are already considered to be a professional. Nevertheless, you are in the initial stages of what will become a lifelong journey of learning more about yourself, about the children in your care, and about the facilitation of the teaching-learning process. You have probably heard the expression "The more you learn, the more you realize you do not know." This is particularly true in early childhood education. We are only beginning to appreciate the impact of research on the brain development of infants and young children. For example, studies indicate that a baby is born with only 25% of its brain developed, but by age 3, 90% of its brain is developed (Benesh, Arbuckle, Robbins, & D'Arcangelo, 1998; D'Arcangelo, 2000; Governor's Commission, 2000; Wolfe & Brandt, 1998). So, as an early childhood educator, you have important opportunities to provide the healthy, stimulating, caring environment children need for a lifetime of success. What an amazing opportunity to shape the future!

Initially, you may have been drawn to the profession of teaching because you want to make a difference in children's lives. Perhaps you will remain in this profession because you enjoy the never-ending fun and challenge of learning along with your children. The simultaneous frustration and joy of teaching young children is that you can indeed make a difference in children's lives, but you may not know for a long time, if ever, the full impact of your influence. Your journey down the road of lifelong

Voices of Reality: Student Teachers Speak

This morning I had the opportunity to lead the class. . . . The students' responses provided ideal springboards for discussions. I absolutely love these moments when I feel so completely "teacher-y!"

Karla S.

One of the boys in my morning class said, "Why does Mrs. K. have to go to school? I thought she already knows everything." I told them that you can always learn something new every day. That had another student say, "Just like you, huh, Miss F.?" And I believe that is true 100%; you do learn something at any point in time on any day, at any age. "Real" teachers are always learning too.

Nancy F.

As I move closer and closer to "professional" status as a teacher, I have found myself viewing a professional as highly dynamic. Being a professional means always striving to be better.

Saul D.

learning and professional development is truly one that can never be fully achieved or fully denied.

During the early weeks of your student teaching, perhaps you are experiencing some of the feelings expressed by these students concerning becoming a teaching professional.

As already stated, you are viewed as a professional from the moment you step into a childcare facility or a school-based early childhood classroom. Accordingly, the expectation is that you will conduct yourself with *professionalism.* This term requires some explanation.

❖ WHAT IT MEANS TO BE A PROFESSIONAL

Consideration of what it means to be a professional is extremely important in early childhood education, just as in any other area of teaching. However, you will be called on not only to teach but also to advocate for the youngest, most vulnerable, and most powerless members of humanity. Therefore, you must be acutely aware of professional standards of practice when making decisions.

Terminology

As recently as the 1990s, some early childhood educators voiced discomfort with the use of the word *professional* as a noun to refer to early childhood teachers. To them, it implied a sense of separation or elitism. Although they called for high standards of practice, they associated the term professional with persons whose work is specialized and selective (Bredekamp & Willer, 1993; Fromberg, 1997). Others, the author included, do not believe that specialization and selectivity are necessarily bad things. Think about how you define the word professional. Does a particular image come to mind? Is this image in tune with your image of yourself as an early childhood teacher?

In contrast, the word professional used as an adjective created positive responses in the past as well as now. No one can argue with the implication that early childhood educators should exhibit ethical conduct and be knowledgeable individuals (Bredekamp & Willer, 1993). Professionalism is behavior characterized by common descriptors (Beaty, 2004; Fromberg, 1997; NAEYC [National Association for the Education of Young Children], 2001b; Whitehead, 1929):

- Adherence to an ethical code of conduct
- Demonstrated sense of commitment and service to others
- Demonstrated mastery of a specialized body of knowledge
- Demonstrated ability to consciously *use* the specialized knowledge acquired
- Attainment of established standards and practices that control entry into the profession
- Membership in a professional organization that affects professional policy and activity
- Commitment to ongoing professional development

You may wish to add your own ideas to this list of descriptors as you reflect on what *becoming a professional* means to you.

Ethical Guidelines and Professional Standards

According to Bredekamp and Willer (1993), a defining characteristic of a profession is a shared code of ethics. As an early childhood professional, you have a code of ethics to guide your own behavior and to monitor the behavior of others. At some point during your early childhood courses, you may have read and discussed the *NAEYC Code of Ethical Conduct*. If not, this is an appropriate time to do so. Even if you have reviewed it in the past, this would be a good time to take another look at the *Code* in Figure 2.1. Certain shared values are inherent in these standards of ethical behavior. One important aspect of becoming a professional is committing yourself to these values. Therefore, as you begin student teaching, you may want to reaffirm your personal commitment suggested in the *NAEYC Code of Ethical Conduct* (Figure 2.2).

Ethical Responsibilities to Children

P-1.1 Above all, we shall not harm children. We shall not participate in practices that are emotionally damaging, physically harmful, disrespectful, degrading, dangerous, exploitive, or intimidating to children. *This principle has precedence over all others in this Code.*

P-1.2 We shall care for and educate children in positive emotional and social environments that are cognitively stimulating and that support each child's culture, language, ethnicity, and family structure.

P-1.3 We shall not participate in practices that discriminate against children by denying benefits, giving special advantages, or excluding them from programs or activities on the basis of their sex, race, national origin, religious beliefs, medical condition, disability, or the marital status/family structure, sexual orientation, or religious beliefs or other affiliations of their families. (Aspects of this principle do not apply in programs that have a lawful mandate to provide services to a particular population of children.)

P-1.4 We shall involve all those with relevant knowledge (including families and staff) in decisions concerning a child, as appropriate, ensuring confidentiality of sensitive information.

P-1.5 We shall use appropriate assessment systems, which include multiple sources of information, to provide information on children's learning and development.

P-1.6 We shall strive to ensure that decisions such as those related to enrollment, retention, or assignment to special education services will be based on multiple sources of information and will never be based on a single assessment, such as a test score or a single observation.

P-1.7 We shall strive to build individual relationships with each child; make individualized adaptations in teaching strategies, learning environments, and curricula; and consult with the family so that each child benefits from the program. If, after such efforts have been exhausted, the current placement does not meet a child's needs, or the child is seriously jeopardizing the ability of other children to benefit from the program, we shall collaborate with the child's family and appropriate specialists to determine the additional services needed and/or the placement option(s) most likely to ensure the child's success. (Aspects of this principle may not apply in programs that have a lawful mandate to provide services to a particular population of children.)

P-1.8 We shall be familiar with the risk factors for and symptoms of child abuse and neglect, including physical, sexual, verbal, and emotional abuse and physical, emotional, educational, and medical neglect. We shall know and follow state laws and community procedures that protect children against abuse and neglect.

P-1.9 When we have reasonable cause to suspect child abuse or neglect, we shall report it to the appropriate community agency and follow up to ensure that appropriate action has been taken. When appropriate, parents or guardians will be informed that the referral will be or has been made.

P-1.10 When another person tells us of his or her suspicion that a child is being abused or neglected, we shall assist that person in taking appropriate action in order to protect the child.

(Continued)

P-1.11 When we become aware of a practice or situation that endangers the health, safety, or well-being of children, we have an ethical responsibility to protect children or inform parents and/or others who can.

Source: National Association for the Education of Young Children. 2005. *The Code of Ethical Conduct and Statement of Commitment*. Brochure. Washington, DC: Author. Available online at *http://www .naeyc.org/org/about/positions/pdf/PSETHO5.pdf*. Reprinted with permission of the National Association for the Education of Young Children.

FIGURE 2.1 Abbreviated Overview of the *NAEYC Code of Ethical Conduct*

As an individual who works with young children, I commit myself to furthering the values of early childhood education as they are reflected in the ideals and principles of the *NAEYC Code of Ethical Conduct*. To the best of my ability I will

- Never harm children.
- Ensure that programs for young children are based on current knowledge and research of child development and early childhood education.
- Respect and support families in their task of nurturing children.
- Respect colleagues in early childhood care and education and support them in maintaining the *NAEYC Code of Ethical Conduct*.
- Serve as an advocate for children, their families, and their teachers in [the] community and society.
- Stay informed of and maintain high standards of professional conduct.
- Engage in an ongoing process of self-reflection, realizing that personal characteristics, biases, and beliefs have an impact on children and families.
- Be open to new ideas and be willing to learn from the suggestions of others.
- Continue to learn, grow, and contribute as a professional.
- Honor the ideals and principles of the *NAEYC Code of Ethical Conduct*.

* This Statement of Commitment is not part of the *Code* but is a personal acknowledgment of the individual's willingness to embrace the distinctive values and moral obligations of the field of early childhood care and education. It is a recognition of the moral obligations that lead an individual to become part of the teaching profession.

Source: National Association for the Education of Young Children. 2005. *The Code of Ethical Conduct and Statement of Commitment*. Brochure. Washington, DC: Author. Available online at *http://www.naeyc.org/org/about/positions/pdf/PSETHO5.pdf*. Reprinted with permission of the National Association for the Education of Young Children.

FIGURE 2.2 Statement of Commitment*

Your cooperating teacher and your college supervisor can provide helpful guidance when you are unsure how to handle a situation to which there is no clear answer. Their perspectives are based on years of experience as well as education.

This affirmation of professional ideals is a good beginning. Your knowledge of the *Code* and your commitment to its values are merely the starting points. You must use these guidelines as the foundation on which you make ethical judgments. As you proceed through your student teaching experience, situations will arise in which your decisions will have consequences for children, families, and perhaps the community. You may have more than one ethical response to problem-solving situations. One source of help is the *NAEYC Code of Ethical Conduct*. Other sources of help include your cooperating teacher and your college supervisor. Although the *Code* does not contain solutions to specific situations, it is a reference point for decision making that was developed by a consensus of professionals in your field (Brophy-Herb, Kostelnik, & Stein, 2001).

The Code of Ethical Conduct and Ethical Dilemmas

You may find that dilemmas requiring ethical judgments occur early during your student practicum. For example, in the second week of the semester, Angie D., a student teacher, reports a situation that makes her uncomfortable. A child in first grade who has been diagnosed with mental retardation is pulled out of the room to receive learning support in math each day. When he returns, the other children are just beginning their math lesson. Current practice has been to occupy the child with a paper to color or to give him the same math worksheet as the more typical students. When he becomes disruptive (which is a daily occurrence), he is removed from class "for the greater good of the remaining students." The student teacher feels bad for the little boy, but she does not want to "rock the boat" with her cooperating teacher. Her peers empathize and suggest the following problem-solving options:

- Ask your college supervisor for advice.
- Talk with your cooperating teacher and brainstorm other ways to handle the situation, such as rescheduling math time, providing adapted activities for the child, and so on.
- Perhaps your cooperating teacher can ask for a team meeting with the special education teacher, the child's parent, and others to brainstorm and develop alternatives.
- Above all, think of the child first and do *something!*

No one in the student teacher support group mentioned the *Code of Ethical Conduct*. Nevertheless, that is perhaps the most important starting point when deciding what to do or say in a difficult situation involving young children. It may help you discover the insights of other professionals. It may help you find the personal courage to make ethical decisions that reflect best practices for *all* children (Feeney, Christensen, & Moravcik, 2001; Freeman, 2000). According to Freeman (2000), the *NAEYC Code of Ethical Conduct* "is specific enough to guide those who need strength to shoulder their ethical responsibilities and those struggling to resolve thorny dilemmas" (p. 14).

In the case mentioned by Angie D., the *Code of Ethical Conduct* is helpful (NAEYC, 2005a). Section P-1.3 reminds us that we should not exclude children from programs or activities for reasons such as difference in ability. Section P-1.4 reminds us that we should involve others, including parents, in the planning process in order to meet each child's needs. These sections and others helped guide Angie D. as she addressed her concerns with her cooperating teacher. In this case, the general education teacher, the student teacher, the special education teacher, and the parents met to brainstorm solutions. As a result, math schedules were modified by the general education teacher, and math activities were adapted by the special education teacher so that this child could be included more effectively with his peers.

Confidentiality

Angie D.'s discussion of her concerns brings to mind another aspect of becoming a professional: the importance of confidentiality. Even if you disagree with your cooperating teacher, another colleague, or a parent, you must not vent your feelings or opinions to others in the faculty room, in the hallway, or outside the facility. If you need to discuss confidential matters that occur in your classroom, wait until you can schedule uninterrupted time with your co-operating teacher or until you can meet with your college supervisor. In the case of the student support group mentioned above, Angie D. was careful not to mention particular names, and students were able to voice concerns with the knowledge that the matters discussed "would not leave that room."

In addition, as present and/or future members of the community of early childhood professionals, you must always keep in mind that confidentiality is an essential component of your commitment to professional conduct. Common examples of confidentiality pitfalls experienced by students include the following:

- **Use of school photographs.** Talk with your cooperating teacher to find out the policy of your center or school regarding taking pictures of children. You may need the written consent of parents or guardians. Using children's photographs in your paper or electronic portfolio or on your own Web site may be considered a serious violation of confidentiality. Discuss this with your college supervisor before using any information in this manner.

- **Conversations at your practicum or student teaching site.** Refrain from engaging in conversations with other students or with professional colleagues that could be interpreted as gossip and/or violations of confidentiality. For example, discussions in the hallway or in the faculty/staff break room about the children, their families, your cooperating teacher, your college supervisor, or your opinions concerning teaching policies and practices should be avoided.

- **Conversations in the community.** In the community, while you are engaged in routine activities such as shopping at the grocery store or the mall, a roommate, a friend, or a family member may ask how things are going at your practicum or student teaching site. Remember that professionalism extends to your behavior in the community. Again, refrain from making any comments that may be considered gossip or violations of confidentiality. Many communities, even those in large cities, are similar to small towns in that people you do not know may recognize you as a student or a teacher in an early childhood center or school. Any comments you make may be overheard and repeated elsewhere.

You do not have to be the one who is initiating the conversation in order to be gossiping. In fact, "listening to gossip is gossiping" (Bruno, 2007, p. 26). In order to help create a work environment that promotes trust and respect, you should refuse to listen to negative comments intended to damage someone's reputation. This viewpoint is consistent with the *NAEYC Code of Ethical Conduct* (2005a). Think about ways that you can respectfully remove yourself from such an unprofessional situation. You may choose to politely express your discomfort with the conversation and make a graceful exit.

You may be able to think of other situations involving confidentiality in addition to those mentioned above. You should discuss any questions regarding professionalism and confidentiality with your cooperating teacher and your college supervisor. These conversations will help you develop the mutual trust and respect that lead to a collaborative partnership.

Written Sources for Professional Decision Making

Although you may not be faced with the same dilemma as Angie D., you will encounter other problems for which you do not have an immediate solution. Therefore, during your student teaching practicum, you may want to start a notebook of relevant guidelines and regulations to help you make professional decisions. A copy of the *NAEYC Code of Ethical Conduct* should certainly be included. You may also locate written policies regarding the reporting of suspected child abuse, school attendance, rights of children with disabilities and their parents, childcare licensing regulations, and educational standards at the national, state, and local levels. You may also find it useful to include NAEYC's Position Statements on a variety of topics. These may be obtained from NAEYC's Web site, *http://www.naeyc.org*. You will feel more comfortable making ethical judgments and discussing best practices for *all* young children when you have easy access to such information.

Knowledge and Critical Reflection

Another aspect of becoming a professional is demonstrated ability to make decisions grounded in sound theory and practice. You must be knowledgeable about current research findings and reflect on the implications of these findings. As you talk with colleagues in the workplace and at conferences, you will discover multiple perspectives concerning what constitutes best practice. You may want to develop a file of ideas on such topics as suggestions for organizing newsletters, recommendations for conducting class meetings, and research-based findings about conflict resolution and peer mediation strategies. Helpful Web sites and locations and phone numbers of community agencies would also be appropriate to keep on file (see Figure 2.3).

As your collection of information and current research grows, you may find that you have uncovered multiple perspectives that differ in their approach to central questions. Therefore, you will have to become a critical,

Figure 2.3 Sample Web Sites for Resources File

- **American Federation of Teachers Educational Foundation (AFTEF),** with which the Center for Childcare Workforce merged in 2002. Now includes a focus on early childhood pre-K issues such as staffing needs and qualifications. *http://www.aft.org*
- **Council for Exceptional Children (CEC)** Web site provides up-to-date information on all aspects of the education and development of students who have disabilities or students who are considered gifted. *http://www.cec.sped.org*
- **Early Head Start National Resource Center @ ZERO TO THREE** with links to resources and information focusing on the first 3 years of life. *http://www.ehsnrc.org*
- **Federal Interagency Coordinating Council** focuses on children ages 0 to 8 who may be considered at risk, and their families, with links to resources and current research. Information is provided in Spanish and English. *http://www.fed-icc.org/*
- **Frank Porter Graham Child Development Center** at the University of North Carolina at Chapel Hill provides research and educational information with a focus on child development and health. *http://www.fpg.unc.edu*
- **National Association for Family Child Care (NAFCC)** Web site focuses on improvement of family and group childcare, with information and assistance for providers. *http://www.nafcc.org*
- **NAEYC** Web site for information on readiness indicators, standards, best practices, and professional development opportunities. *http://www.naeyc.org/childrens_champions/issues.asp*
- **National Child Care Information Center** Web site provides a national clearinghouse, technical assistance, and links to information about early childcare and education. Links include faith-based initiatives, fatherhood, rural families, welfare reform, and many other priorities. *http://www.nccic.org*

reflective practitioner as you make decisions based on the context of your particular early childhood community. Your cooperating teacher and your college supervisor will be helpful resources as you assimilate these perspectives and formulate your own reflective approach to teaching.

Identification and Involvement

An important step in becoming a professional is to involve yourself with others who share your interest in the early childhood field. You need to become identified with colleagues who understand what being a professional means. One of the best ways to do this is to join a professional organization such as NAEYC. Students generally have limited financial resources, but student memberships are available at a reduced rate. It is not too late to join at the student rate if you have not already done so.

This connection with your professional organization identifies you with over 100,000 teachers, administrators, parents, and others who share your commitment to high-quality education and care of young children. The benefits for students outweigh the costs. For example, membership entitles you to receive a journal describing the most recent developments in your field and access to a members-only Web site at no extra charge. Other opportunities, such as attendance at conferences and seminars, are available at a reduced fee. Perhaps the most important benefit of student memberships is the heightened awareness that you share a knowledge base and a history with respected professionals worldwide.

Figure 2.4 is but a small sample of the organizations available to offer information, advocacy, and support for you as an early childhood teacher as well as for the parents and community agencies with which you come in contact.

Figure 2.4 Examples of Professional Organizations

American Montessori Society (AMS)
281 Park Avenue South
New York, NY 10010
http://www.amshq.org/
(journal: *Montessori Life*)

Association for Childhood Education International (ACEI)
17904 Georgia Avenue, Suite 215
Olney, MD 20832
http://www.acei.org/
(journal: *Childhood Education*)

Child Welfare League of America (CWLA)
2345 Crystal Drive, Suite 250
Arlington, VA 22202
http://www.cwla.org/

Council for Exceptional Children (CEC)
1110 North Glebe Road, Suite 300
Arlington, VA 22201-5704
http://www.cec.sped.org/
(journal: *Teaching Exceptional Children*)

National Association for Bilingual Education (NABE)
1313 L Street, NW, Suite 210
Washington, DC 20005-1503
http://www.naeyc.org/
(journal: *Bilingual Research Journal*)

National Association for the Education of Young Children (NAEYC)
1313 L Street, NW, Suite 500
Washington, DC 20005
http://www.naeyc.org/
(journal: *Young Children*)

You can check out the professional development opportunities by going on-line or by writing to these organizations and others with similar goals. You may soon find that your work with diverse young children and their families will lead you in many different directions of professional development.

Professionalism and Lifelong Learning

Another aspect of becoming a professional is the recognition that you are embarking on a process of lifelong learning. Your student teaching practicum is a milestone in your career development, but it is only the beginning of your professional growth. Presumably, throughout your education courses, you have engaged in collaborative learning with other students, your professors, and the cooperating teachers from previous field experiences. This exchange of ideas with colleagues will continue to be an integral part of your professional development.

Throughout your student teaching practicum, avail yourself of all opportunities to learn from colleagues. Attend inservice training experiences. If possible, accompany your cooperating teacher to educational workshops and/or conferences.

Equally important, form connections with professionals from disciplines related to early childhood education. This may sound like unusual advice at a time when you may be just starting to know your cooperating teacher, the children, and their families. Nevertheless, you need to know the specialists who serve your diverse population of children. If you understand the roles of these other professionals, you will know when and how to access the skills and expertise they offer. Therefore, ask your cooperating teacher for assistance in meeting the special educators, the reading specialist, the school psychologist, the English as a second language specialist, the speech and language therapist, and others. Because many children who have special needs are now included in early childhood programs with their typically developing peers, your collaboration with colleagues in other disciplines is more critical than ever before.

Professional Growth as a Team Member

During your student teaching practicum, seek opportunities to observe and/or participate in any transdisciplinary team meetings that are held. These are meetings attended by people across *(trans)* various disciplines who come together with a child's parents or guardians to coordinate services and develop plans for improving the child's functioning. One significant characteristic of transdisciplinary teams is that people share information and learn from each other; services are coordinated with each other rather than provided in isolation.

Participating as a team member is one of the most important experiences you can have as a student teacher. You will observe how educators and parents learn from each other, solve problems, and make decisions as a team.

Therefore, you may be sitting around a table with the child's parents, your cooperating teacher, a communication disorder specialist, a nurse, an administrator, a psychologist, a behavior specialist, and other support staff. Such teaming may occur for the purpose of developing an Individual Family Service Plan (IFSP) for a child below the age of 3 or an Individual Education Plan (IEP) for a child beginning at age 3 who has special needs. A transdisciplinary team meeting may also be held to discuss observations or formal assessment results of a child who seems to be developing in an atypical manner.

If you have a chance to participate in a transdisciplinary team meeting, you will see how team members share information, resolve conflicts of opinion, generate creative ideas to find solutions, and collaborate to make decisions. You may even be called on to share your observations. You will see for yourself how effective communication skills can lead to positive relationships between parents and professionals. You may also take some comfort in the knowledge that "no one person assumes more responsibility than another; all are held accountable together" (Westling & Fox, 2000, p. 52). In addition, you may learn helpful information that you can implement right away. An effective team approach is therefore beneficial to all participants. It can be an opportunity for learning and professional growth.

Becoming a Professional Member of the Workplace

Your overall appearance, including your clothing, your grooming, and your demeanor, contributes to your image as a member of the professional workplace. Some schools or child development programs have written dress codes. Others do not. If you are not sure how to dress, then choose conservative clothing.

Although most student teachers dress appropriately in the workplace, once in a while they make inappropriate choices. These unfortunate choices may result in embarrassment for the student and for the person who finds it necessary to discuss the matter with the student. This difficulty can be easily avoided by following a few guidelines. Figure 2.5 lists typical guidelines for dressing professionally. You may be able to add to these suggestions or alter them as you talk with your cooperating teacher or college supervisor.

In addition, you should be aware of your grooming and your demeanor. Hairstyles, for example, should, like clothing, be conservative. A smile on your face even if you do not feel well sends a positive message to others. These personal areas of dress, grooming, and demeanor can go a long way toward helping you become an accepted member of the professional community.

In the early days of your field experience or student teaching, you are told about attendance policies. Make sure that you remain vigilant about

Figure 2.5 **Typical Guidelines for Professional Dress**

- Make sure that when you bend over, your shirt or sweater does not rise up to expose bare skin.
- Make sure that if you wear white or light-colored clothing, no undergarments show through the fabric.
- Generally, avoid perfume, cologne, or aftershave. They may be distracting or cause allergic reactions.
- Generally, remove nose rings, eyebrow rings, lip or tongue rings, or any other piercings that may be a distraction.
- Women should observe the accepted practice regarding hemlines on skirts or dresses and wearing pants or jeans at the field experience site. Men should observe the accepted practice regarding ties, dress pants, or jeans.
- Some schools have a policy prohibiting sneakers, sandals, and flip-flops. Check with your cooperating teacher to find out the policy at your location.
- Avoid clothing or jewelry that makes a political or religious statement. For example, some schools will not allow religious jewelry to be worn by either children or adults.

your punctuality and attendance. Teachers with a professional attitude usually prefer to work even when they do not feel well. They frequently arrive early and stay late. You may find that you do likewise as you progress through the weeks of your student teaching experience.

Professional Behavior in the Workplace

Professional behavior is also a critical component of a successful practicum or student teaching experience. Be mindful of behaviors that you may take for granted, such as carrying a cell phone. The safest practice is to leave your cell phone in your car or at home. Even if you have every intention of turning your phone off, omissions happen. You do not want your cell phone to start ringing when you are assisting children, teaching a lesson, or talking with parents or professional colleagues. Even if you are on a break or at lunch, many centers and schools do not want you to use your cell phone for chatting or text messaging. Another behavior you may take for granted is chewing gum. Many programs have a policy forbidding children from chewing gum; you need to be a role model by not chewing gum yourself.

Your use of appropriate language is also an important component of professional behavior. Language that may be acceptable on a college campus, at home, or in a gathering of your friends is not necessarily acceptable in the center or school where you work with children. Therefore, you must refrain from the use of profanity, even if you think you cannot be overheard. Be cautious about the use of slang terms. Your language should be professional and respectful of human dignity at all times (Baptiste & Reyes, 2008). Think about how you refer to the children in your care. For example, if a child in your program has a disability, use people-first language. The girl who has a learning disability (LD) is not "an LD child"; she is "a child who has LD" (Friend & Bursuck, 2009; Hallahan & Kauffman, 2006). Also, notice how your cooperating teacher refers to the children, and follow her example. When she talks to them, she may say "boys and girls" rather than "kids" or "guys."

If you are unsure of what professional behaviors are expected, talk with your cooperating teacher and your college supervisor. By your willingness to follow the guidelines for professional behavior at your practicum or student teaching location, you will demonstrate the positive attitude that will help you have a successful experience.

Becoming an Informed Professional

One final element of becoming a professional involves keeping abreast of current issues and the policy-making process. As a student teacher, you should be cognizant of societal concerns regarding the quality of early childhood programs. These concerns will affect you in areas such as financial compensation, assessment, and standards. Therefore, it is in your best interest to know who makes these decisions and how these policies are implemented.

One way of keeping informed is to maintain your connection with your early childhood professional organization, NAEYC. Periodically, check their links regarding advocacy and recent developments. For example, the NAEYC home page maintains a site called Children's Champions through which you can access an Action Center. This Action Center allows you to e-mail your state's members of Congress regarding critical issues impacting early childhood education. Through this link, you may also discover federal and state policies and legislation that affect young children. As a student teacher, your time is severely limited, but you may find it worthwhile to be aware of issues that impact your life in such a direct manner. In addition, your advocacy can make a difference in the lives of young children who have no voice in these matters.

❖ PROFESSIONAL ISSUES RELATED TO EARLY CHILDHOOD

You are entering the field of early childhood education at an exciting time of change. You have an obligation to yourself, your colleagues, and your children to be acutely aware of trends and current issues affecting your field. Your future depends on your awareness and your professional involvement.

Public Perception

Early childhood education has been called "a public relations nightmare" (Fromberg, 1997, p. 188). A common misperception is that anyone who is nurturing and motherly can use common sense to care for infants and young children. So-called dual systems of early childhood care through public schools and nonpublic settings may have contributed to this viewpoint (Fromberg, 1997).

Thankfully, the status of early childhood care is gradually changing as nonpublic settings are becoming accredited. For example, many families choose family childcare for their young children. More and more of these home providers are becoming so-called master providers who are regulated by organizations such as the National Association for Family Child Care (NAFCC). NAFCC accreditation is a voluntary commitment to professionalism that at least 1,500 family childcare providers undertook in 2001 (Eaton, 2002). NAFCC (2009) reports that 8,000 members are currently caring for "an estimated 60,000 children in 45,000 house-holds" (p. 2). These providers consider themselves to be lifelong learners who are committed to providing high-quality childcare (Weaver, 2002). They still represent a minority of providers, however. Therefore, your challenge will be to act as an advocate for your profession as you interact with the public.

Compensation

Another area of concern in pre-K early childhood education is inadequate compensation for qualified teachers. According to the U.S. Department of Labor Bureau of Labor Statistics (2007), the average childcare worker earns an average of $19,670; preschool teachers earn an average of $25,800; elementary school teachers earn an average of $50,040. These figures indicate that childcare workers, including those in childcare programs, receive less than half of what the average elementary school teacher earns during the same period; preschool teachers earn barely half of an elementary teacher's salary. In fact, "as a nation, the United States pays about as much to parking-lot attendants and dry-cleaning workers as it does to early-childhood educators" (*Executive Summary*, 2002, p. 9). No wonder the profession is plagued by high turnover rates of personnel!

The U.S. government's support of childcare is ranked among the lowest in the civilized world (NAEYC, 2001a). Now, before you despair and consider changing your career choice, you should know that there are some positive examples of financing childcare. For example, in the 1980s, the military implemented an affordable, high-quality, well-financed childcare system funded by Congress. In the 1990s, North Carolina implemented the Teacher Education and Compensation Helps (T.E.A.C.H.) Project to provide funding for education of employees in regulated childcare programs. The T.E.A.C.H. Model, linking scholarship to increased compensation, has now been implemented in at least 22 states (*Executive Summary*, 2002).

As a professional beginning your career, what can you do? NAEYC suggests the following:

- Read position papers and join the NAEYC interest forum on financing so that you will be knowledgeable enough to engage in discussions of early childcare financing options.
- Attend professional conferences and attend sessions on finance.
- Join with others in your state to call for a well-financed system of early childhood care.
- Join with other organizations that call for a national dialogue on what is needed to adequately finance childcare.

In other words, consider becoming an advocate for your profession.

Increased Demand for Early Education

The good news is that early childhood education is receiving more and more attention as research continues to document its benefits (Barnett, 1998; Barnett & Camilli, 2002; Olson, 2002). In fact, "Senator Zell Miller, the former governor of Georgia, has called preschool 'the most important grade'" (Barnett & Hustedt, 2003, p. 57). His sentiments are echoed by others across the country.

Georgia mandates statewide universal pre-K education for all 4-year-old children, regardless of income. Other states are beginning to follow suit, including New York, Oklahoma, and Florida. The United States has a long way to go on this issue, but at least progress is being made. You, as a new professional, have an opportunity to be an important part of this change in the public's perception of early childhood education.

Shortage of Early Childhood Teachers

According to the American Association of State Colleges and Universities (AASCU), there is no longer a clear answer to the question of whether or not a teacher shortage actually exists. Challenges identified by AASCU include how to agree upon what makes a teacher qualified and how to retain teachers (2005). The turnover rate is approximately 30%, due in part to low wages. The current movement toward universal pre-K classes will only increase the demand for qualified personnel (Whitebook, Sakai, Gerber, & Howes, 2001).

Meeting this demand will take time. In order to become qualified early childhood professionals, people need to complete courses or programs of study, pass standardized tests, and obtain varying amounts of experience. Then they may receive professional credentials. NAEYC lists six different levels of early childhood professionals (see Figure 2.6).

Examine these levels and determine where you will be when you complete the program in which you are currently enrolled. These levels also indicate opportunities you may want to consider for future growth as well. They represent one approach to increasing awareness of early childhood education as a profession.

❖ FINAL THOUGHTS

As you can tell, living the life of a professional is a complex mission. Professionalism affects every aspect of your life. You will be holding yourself to high standards of dress, behavior, punctuality, attendance, professional development, and communication with children and their families, colleagues,

Level I

- Working under supervision in an early childhood professional role. Participating in training leading to assessment of competencies or degree.

Level II

- Successful completion of Child Development Associate (CDA) Professional Preparation Program or successful completion of training program leading to CDA Credential through direct assessment.
- Successful completion of one-year early childhood certificate training program.

Level III

- Successful completion of associate degree from NAEYC approved program, or
- Successful completion of associate degree plus 30 units of early childhood development studies or education with 300 hours supervised teaching experience in early childhood, or
- Successful demonstration of meeting outcomes of associate degree program conforming to NAEYC guidelines.

Level IV

- Successful completion of baccalaureate degree from NAEYC approved program, or
- State certification meeting NAEYC or NCATE guidelines, or
- Successful completion of baccalaureate degree in another area with at least 30 units in early childhood development/education including 300 hours of supervised teaching experience, including 150 hours each for at least two of the following age groups: infants and toddlers, 3- to 5-year-olds, or primary grades, or
- Successful demonstration of meeting outcomes of NAEYC approved baccalaureate degree program.

Level V

- Successful completion of master's degree in prescribed program conforming to NAEYC guidelines, or
- Successful demonstration of meeting outcomes of NAEYC approved master's degree program.

Level VI

- Successful completion of a Ph.D. or Ed.D. in prescribed program meeting NAEYC guidelines, or
- Successful demonstration of meeting outcomes of NAEYC approved doctoral degree program.

Source: The Levels of Early Childhood Professionals are adapted from *A Conceptual Framework for Early Childhood Professional Development*, a position statement of the National Association for the Education of Young Children, 1993. Washington, DC. Copyright 1993 by the National Association for the Education of Young Children. Reprinted with permission of the National Association for the Education of Young Children.

FIGURE 2.6   Levels of Early Childhood Professionals

Voices of Reality: Student Teachers Speak

When I think of the word professional I think of being the best that someone can be. The criteria would be as follows: (1) Act professionally, (2) dress professionally, (3) give up some of your college habits . . . hmm . . . , (3) keep children's names/ gossip to yourself even though it might be hard. The list could go on and on. I believe that everyone has their own way of being a professional, but my question is, "Is there a right way or a wrong way to be a professional?"

Jackson L.

Teaching is an interesting profession in that we are not always seen as professional, despite training and knowledge. Being a professional teacher involves so many different facets, including teacher, counselor, nurse, and, unfortunately, sometimes parent.

Krista U.

A professional manages and balances responsibilities to students, parents, fellow teachers, administrators, and the district at large.

Saul D.

A professional is someone who is involved in a particular line of work for their livelihood.

Nancy F.

and members of the community. In many respects, you will be held to a higher standard of expectations than people in the general workforce. Many educators, including the author, believe that you are not preparing for a job; you are preparing for a profession. Think about why such a distinction might be made.

As you read the chapters in this textbook, keep in mind what it means to be a professional and how you can relate your sense of professionalism to every aspect of teaching young children. You may develop your own definition of what it means to be a professional. Perhaps you can relate to the comments made by the student teachers.

ACTIVITIES FOR REFLECTION AND ACTION

1. Create your own definition of what it means to be a professional. Look back at this definition at the end of your student teaching practicum and see if your perspective has changed.
2. Put a copy of the *NAEYC Code of Ethical Conduct* in your student teaching notebook or journal. Refer to it when in doubt as to the right thing to do in a given

situation. Keep a record of any dilemmas or tough decisions you encountered and how you handled them.

3. Keep a record of any dilemmas or tough decisions you encountered and how you handled them in the context of the *NAEYC Code of Ethical Conduct*.

4. *Portfolio*: A discussion of and reflection on a situation in which you made a decision based on ethical guidelines for professionals can be included in your portfolio.

5. Visit the Web sites of two or three professional organizations that you might consider joining. List the benefits of each organization. For example, do they offer journals, newsletters, and books to their members? Do they have local, state, and/or national conferences? Do they offer discounts on services of any kinds? What fees are charged for memberships?

CHAPTER 3

Establishing Effective Professional Relationships

In seeking knowledge, the first step is silence, the second listening, the third remembering, the fourth practicing, and the fifth—teaching others.

Solomon Ibn Gabirol

Solomon Ibn Gabirol's words may seem somewhat enigmatic. They contain, however, basic elements necessary for a successful student teaching experience. As you begin the most important field experience of your education so far, you are obviously seeking knowledge that you cannot gain from a textbook alone. Part of your first few days will be spent in watchful silence. You will listen to the sounds of learning as children interact with each other and with the teacher. You will remember your education courses and compare theory to practice. You have the core knowledge necessary to be successful. Now you will practice the application of your skills as you begin teaching children and reflecting on the teaching-learning process. You are beginning your lifelong journey along the path of becoming a skillful teacher.

In the early days of your student teaching practicum, you may be wondering how to optimize your relationship with the one person you will be spending most of your waking life with over the next few months—your cooperating teacher.

❖ ESTABLISHING A POSITIVE RELATIONSHIP WITH COOPERATING TEACHERS

Your relationship with your cooperating teacher is perhaps the single most important factor in determining whether or not you will have a successful student teaching experience. It can be a source of joy or extreme anxiety

Voices of Reality: Student Teachers Speak

Ah, the first days of school. So many questions and decisions. What should I wear? Will my teacher like me? What should I take? Not only were these questions running through the minds of the students, but also me! Once I calmed myself down, I was ready to walk through the doors of the school as an official student teacher!

First person I saw when I walked in the office was none other than my co-op with a smile on her face. Although I had met her several times before, it was still great to see her bright and early in the morning!

Rosa K.

(Morris & Morris, 1980). Increasing your awareness of several key issues will help you develop the productive working relationship you desire (Knowles & Cole, 1996).

Differing Types of Cooperating Teachers

You cannot assume that your current cooperating teacher will have the same perspective as teachers in your previous field placements. In fact, you will quickly discover that your cooperating teacher may even have a different outlook on the student teaching process than the teacher down the hall. Sudzina, Giebelhaus, and Coolican (1997) distinguish between two mentoring styles of cooperating teachers. Mentors characterized by Style One may view themselves as older and wiser guides who are in control. With this control-style mentor, the student teacher's role is one of being an attentive follower who models the mentor's teaching style. She is expected to accept constructive criticism amiably, work hard, and gradually assume more responsibilities within the classroom. In contrast, Style Two mentors may characterize themselves as supportive partners who share their classrooms, their children, their knowledge, and their responsibilities. This partner-style mentor may be attentive to the student teacher's feelings while still expecting cooperation and a willingness to accept criticism. Both parties negotiate and accommodate their needs. The student teacher's role, therefore, is one of being a learner who also has valuable resources to share with the teacher (Machado & Botnarescue, 2001; Sudzina et al., 1997).

Invited Guest/Participant

Although you may encounter other types of cooperating teachers, you must realize the need to be flexible and adapt your behaviors. You are, after all, being invited into your cooperating teacher's classroom with the understanding that you will take every opportunity to learn from that person. You are a guest who is expected to be an active participant. Your awareness of this guest/participant status may be particularly crucial if you are placed with a teacher whose philosophy of teaching differs from your own.

Cooperating teachers are experienced educators who are often motivated by a desire to mentor a student just as someone once mentored them. Your cooperating teacher may have volunteered to mentor you or she may have been selected by the director of the center or the principal of the school based on her record of excellent performance. She will be investing her time and energy in helping you learn, usually with no monetary compensation or with only a minimal honorarium from the college or university. Keep in mind that someday you yourself may want to be a cooperating teacher. You may find it helpful to keep a journal as you reflect upon your feelings and your learning throughout this process. Accordingly, much of the success of this experience ultimately depends on you.

Establishing a Successful Mentoring Relationship

Think about the kind of relationship you want with your cooperating teacher. Do you want her to be your teacher, your encourager, your role model, your friend, your advisor? With careful thought, attention to some

Meetings with your cooperating teacher allow you to discuss events of the day and plan your future activities. This is an opportunity for you to receive feedback and ask for advice.

Figure 3.1 Sample Topics to Encourage Dialogue

- One of your successes as a student teacher this day/week
- Your greatest concern at this time
- What you are doing to create a warm, caring environment for children
- How you can tell when children are learning
- Insights gained about the art of teaching, in other words, your own "aha moments"

(Boreen et al., 2000)

basic communication skills, and planning, you will improve the likelihood of building the kind of relationship you desire.

You may be able to negotiate a regular time to meet and discuss questions and concerns. This planning will also promote the conversation necessary to develop a collaborative mentoring relationship with your cooperating teacher in which the two of you can learn from each other.

Remember that the mentoring relationship is not limited to you and your cooperating teacher. Your college supervisor can also be a mentor to both of you. She is available to provide support and professional development. This can be a three-way partnership in which all of you benefit from reflective discussions (Boreen, Johnson, Niday, & Potts, 2000).

Mentor refers to a person who serves as a trusted guide, an advisor, a teacher, and an encourager of reflective thought (Schon, 1983).

When you and your **mentor** begin these reflective discussions, you may find it helpful to have a specific topic on which to focus. The suggestions in Figure 3.1 may give you the starting point needed to commence the conversational flow and exchange of ideas.

Beginning these conversations may not always be easy. Experienced teachers often make decisions intuitively, without taking the time for a formal problem-solution process (Bey & Holmes, 1992). Nevertheless, talking about the process of teaching and learning is important. As noted by Richert (1992), when "teachers talk about their work and 'name' their experiences, they learn about what they know and what they believe. They also learn what they do not know. Such knowledge empowers the individual by providing a source for action" (p. 197). Therefore, such dialogue may prove to be mutually beneficial.

❖ ESTABLISHING A POSITIVE RELATIONSHIP WITH YOUR COLLEGE SUPERVISOR

Although many educators believe that your cooperating teacher has more of an impact on your performance than anyone else, your college supervisor is another person who plays an important role in promoting a successful

> # Figure 3.2 Typical Functions of College Supervisors
>
> - Act as liaison between the school or child development center and the college
> - Act as mentor to the student teacher
> - Act as mentor to the cooperating teacher, providing support and professional development
> - Hold seminars for student teachers as desired
> - Provide immediate feedback to encourage student teacher's professional development
> - Hold individual and three-way conferences with the student teacher and the cooperating teacher to discuss needs and progress
> - Write final evaluations and letters of recommendation to school districts and college placement offices
> - Review portfolios and lesson/unit plans
> - Recommend state certification or, if necessary, recommend termination, reassignment, or extension of the student teaching experience
>
> (Blair & Jones, 1998; Boreen et al., 2000)

student teaching experience. Your supervisor will interact with you and your cooperating teacher to define your roles, to set expectations for your performance, and to establish procedures for your evaluation. Figure 3.2 outlines the typical functions of your college supervisor.

When visiting to observe your teaching, the supervisor may use techniques to encourage you to analyze your behavior and solve problems yourself. One common practice is to hold a preconference in which you will specify an area where you would like to have feedback. Then, at the end of the lesson or activity, she may ask you to write down your strengths, areas that need improvement, and things to do differently next time. In so doing, you will be developing the skills of critical reflection that you will use throughout your professional career (Valli, 1992). This process, called *nondirective supervision*, may seem frustrating at first because it is much easier to have someone just tell you directly what you are doing well and what you can improve on. Nevertheless, it is a highly effective approach that is commonly used (Glickman, 1981). Different supervisors use different techniques. This is something you can discuss during your conferences.

An important aspect of your college supervisor's role is to provide constructive criticism in order to help you grow as an early childhood teacher. She will talk with you about your planning: what you are doing, why you are doing it, and how you are accomplishing your goals. She may want to see your written lesson plans and discuss how they address specific standards. She will observe the implementation of these plans as well as your interaction with children, support staff, and others. Your college supervisor will provide you with the feedback you need to improve your skills and develop your confidence. (**Note:** Lesson planning will be discussed in more detail in Chapter 8.)

In addition, your supervisor is the liaison between you and your cooperating teacher. If a situation should arise that you do not know how to handle regarding interactions with your cooperating teacher, with children, or with others, call on your college supervisor for assistance. For example, some students desire more written feedback from their cooperating teachers, but they are hesitant to ask for it. Other students want to try out their own ideas, but they are hesitant to deviate from the activities their cooperating teacher has suggested. In each case, the college supervisor may offer suggestions or arrange a three-way conversation to discuss expectations and goals. (**Note:** Observations and assessments of several types will be discussed in Chapter 6.)

You may also want to invite your supervisor to observe special activities in addition to her regularly scheduled visits. The more collegiality there is among you, your cooperating teacher, and your college supervisor, the more comfortable you are likely to feel in your practicum site. Therefore, effective communication skills will be a key ingredient in developing positive relationships.

❖ EFFECTIVE COMMUNICATION AND BUILDING RELATIONSHIPS

One of the keys to a successful student teaching practicum is effective communication. In fact, studies indicate that interpersonal communication is so important that it is considered to be a major factor in determining the effectiveness of coteaching relationships (Dieker & Barnett, 1996; Thomas, Correa, & Morsink, 2001; West & Cannon, 1988). Bruneau-Balderrama (1997) emphasizes the importance of "open and frequent communication" (p. 329) in the successful implementation of inclusion. The development of mutual understanding resulting from effective communication is equally important to a positive student teaching experience.

You cannot assume that you and your cooperating teacher are skilled at the communication process just because you are both nice people. Effective communication is an ongoing endeavor that takes conscious effort as well as considerable patience and maturity. According to Covey (1992), communication, or mutual understanding, "is a prerequisite to problem-solving and one of the most fundamental skills in life" (p. 138). Therefore, you must heighten your awareness of the words you speak, the message you intend to send, and how well you are understood (Knowles & Cole, 1996).

Developing Effective Communication Skills

The need for you and your cooperating teacher to achieve an understanding regarding "the purposes, roles, and responsibilities during supervision is generally accepted in principle, yet it is hard to achieve" (McIntyre & Byrd, 1998, p. 412). A critical component in developing this understanding with your cooperating teacher is **trust.** In fact, according to Williams (1989), trust is necessary in order to develop the positive interpersonal relationship with your cooperating teacher, your supervisor, and others that you need in order to receive approval and recognition.

> **Trust** is equated with the confidence and integrity, commitment, and caring that are inherent in professionalism.

   Development of trust takes a commitment of time and energy, but it is worth the effort. According to Covey (1992), "When trust is high, communication is easy, effortless, instantaneous, and accurate. When trust is low, communication is extremely difficult, exhausting, and ineffective" (p. 138). We acknowledge that communication is a shared responsibility. However, you can develop skills that will enable you to go a long way toward creating the sense of trust and openness you desire in a support relationship. These skills will be valuable in building effective relationships with your children and their families; these relationships will be discussed in Chapter 9.

Effective Communication and Nonverbal Behaviors

Research indicates that your **nonverbal behaviors** may enhance or impede the communication of your spoken language. This concept is particularly important when you consider that between 65% and 90% of all communication is transmitted nonverbally (Bowers & Flinders, 1990; Ornstein & Lasley, 2000; Thomas et al., 2001). In fact, nonverbal messages may represent the speaker's intent more accurately than her spoken words (Pugach & Johnson, 1995). Therefore, as you speak with your cooperating teacher and others, you must be aware of what messages you are inadvertently sending with your body position, facial expression, and movements.

> **Nonverbal behaviors** refer to the silent messages transmitted to others by body language.

   For example, posture, gestures, intonation, and rate of speech can all enhance or impede the communication process. You may even want to have yourself videotaped as you communicate with children and teachers. Think about nonverbal communication signals and their possible implications, such as those listed in Figure 3.3, as you observe yourself and others (Olsen & Fuller, 1998). Of course, you do not want to be in the position of second-guessing every movement, but increased awareness on your part can help prevent misunderstandings. Therefore, appropriate nonverbal behaviors can help you establish effective relationships.

Behavior	Implication
Leaning forward	Interest and cooperation
Arms folded across chest	Defensiveness or suspicion
Open or "steepled" hands	Cooperation and confidence
Picking or pinching flesh	Frustration or insecurity
Throat clearing; rapid speech	Frustration or nervousness
Chin stroking; tilted head	Evaluation or judgment
Coat unbuttoned	Cooperation and confidence

FIGURE 3.3 Nonverbal Communication Signals

In addition, you must be aware that nonverbal communication is symbolic in that it changes meaning, depending on cultural experiences (Martin & Nakayama, 2000). Gestures and movements that are acceptable in one culture are taboo in another. Therefore, it is important to understand the cultural background of the children in your care and their families. These matters will be discussed in later chapters.

Importance of Verbal Behaviors and Active Listening

Because language can be ambiguous at best, active listening skills are critical to the process of effective communication. The positive professional relationships you desire require that you achieve mutual understanding with others. Effective listening skill can serve as "a 'bridge' between the nonverbal and verbal forms of communication because it incorporates elements of both and affects both" (Thomas et al., 2001, p. 172). Therefore, active listening will improve interpersonal communication.

The active listening skills listed in Figure 3.4 will help you improve the quality of your communication as you listen carefully to what is being said. Each step does not have to be followed in every conversation you have.

Figure 3.4 **Active Listening Skills**

- Respond by restating what you hear in your own words.
  "You are saying that . . ." or "You are feeling . . ."
- Clarify your understanding by asking the speaker to restate his words.
  "I'm confused about . . ." or "Let me try to explain what I think you are saying."
- Check your perception of the speaker's feelings
  "Am I correct in thinking that you feel . . . about . . . ?"

(Based on Thomas et al., 2001)

However, you may find that through practice, you will use many of these skills automatically.

Active listening skills generally encourage further communication. It has been said that we communicate who we are, and as individuals we differ markedly. Therefore, we should not be surprised that the words and phrases we use may become so distorted that the messages we intend to convey are not necessarily those that are received. Active listening is a valuable means of helping us achieve common understanding (Brill & Levine, 2002; Egan, 2002; O'Hair, Friedrich, Wiemann, & Wiemann, 1995; Olsen & Fuller, 2003).

You may consider yourself a good listener. Perhaps you have never really thought about this. Reflect for a moment on how you would evaluate your own skills as a listener or as a communicator. The questions in Figure 3.5, adapted from O'Hair et al. (1995), may give you some insights.

You may find it interesting to have someone who knows you well rate you on these same items and compare the results. Your actual listening skills may differ from your perceived skills. There may be some listening skills that you want to improve as you interact with others in a professional environment or you may be a better listener than you realized. The results of the self-assessment in Figure 3.5 may give you some insights. Use them as you develop your effective communication skills.

As you answer these questions, respond with your initial reaction. Put a check in the box that most closely characterizes how you see yourself.

Statement	Yes	No	Unsure
1. People tell me that I am a good listener.	☐	☐	☐
2. I tend to interrupt people when they are speaking.	☐	☐	☐
3. I am good at letting people know that I understand what they are saying.	☐	☐	☐
4. I need to have information repeated.	☐	☐	☐
5. I can tell when people are really listening to me.	☐	☐	☐
6. I consider myself to be a good listener.	☐	☐	☐
7. I can remember what people are saying to me.	☐	☐	☐
8. My mind tends to wander when people are talking to me.	☐	☐	☐
9. I am a better listener in some situations than in others.	☐	☐	☐
10. I am good at asking questions when I don't understand what is being said.	☐	☐	☐

Source: Selected statements adapted from *Competent Communication* by O'Hair, D., Friedrich, G. W., Wiemann, J. M., & Wiemann, M. O., 1995. New York: St. Martin's Press. Copyright 1995 by St. Martin's Press.

FIGURE 3.5 Listening Skills Self-Assessment

Another approach to developing effective communication is a behavioral model developed by Bergan (1977). This model can be used in conjunction with the active listening skills previously discussed. Bergan describes three dimensions of communication, the second of which includes five verbal prompts:

1. Specification: "Tell me more about . . ."
2. Evaluation: "How do you feel about . . . ?"
3. Inferences: "It seems to me . . ."
4. Summarizations: "Let's review my understanding of . . ."
5. Validation: "Can we conclude that . . . ?" (Kampwirth, 2003, p. 113)

Each of these prompts can be worded as a question in order to gather information and clarify understanding. Although the model was originally developed for behavioral consultation, it is useful for developing mutual understanding in many settings.

While you are engaging in dialogue, do not be afraid of silences in your conversation. Silences may indicate confusion or they may be opportunities for reflection. So, as you listen, "hear the silence, [and] observe the nonverbal responses" (Zachary, 2000, p. 27). Remember that active listening is also an attitude, not just a collection of scripted skills. It embodies a nonjudgmental desire to hear and understand, and it can lead to mutually supportive relationships.

❖ "GROWING PAINS": STAGES OF DEVELOPMENT

As you progress through your student teaching experience, you may find that your relationship with your cooperating teacher passes through several stages of development. While moving through these stages, you will have opportunities to establish boundaries and to negotiate your responsibilities. Knowing the challenges other student teachers typically encounter may help you navigate through the exciting but often turbulent waters of your own experience.

Stages of Student Teaching

Stages of student teaching development have been a topic of interest since 1925, when Bagley first described seven distinct stages that focused on the student's performance of classroom tasks (Armentrout, 1927). Interest in this topic continued throughout the 20th century; various authors outlined three to seven stages (Piland & Anglin, 1993). For example, according to

Schwebel, Schwebel, Schwebel, and Schwebel (1996), elements of the following four stages and characteristics are typically described by students in their journals:

- Stage 1: *The Early Days* may be somewhat overwhelming because so much information about children, teaching materials, and procedures must be absorbed in a short amount of time.
- Stage 2: *Becoming a Member of the Teaching Team* is a period of rising morale and establishing a sense of belonging to the class and the teaching team.
- Stage 3: *Soloing as a Teacher* is a time for solo teaching; morale may fluctuate, depending on feedback received from cooperating teachers, supervisors, and students.
- Stage 4: *Feeling Like a Teacher* is a settling-down period that focuses on working with the children and building confidence (pp. 23–26).

Interestingly enough, theories describing stages of development have been applied not only to student teachers but also to beginning teachers within the first 3 years of their careers. Both student teachers and beginning teachers share the same three stages of concerns that were originally described by Fuller and Brown (1975): survival, task, and pupil. During the *survival* phase, teachers and student teachers focus on issues of control and perception, such as their ability to provide classroom management and discipline and whether or not the children and supervisors like them. During the *task* phase, their concerns center primarily on the work to be accomplished. For example, they focus on their own knowledge of appropriate teaching strategies, whether or not they have the necessary materials and supplies, and their ability to manage time.

Finally, during the *pupil* phase, their concerns shift from their own performance to the well-being of others. They focus on the children's academic, emotional, and physical needs. This progression through stages of concerns is not linear; it has been described as overlapping, cyclical, and complex (Martin, Chiodo, & Chang, 2001; Smith & Sanche, 1993). As you progress through your own student teaching practicum, you will be asked to reflect on your development as a teacher. You may consider where your own concerns fit into the stage theory of teacher development. At some point on your way to "feeling like a teacher," you may discover that your concerns shift from being self-directed to being other-directed.

As you become more accustomed to your new teaching role, you may begin to feel a little pressured by fatigue and time constraints. You will benefit from taking a few moments to maintain contact with peers who are also dealing with the turbulent highs and lows that accompany this adventure. The early childhood student teachers who meet as a peer support group often comment that it helps them to hear what others are experiencing. Some of their reflections may be helpful to you as well.

Comments During the Early Days

Students typically express a feeling of exhaustion tempered with a desire to do more in the classroom. What are you feeling in the early weeks of your student teaching experience?

Comments on Becoming a Member of the Teaching Team

Generally, after a few days or weeks, students express elation as they develop a sense of belonging. At the same time, they begin evaluating their environment and the people in it. If you are feeling a mixture of emotions right now, this is normal.

Comments on Soloing as a Teacher

This is the time period you have been anticipating throughout your months and/or years of preparation. The dream is that you will have a perfect experience in which your students demonstrate their learning. Furthermore, your students and their parents, your cooperating teacher, and your college supervisor will appreciate your efforts. This is often true, but unfortunately, the reality is sometimes quite different. You may struggle with unexpected discipline issues or with a cooperating teacher who provides little or no feedback. Student teaching, like life, rarely follows the prescribed plan.

Comments on Feeling Like a Teacher

This is the phase in which you may feel that you are coasting through relatively calm waters. You may find yourself worrying less about your own success or failure. Tasks such as planning lessons and maintaining discipline become routinely manageable. Your focus may become more child-centered. In other words, you concern yourself primarily with helping each child learn and feel successful in your classroom. As one student phrased it during the final weeks of student teaching, "During our time together in the classroom, it's all about *them*, not about me." When you reach that point, you will know that you are indeed a real teacher.

Voices of Reality: Student Teachers Speak

I am feeling slightly overwhelmed as I listen to conversations peppered with such alphabet soup ingredients as I.L.S., T.S.S., and O.D.D., and as I peruse the encyclopedia-sized curriculum that is to be [taught] in a mere 180 days, but I suppose that my current state of confusion is a normal part of this stage of the training process. . . . I feel like I'm becoming a hermit, kind of like "Shrek"! While my friends are out flitting around, I'm holed up in the quad, lounging around in my pj's at 7:00 in the evening. I'm having a severe energy drought.

Karla S.

I have a package at the post office that's been there for 3 days and I can't pick it up because I get home late! Right now I'm just worried about how long I'll be able to keep up this momentum and patience for teaching.

Keeley N.

I am anxious to start my "full-time" [teaching]. I can't wait to see my successes and failures. I am frustrated that I cannot help the kids with their personal life because of all their problems (divorce, violence, abuse, etc.).

Angie D.

❖ FINAL THOUGHTS

You may begin to breathe a little more easily as you consider the thoughts of other student teachers in relation to your own experiences. Therefore, your mixed feelings are normal as you navigate the turbulent waters of your teaching career. In fact, Brookfield (1990) states the following:

> Teaching is the educational equivalent of white-water rafting. Periods of apparent calm are interspersed with sudden frenetic turbulence. Boredom alternates with excitement, reflection with action. As we successfully negotiate rapids fraught with danger, we feel a sense of self-confident exhilaration. As we start downstream after capsizing, our self-confidence is shaken and we are awash in self-doubt. All teachers sooner or later capsize, and all teachers worth their salt regularly ask themselves whether or not they are doing the right thing. (p. 2)

Although Brookfield's work is directed to the teaching of adults in higher education classrooms, his perspectives on the teaching-learning process apply equally well to students and cooperating teachers in early childhood settings. Therefore, if you feel yourself capsizing from time to time, you should consider these mishaps to be opportunities for reflection and learning.

ACTIVITIES FOR REFLECTION AND ACTION

1. Keep an anecdotal communication log. Note a time when you feel good about the communication between you and your cooperating teacher. Note a time when you think the communication could be improved. Reflect on the verbal and nonverbal communication strategies employed in each instance.

2. As you progress through your practicum or student teaching experience, try to decide where you fit into each of the four stages of student teaching: Stage 1: *The Early Days*, Stage 2: *Becoming a Member of the Team*, Stage 3: *Soloing as a Teacher*, and Stage 4: *Feeling Like a Teacher*. Do you spend more time in one stage than another? Do you complete all four stages? What examples can you think of from your experiences that determine your current stage? Perhaps you would label the stages differently. You may wish to develop your own descriptors for the stages you experience.

3. During your practicum or student teaching experience, you will have opportunities to interact with people who have differing viewpoints. During these interactions, reflect upon a time when you used your active listening skills to understand someone else's viewpoint. Write a description of the conversation that includes the following: how you paraphrased what you thought the other person was saying, how you clarified your understanding by asking the person to restate her view if there was still confusion, and how you checked your understanding by summarizing the key points of the discussion.

4. *Portfolio*: This written example of your effective communication can be included in your portfolio.

CHAPTER 4

Guiding Young Children in the Classroom

One looks back with appreciation to the brilliant teachers, but with gratitude to those who touched our human feelings. The curriculum is so much necessary raw material, but warmth is the vital element for the growing plant and for the soul of the child.

Carl Gustov Jung

Carl Jung's sentiments relate well to a discussion of classroom management and discipline. The young children whose lives you touch will remember whether or not they believed you cared about them much more than the perfect lesson you taught or the beautiful visual aid you spent hours creating. The learning environment you create will speak to your children. Is it warm and inviting? Is it aesthetically pleasing? Does it contain child-centered organized spaces accessible to all children, including those with special needs? Equally important, do you create a safe learning climate that communicates your concern for each child entrusted to your care? Your ability to develop supportive relationships with your children will enable you to guide individual and group behavior constructively. Although the curriculum, the instruction, and the planning skills are important, you must create a climate of warmth in which the souls of your young children can flourish. Only by touching their human feelings can you impact their lives in profound ways.

Metaphorical Perspective

Many student teachers want their classroom to be a warm, nurturing environment characterized by mutual respect, a sense of caring, and friendship. Then they encounter the reality of excitable, potentially disruptive young children. Frequently, these children may alter the student teacher's perspective from that of a nurturing caregiver to that of a custodial controller (Weinstein,

Voices of Reality: Student Teachers Speak

When I think of my class, I think of twenty happy little springs tightly coiled, ready to unwind and start bouncing all over the room if I let my guard down even a little. I'm having fun though!

Angie D.

I am concerned about not having control of the class. Sometimes, especially in the afternoon, I feel like this is a zoo, and I am a zookeeper. But I want them to respect me and also see me as their friend.

Jamal D.

Woolfolk, Dittmeier, & Shanker, 1994). As you progress through your student teaching, you may want to consider the metaphors you use to describe your children and your role as a student teacher. For example, do you view yourself as a circus ringmaster, a guard, a parent? How do the metaphors you use reflect your approach to classroom management and discipline?

❖ EMPHASIS ON CLASSROOM MANAGEMENT

Classroom management is usually an area of concern for student teachers. Teachers are expected to be good classroom managers. Administrators, parents, and others may equate good teaching with good classroom management. In fact, you may be tempted to judge your ability to be a good teacher by your skills in the area of classroom management alone. Thus, the significance of this topic cannot be downplayed.

How will you prevent disobedience? You may wonder what you will do, for example, if a student tells you "no" or "shut up" or worse. How will you manage all the little details inherent in the daily schedules of young children? Are you adept at multitasking? Can you keep track of daily classroom routines, including nonacademic tasks such as attendance, snack and/or lunch routines, and special areas such as art/music/library/computer lab/physical education, as well as regularly scheduled support services such as speech/language therapy for children with special needs? Scheduling alone becomes a challenge. On top of that, you must keep transitions short and smooth so that little if any time is lost, plan and carry out creative activities that meet the needs of all children, keep everyone on task, and make sure that everyone cooperates pleasantly, with few if any disruptions. If you think this is a challenge, you are correct. Do not be overly concerned, however. This is a challenge you can manage and enjoy!

You will find your own style of classroom management. You may not be a cheerleader like Jackson L. or a zookeeper like Jamal D., but you will discover strategies that work for you as you learn to guide children's behavior and manage their environment.

Distinct Areas of Classroom Management

Some differences exist among the various definitions of classroom management. Generally, however, classroom management includes both the preventative and reactive measures a teacher uses to create an environment in which effective teaching and learning can take place (Duke, 1987). People commonly think of a well-managed classroom as one in which children cooperate with the teacher and conduct themselves appropriately (Brophy, 1988). However, Machado and Botnarescue (2001) favor a more comprehensive definition that includes five separate areas: "(1) the physical arrangement of the classroom(s); (2) curriculum choices; (3) time management; (4) managing classroom routines; and (5) the guidance function" (p. 183).

For our purposes, we will address these areas in reverse order. We will begin by discussing guidance and discipline because this will probably be an area of immediate concern to you, at least initially. Next, we will address classroom routines and time management, areas of concern for many student teachers. We will consider curriculum choices and physical arrangement of the room last because those are areas you will probably have little control over as a student teacher.

❖ DISCIPLINE AND GUIDANCE

Teachers have reported that misbehavior by individual children is their primary cause of job-related stress (Feitler & Tokar, 1992). They may judge their own effectiveness by the degree of cooperation they receive in the classroom. The absence of misconduct, however, does not guarantee effective professional practice.

Definition of Terms

The term *discipline* is commonly defined as whatever teachers do to help children behave in an acceptable manner in school (Charles, 1996, 2002). Unfortunately, "whatever teachers do" is often viewed as punishment to force children's obedience. Punishment may cause children to obey, but it can also teach disturbing lessons about the use of power (Clewett, 1988; Gartrell, 1995; Kohn, 1996; NAEYC, 1998).

In contrast, a more humane and perhaps more effective approach to behavior management stems from the derivation of the word discipline. Consider that it "comes from the same root as disciple, and the implication is that to discipline is to guide and teach" (Betz, 1994, p. 14). Knowing the derivation of the word may help focus your thoughts on guidance rather than on punishment as you develop your own philosophy of discipline.

One of the questions you will inevitably be asked when you interview for a teaching position is "What is your philosophy of discipline or behavior management?" You should have at least a tentative response to that question in your mind right now as you observe and assume more and more teaching responsibilities. You may find it helpful to consider your answers to several questions as you formulate your philosophy (see Figure 4.1). Reflecting on these questions and talking with your cooperating teacher and college supervisor will help you articulate your own approach to behavior management.

Guidance Approach

If our starting point for discussion is the root of the word discipline, then we should adopt a guidance approach to teaching children in a positive manner. This guidance approach develops from observing your children, knowing your children, and understanding their developmental levels. The value of careful observation or "kid watching" has been documented

Figure 4.1 Sample Questions to Guide Goal Development

- What is the purpose of discipline?
- What does effective discipline look like? Feel like?
- Do you believe that children are innately good or bad?
- Do you believe that children are innately motivated?
- What is your attitude concerning conflict?
- How should problems between children or between children and adults be solved?

repeatedly as a means to meet children's developmental needs (Beaty, 2002; Flicker & Hoffman, 2002; Nicholson & Shipstead, 2002).

As you observe, you may want to consider the following questions based on Nelson, Erwin, and Duffy (1998b):

- How can I help this child feel capable?
- How can I help this child feel a sense of belonging and significance?
- How can I help this child learn respect, cooperation, and problem-solving skills?
- How can I get into this child's world and understand his developmental process?
- How can I use problems as opportunities for learning—for both this child and me? (p. 181)

Focus on the Child

Notice that the focus of these questions is the child. We are reflecting on what is best for the child's development rather than what will enhance your performance as a teacher. This is an important change in focus for most student teachers at a time when they want to shine and perform at their best.

Individual guidance talks with a child are a positive way to reduce mistaken behavior.

Teaching Self-Discipline

Gartrell (2002) recommends replacing discipline with a comprehensive guidance approach in order "to reduce mistaken behavior by holding developmentally appropriate expectations for children and by teaching democratic life skills" (p. 36). The goal of discipline, then, is to teach the child to regulate her own behavior. Brazelton and Sparrow (2001) provide an example of appropriate responses to a child's biting when at age 1 the child bites a caregiver and at age 2 she bites a friend. In both instances, this behavior may be characterized as exploratory behavior typical of the developmental age. When teachers or parents either ignore the behavior or overreact, the child will continue biting "as if to say, 'I'm out of control. Help me!'" (p. 40). This situation provides a teachable moment for guidance. The child may be receptive to learning a replacement behavior when she feels the urge to bite. Brazelton & Sparrow (2001) gives examples of suggesting to the child that she bite a "lovey" or even a rubber dog bone instead. The suggestion to use a rubber dog bone may seem a bit insensitive, depending on your attitude about teaching a child to bite a bone like a dog, but the general concept of replacement behaviors is helpful.

Guidance for Infants and Toddlers

Some of you will be caregivers and early childhood teachers in various settings with infants and toddlers. The supportive care you give includes helping children regulate their emotions as they develop an understanding of their environment and the people with whom they interact. The responsive guidance you provide must be developmentally appropriate for these young learners.

As an infant-toddler teacher, you must plan and monitor the learning environment to ensure the safety and emotional well-being of the children. A discussion of how to manage the physical space, the emotional climate, and the daily routines will be presented in Chapter 5. An appropriate environment will contribute to your ability to provide children with positive behavioral guidance.

Accordingly, an appropriate environment will allow the infant or toddler to explore her environment safely. The child can initiate her own learning by interacting with people and objects. You can help the infant or toddler develop a positive sense of self by creating a nurturing environment in which she feels liked and accepted. In fact, "creating a warm, caring, subjective relationship with the infant [or toddler] is more than nice; it significantly contributes to a child's positive sense of self" (Lally & Mangione, 2006, p. 18). Therefore, the physical and emotional environment itself can be considered an important part of the developmentally appropriate curriculum.

As the infant or toddler becomes mobile, you will have opportunities to guide behavior. However, keep in mind that, for the most part, you cannot control a child's behavior. You can, however, control your reaction to that behavior. If you "feel responsible for a child's behavior, you set up a no-win situation, wherein you must try to control the child, which is impossible" (Watson & Swim, 2008, p. 150). For example, if an infant or a toddler in your care cries despite your best efforts to assess her needs and to calm her, you may feel yourself getting tense and upset. You may not be able to stop the crying, but you can alter your reaction to it by asking another caregiver to take responsibility for the child for a few minutes. Often, a short break is all you will need to calm yourself. If the child's crying continues, then consult with your cooperating teacher. She may be able to determine the cause of the child's distress and offer suggestions or she may decide that the child's family should be contacted (Watson & Swim, 2008).

Guidance of toddlers often takes the form of setting limits, establishing appropriate consequences, providing choices, and redirecting the child's attention. You may set limits by saying "no" to behaviors that could cause harm to the toddler, to others, or to property. Try to anticipate what these behaviors may be and keep the list short for young children. Keep in mind that you should guide the child using positive words (Hearron & Hildebrand, 2009; Watson & Swim, 2008). For example, a toddler may try to climb up on a chair. Instead of telling her not to stand on chairs, tell her that chairs are for sitting. You may model the appropriate behavior and then redirect her to a more appropriate activity.

As you guide young children, consider the natural and logical consequences of behavior. A *natural consequence* is a naturally occurring result of a particular behavior. For example, if a toddler adamantly refuses to wear gloves or mittens on a cold day, then the natural consequence is that her hands will get cold. If she runs in a play area strewn with blocks, then the natural consequence is that she may fall. You must monitor her behavior so that the potential natural consequences do not jeopardize her safety and well-being. A *logical consequence* is a result of a particular behavior that would not occur without the intervention of yourself or someone else. For example, if a child refuses to help at clean-up time, then the logical consequence may be that she waits to choose another activity until after she helps to clean up (Dreikers & Cassel, 1972; Kaiser & Rasminsky, 2007; Marion, 2007; Watson & Swim, 2008). You can also encourage participation by making clean-up an enjoyable activity with a song.

Even so, you may expect that toddlers will say "no" to you at times. This is a typical developmental phase that you have probably heard described as the "terrible twos." You cannot control this behavior. Saying "no" is part of the child's developing sense of self and independence, and, as such, it is a positive rather than a negative behavior. You may find that some toddlers will say "no" to every directive or suggestion you give. In that case, you may want to try giving choices. For example, at snack time, ask, "Do you want a cracker or an apple slice with your juice today?" Throughout the day, there will be opportunities for choice-making. Just make sure that each choice you give is a positive one that is acceptable to you. Children will become confused if you offer a choice and then refuse it later (Hearron & Hildebrand, 2009).

Supportive Time Away

The child at age 3 needs help in setting limits. Reminders and patient repetition are appropriate. You may find that a child, by age 3, needs to be removed calmly from an excitable situation and reassured. Some early childhood teachers set aside a quiet area in their room for one or two chairs. If a child becomes upset and needs to be removed from a group activity to calm down, she is accompanied by a caring adult who will sit with her, help her talk about her feelings, and provide guidance related to appropriate behaviors (Hearron & Hildebrand, 2009). Other teachers provide a *time-away* area or a *thinking chair* that the child can retreat to until she feels more cooperative. The author prefers *talk-it-over chairs* to an isolated time-away area or a thinking chair. Isolation can too easily feel like punishment or abandonment to a young child, and that is never acceptable. Accordingly, a time-away area can be an effective place for the out-of-control child to take a break, but she will benefit more from a caring adult who accompanies her to that area for support and guidance (Cook, Klein, & Tessier, 2008; Miller, 2007).

Time-out is sometimes used by educators and parents as a well-intentioned means of helping a child reduce disruptive or undesirable behaviors (Henniger, 2002; Porter, 1999). For example, this author has observed teachers warn a child, then remove her from a group activity, and then sit her in a time-out chair for a brief period to calm down. Other teachers have a quiet, private corner of their room called the *time-out corner* that serves the same purpose (Fields & Boesser, 2002; Nelson, Erwin, & Duffy, 1998a). The idea is that removing the child from participation in a desired activity will cause a decrease in the unwanted behavior; the child will have the opportunity to calm down and determine when she is ready to return to the group (Crosser, 2005; Jones & Jones, 2004; Kyle & Rogien, 2004).

However, there is great potential for misuse and abuse of a time-out strategy. Keep in mind that some children may enjoy leaving an activity that they find unrewarding; for example, some children may not enjoy sharing news in circle time or interacting with others in group activities. They may prefer the quiet isolation of a time-out corner (Friend & Bursuck, 2009; Vaughn & Bos, 2009). Any time you isolate a child, you are denying her an opportunity to learn from you and others. A young child may not even understand why she is being isolated (Hearron & Hildebrand, 2009; Kaiser & Rasminsky, 2007). Worse, she may "develop a [negative] image, in her own eyes and in the eyes of other children that becomes a self-fulfilling prophecy" (Hearron & Hildebrand, 2009, p. 179). Furthermore, the isolation associated with time-out can be particularly damaging to a child from a culture that strongly values the sense of belonging to a community (Gonzalez-Mena, 2002, 2007). Sadly, there have been reported incidents in which time-out has been abused by isolating children for extended periods of time in confined spaces, such as the case of the ethical dilemma discussed later in this chapter. Therefore, time away with a caring adult is, in the author's opinion, a preferable choice.

In addition, if you have a child with special needs of age 3 or more in your program, you should ask if the child has an **Individual Education Plan (IEP).** Your cooperating teacher will share information that you need in order to interact appropriately with a child who has a diagnosed disability. You may be allowed to read the IEP. This document contains important information. Some IEPs specify what strategies may or may not be used to guide the behavior of a particular child. Similarly, children from birth to age 3 who have special needs and qualify for early intervention services may have an **Individual Family Service Plan (IFSP).** This document contains important information about assessment, services to meet the child's individual needs, implementation of services, and monitoring the child's progress. Just as in the case of an IEP, if a child in your care has an IFSP, you should know the contents of the document and discuss them with your cooperating teacher. The families of *all* children should be involved in discussions about issues of behavioral guidance as part of your frequent and regular communication process. Matters related to communication with diverse types of families will be discussed in more depth in Chapter 9.

You should follow the behavior management system of your cooperating teacher and the policies of your center or school. If you have any questions or concerns, always discuss them with your cooperating teacher and your college supervisor.

Modeling Effective Strategies

You must model the behaviors you want children to emulate. For example, you may get tired or stressed after dealing with children whose temperaments cause occasional difficulties. During these times, remember that children can sense your emotions, and they will be observing your behavior.

Individualized Education Plan (IEP) refers to an individualized written service plan that results from a collaborative process to provide education and support services for children from age 3 to age 21. It is a child-centered plan that contains information such as the child's current levels of functioning, special services to be provided, annual goals, short-term objectives, and methods of assessment.

Individualized Family Service Plan (IFSP) refers to an individualized written service plan that results from a collaborative process to provide early intervention services for children from birth to age 3 and their families who have identified special needs. The focus is on the priorities, the strengths, and the needs of the child's family.

You may have to model positive self-talk and restraint to remain calm when teaching children whose temperaments clash with your own.

One effective strategy to model for your children is the use of "I messages" (Gordon, 1974). Use of the pronoun *I* allows you to communicate your feelings about a behavior as well as an explanation of why your feelings are important. For example, a child interrupts you when you are reading a story to the class. You can say, "I get frustrated when you interrupt me while I am reading aloud. You distract the other children, and they cannot listen to the story." This process allows you to identify your feelings and help the child understand the effect of her behavior on others.

As you are learning to use I messages effectively, you may wish to practice stating your feelings by using a formula. The three basic parts of this formula are as follows (based on Gordon, 1974):

1. **I feel...** (happy, sad, frustrated, etc.)
2. **when you...** (interrupt, yell, call out, etc.)
3. **because...** (I cannot hear others, children cannot listen to the story, etc.)

This is a skill that you can use in your professional life as well as in your personal life to confront your feelings about a person's troubling behavior in a nonjudgmental manner. Activities at the end of the chapter provide opportunities for you to practice giving and receiving I messages.

At the same time, you need to focus on the feelings of the children in your care. As Faber and Mazlish (1982) emphasize, children "need to have their feelings accepted and respected" (p. 27). That does not mean, however, that you must accept the actions that go along with those feelings. For example, if one child hits another, you can tell her that you see how angry she is. Then you can tell her to use words to say what she wants and to keep her hands to herself. By telling her *what to do* rather than *what not to do*, you are coaching her in a positive manner. You are giving a name to the child's feeling; you are also providing her with guidance (Faber & Mazlish, 1982).

Behavior as Communication

Children communicate to us through their behavior. If you know your children, you can use the messages they are sending to discover their needs and feelings. Then you will be able to choose appropriate guidance strategies for each child.

Some of these behaviors are indicators of serious problems (see Figure 4.2). If you have reason to believe that a child may be in potential danger, discuss your concerns with your cooperating teacher. As the *NAEYC Code of Ethical Conduct* indicates, you have a professional obligation to advocate for young children who cannot advocate for themselves. At the same time, you

Figure 4.2 Sample Behaviors as Communication Messages

Signs of Stress	Signs of Abuse	Signs of Unmet Need	Signs of Skill Deficit
Fearful	Passive	Fidgeting	Difficulty following
Withdrawn	Withdrawn	Fussiness	directions
Aggression	Inability to play	Inattention	Difficulty with
Nail biting	Food hoarding	Disruptive (unmet	social interactions
Nervous laughter	Lack of empathy	needs such as rest,	Easily distracted
Self-injurious behavior	Regression	food, exercise,	Impatient
		security, acceptance)	

(Based on Marion, 2003, pp. 74–78)

must be careful not to judge a situation too quickly. Your cooperating teacher's judgment and professional guidance will be invaluable in these matters.

❖ GUIDANCE STRATEGIES

The guidance approach to discipline involves teaching children social problem-solving skills. Social skills are not innate. Children must be taught to share, to get along well with others, to name their feelings, and to handle anger appropriately. As young children learn these skills, there will inevitably be mistaken behaviors that provide teachable moments for the development of self-regulation.

Conflict Resolution

Although many models of conflict management exist, Gartrell (2002) recommends using a simple plan that he calls the *five-finger approach* (see Figure 4.3). This plan may be applied in both preschool and early primary settings.

The five-finger model can be used as part of the process in a number of guidance situations. For example, instead of the old-fashioned lecture *at* a child, this model can be part of a private guidance talk *with* a child. In a conversation with a child, you can encourage empathy for other people's feelings. You can also help her brainstorm other behavioral choices to use the next time a similar situation occurs (Gartrell, 2002, 2006a).

Figure 4.3   Five-Finger Problem-Solving Model

- **Thumb: ("Cool off")**   Calm down to set the stage for the process of mediation.
- **Pointer: ("Identify")**   Children use words to identify the problem. Teacher may help as needed.
- **Tall guy: ("Brainstorm")**   Children brainstorm ideas for problem solution. Teacher may help as needed.
- **Ringer: ("Go for it")**   Children choose a solution to try.
- **Pinky: ("Follow-up")**   Teacher monitors children as they try the solution. Teacher may encourage and guide as needed.

(Based on Gartrell, 2002, p. 37)

Class Meetings

The five-finger model can also be part of the class meeting process. Class meetings have become customary in many primary grades, but older preschool children are not too young for class meetings, too. In fact, class meetings, sometimes called *community meetings,* are often encouraged as a means to reduce a young child's anxiety, provide a reassuring sense of belonging, develop language skills, and encourage the development of empathy (Gartrell, 2006b; McClurg, 1998).

Class or community meetings are an appropriate forum for encouraging children to develop problem-solving and self-regulation skills. Some teachers hold these meetings daily, others weekly. The frequency is not as important as the process, although regular meetings are recommended. Benefits include the following:

- Awareness of other people's perspectives, feelings, and experiences
- Development of empathy
- Self-awareness
- Empowerment of children
- A sense of inclusion rather than exclusion
- Development of consensus-making ability
- Development of positive social skills
- Development of listening skills
- Development of problem-solving skills

The guidelines in Figure 4.4 have been suggested to maximize the benefits of effective meetings (Gartrell, 2002; McClurg, 1998; Styles, 2001). These are

---

Figure 4.4 **Guidelines for Class/Community Meetings**

- Children and teacher sit in a close circle
- Teacher's role: group member, coach when necessary, secretary
- Agenda set by the children
- Shared leadership of the meeting
- Group members give and receive compliments or "appreciations"
- Five-finger problem-solving steps followed
- Questions for clarification
- Summarize choices made by consensus

---

only guidelines; they can be adapted to meet the needs of your children and your teaching situation.

Class meetings are more commonly used with school-age children. However, even preschool children can learn simple strategies of conflict resolution. An effective model involves the use of the **Peace Table** (Gillespie and Chick, 2001; Peace Learning Center, 1997).

Peace Table

Gillespie and Chick (2001) believe that preschoolers can learn to negotiate solutions to their problems and resolve conflicts peacefully. Use of the Peace Table is an effective strategy to help children develop positive social skills in a caring community. The Peace Table is a calm place in a neutral location where children and a caring adult talk, listen, and develop a plan for solving a conflict. You can help young children give words to their feelings and develop empathy for the feelings of others. You model the speaking and listening skills that you want them to use as you facilitate this process. With assistance, young children can learn to identify the problem, suggest possible solutions, choose a solution to try, and decide if their solution works.

From time to time, you will find young children whose problems are more serious than you or your cooperating teacher will be able to handle through positive guidance practices alone. At these times, do not hesitate to ask for assistance. Part of your role as an early childhood educator is knowing when and how to be an advocate for the child and her family. A collaborative effort involving the child's family, senior staff, and support personnel such as mental health professionals and/or special educators may be necessary.

Peace Table refers to a quiet area in which children learn peace-building skills of respecting another's point of view, communicating to discuss the cause of the problem, and collaborating to solve a problem.

❖ ADDITIONAL BEHAVIOR MANAGEMENT TECHNIQUES

As you have observed in various field experiences prior to student teaching, a wide variety of behavior management strategies are being used. Although the author favors using the positive guidance approaches previously discussed, a brief overview of other strategies may be helpful to you.

Assertive Discipline

This behavior management system has been used for over 30 years in early childhood primary classrooms and with older children. It focuses on teachers' rights and children's rights. In other words, teachers have a right to require appropriate behavior from children, and children have a right to learn in a disruption-free environment. Teachers must be consistent, specific in their expectations, and provide clear, predetermined consequences. Teachers also use I messages such as "I like the way you raised your hand and waited to be called on" or "I don't like it when you run in this room" (Canter, 1976; Canter & Canter, 1992).

Although it can be effective, this approach has come under attack by critics who suggest that "it ignores methods for improving the quality of instruction and discourages the teacher from examining the specific classroom events that may be involved in the child's challenging behaviors" (Newcomer, 2003, p. 273). Even so, assertive discipline strategies allow the teacher to communicate positive behavioral expectations in a specific manner. An assertive teacher also knows exactly what appropriate consequences she will provide for inappropriate behavior in order to maximize her influence. She is in control (Canter, 1976).

Logical Consequences

The concept of *logical consequences* was developed by Rudolph Dreikurs, an Austrian psychiatrist. Dreikurs considers logical consequences to be the reasonable results of any behavior. The child's action must make sense in terms of the adult's reaction (Charles, 1996). The logical consequences must be developed cooperatively with the children and must be applied consistently. Accordingly, children choose the consequences of their appropriate or inappropriate behaviors (Newcomer, 2003). For example, a child who throws sand at the sand table center will be allowed to play somewhere else so that the other children will be safe. She will not be sent to a time-out chair to think about what she has done wrong because that would be a form of punishment.

Dreikurs maintained that children generally misbehave for four reasons: to get attention, to get power, to get revenge, or to withdraw (Machado & Botnarescue, 2001; Porter, 1999). Through careful observation of the child's reaction to being corrected, you can generally identify the child's goal. For example, a child whose goal is to get attention may snap her fingers and wave her arm in the air repeatedly. You can choose to ignore or extinguish the behavior. She may increase her finger snapping or arm waving for a while before reducing the behavior and ultimately stopping it. You must be prepared to continue ignoring the behavior and not get discouraged (Martin & Pear, 1999).

A child whose goal is to get power may become confrontational when corrected. One whose goal is revenge may become hostile or aggressive. If a child feels inadequate or hopeless, her goal may be withdrawal. You can often prevent undesirable behaviors by giving children choices, by making your expectations specific and clear, and by having children participate in developing the rules and their logical consequences (Machado & Botnarescue, 2001).

Glasser's Choice Theory

William Glasser is a psychiatrist whose early work includes *Reality Therapy* (1965) and *Schools without Failure* (1969). He emphasizes the idea that people are rational beings who can control their behavioral choices. Children can be taught to behave in a responsible manner that reflects society's standards. Accordingly, teachers must help children make appropriate choices by suggesting alternatives if the child cannot do so for himself (Glasser, 1986). In his later writings, Glasser changed his focus from control to choice—for example, in *Choice Theory in the Classroom* (1988) and *Choice Theory: A New Psychology of Personal Freedom* (1998). Glasser's approach hinges on the belief that everyone has four equally important needs in addition to the basic need for survival:

- Need for belonging
- Need for power
- Need for freedom
- Need for fun

Glasser believes that these needs are so strong that we will behave in such a way as to have them met. He promotes the use of cooperative learning groups of no more than five students. These groups should be heterogeneous and changed periodically by the teacher. Children will develop a sense of belonging; the strong can help the weak; the children can make choices; and they will enjoy the process of learning together. Glasser calls this process *positive interdependence* (Glasser, 1988).

Limits or Class Rules

All effective teachers have a set of limits or classroom rules that they believe are essential. These rules may vary somewhat from teacher to teacher, but generally they are few in number (four to six) and they are stated in positive rather than negative terms. They are usually posted and visible. If the children are too young to read, the rules may consist of pictures.

Your cooperating teacher will have already established her limits with the children before you assume teaching responsibilities. Generally, you will be continuing the management policies she has put in place. Even so, the children are likely to test you to see if your limits are truly the same as your cooperating teacher's. You may need to give frequent reminders before they accept these limits from you. Student teachers often feel torn between their desire to be liked and their desire to have good classroom management.

Behavior Modification

Although the term *behavior modification* sometimes has a negative connotation, we all use behavior modification techniques to some extent. For example, we may clap a rhythm or flick the lights in a room to get everyone's attention. When we look at a child and smile, we are actually practicing behavior modification.

Proponents of behavior modification call our attention to critical aspects of good teaching such as the nature of teacher-child interactions, proximity, transitions, and reinforcement. Perhaps the most critical aspect of behavior modification is the positive feedback or constructive feedback that you give children. All children want attention. If they do not get it for appropriate behavior, they will get it any way they can. Research indicates that "effective behavior managers tally a 5:1:0 ratio of positive to corrective to negative feedback" (Newcomer, 2003, p. 254). Generally, you should give four to five times more social approval than social disapproval (Madsen & Madsen, 1974). That is why some teachers make a point of catching children being good. The social approval you use may be as simple as a smile, a nod, a glance, or a pat on the shoulder. This positive attention is usually a strong reinforcement for children.

Another aspect of behavior management involves the use of proximity and "withitness." You need to be moving throughout the room, aware of what each child is doing at all times. Your proximity allows you to give children continual verbal and nonverbal feedback. Some cooperating teachers will actually draw a diagram of your movements throughout the room to help you see where you spend most of your time. This is helpful in determining if you are circulating throughout the room or staying in one place too long.

What to Do When All Else Fails

There will be occasions when all your best plans do not work out as you wish. You tried Plan A and Plan B; your guidance efforts did not work, and perhaps you have already tried positive and corrective feedback. Now what?

This is the time to call for assistance. When you have a child who is not responding to the typical behavior management approaches already discussed, you should ask for suggestions before she creates a dangerous situation for herself and others. A team approach works best. Involve the child's family, an administrator, support personnel such as a mental health or behavior specialist, a social worker, and anyone else that you and your cooperating teacher believe would be appropriate. Time is of the essence. A meeting should be arranged as soon as possible. Describe the child's behavior in specific terms, and describe what you have tried and the results. The team can then brainstorm alternative approaches and appoint an objective person to observe the child.

In some cases, you may need to have a crisis intervention plan in place. This is a written plan developed by the team that states what should be done, by whom, and under what circumstances if the child creates a situation potentially dangerous to herself or others. All members of the team, including the child's family, should reach a consensus.

You may think that you do not need something as drastic as a crisis plan for children in the early childhood years, but unfortunately, occasions arise when it is necessary. One cooperating teacher and student teacher reported the following event during the college supervisor's visit. It occurred in rural Pennsylvania, but the same situation could have happened anywhere. Picture this:

Place: A primary class of 22 children, ages 6 and 7; 1 cooperating teacher and 1 student teacher.

When: Early spring day after lunch and a brief outdoor recess; no unusual or precipitating events.

Who: Child B, age 7, recently diagnosed as bipolar, with a history of defiant behavior. Placed on medications by a local physician.

What: Class returns from recess and is told to get ready for the math lesson. Child B refuses to sit down. Runs to the floor-to-ceiling bookcase and begins climbing on the shelves and throwing books off them.

Act: Activate Crisis Intervention Plan.
(a) Student teacher immediately removes the other children from the room and takes them to a designated area. Cooperating teacher uses the phone in the room to call for immediate assistance, then remains with child B and tries to talk calmly and reassuringly with the child. The child climbs down.

(b) Administrator arrives. Parent of Child B arrives. Child is removed to a medical facility for reevaluation of medications.

Next: Child B is returned to school with the support of a part-time teaching support staff (TSS) person.

The situations you encounter may not be as drastic as this one. Nevertheless, be prepared in advance with a backup plan, seek assistance from a team if necessary, and develop a crisis intervention plan if appropriate. No one expects you or your cooperating teacher to have all the answers.

❖ REAL-LIFE ETHICAL DILEMMAS

Unfortunately, as you proceed through your student teaching experience, you or someone you know may encounter an ethical dilemma regarding classroom management and discipline. How you handle these difficult situations and the lessons you learn from them will be important to your professional development. The following scenario is an actual story of a student teacher who recently found herself in the awkward position of wanting to please the cooperating teacher from whom she needed a positive evaluation and wanting to do the right thing for a young child. She turned to her college supervisor for help. As you read the scenario, you may want to refer to the *NAEYC Code of Ethical Conduct* (see Appendix A).

Setting the Stage

Miss A. is a student teacher in a second-grade classroom of a suburban school district. She has been in her placement for only 3 weeks during the fall semester. She gets along well with Mrs. B., her cooperating teacher, who is a well-respected teacher with 12 years' experience. When Miss A.'s college supervisor, Dr. R., makes her regular visits to the room for an observation and a conference, she routinely asks how things are going. This time, the student's reply is disturbing. Think about what you would do in this situation.

Student Teacher's Response

Miss A. relates the following:

All the children in this class are really great . . . except this one . . . J. At first, I thought he was charming. He always wanted to be near me. But now that I've been here awhile, I see that he is manipulative. We keep his desk separated from the rest because he is always disrupting the class. He chatters all the time, and he laughs inappropriately for no reason. . . . He demands immediate attention. When he doesn't get his way, he steals or lies or destroys the property of other children. I could go on and on. . . . Mrs. B. has started locking him in the closet for time-outs. Yesterday, he was in there for 40 minutes, and he wouldn't stop sticking his fingers out from under the door to bother the other children in the room. I'm not sure what to do. I'm not comfortable with having a 7-year-old locked in a dark closet at all, especially for a long time like 40 minutes. He has been in there 3 days so far this week for anywhere from 10 minutes to 30 or 40 minutes. I don't think that's the right thing to do, but I don't want to get my coop mad at me either. I feel like I have to choose between my coop and the child.

College Supervisor's Response

After the formal observation of the student teacher's lesson, the college supervisor decided to stay longer to observe the children and return later for a three-way conference with both the student teacher and the cooperating teacher. The cooperating teacher's comments and discussion of the dilemma stem from that conference.

Cooperating Teacher's Response

I'm pulling my hair out with J. I've tried everything I can think of. Time-outs help for a little while, but I don't think he really cares about anything. He won't work for tangible rewards; he doesn't care if he loses his recess. In fact, I think he likes staying inside with me . . . then I end up being the one who gets punished. Praise doesn't faze him; in fact, it makes him worse. None of the other children want anything to do with him, and they've tried to be his friend. His schoolwork is below grade level, although his test scores show he can do the work if he wants to. . . . He has been in five foster homes since birth. This latest foster mother wanted to adopt him, but now she's not so sure. She has to pick him up every day at my door because the school won't allow him to ride the bus anymore. I genuinely like the kid; he can be sweet. In fact, when no other second-grade teacher wanted him this year, I volunteered. I had him last year when I taught first grade, so I knew him and the family already.

Ethical Dilemmas and the Decision-Making Process

The college supervisor had several ethical factors to consider. To complicate matters, the college needed to maintain a good rapport with the cooperating teacher and the school so that they would take student teachers in the future. This became a teachable moment. Somehow, there had to be a positive outcome for the child, the child's family, the student teacher, the cooperating teacher, and the college supervisor.

When in doubt about how to handle an ethical dilemma, look to the *NAEYC Code of Ethical Conduct* as a guide for reflection to help you think through a course of action (Greenberg, 1999). The college supervisor relied on the principles stated in the *Code of Ethical Conduct* as the basis for guiding the discussion. Several parts of Section I: Ethical Responsibilities to Children were particularly helpful. For example, P-1.1 says that above all else, we must do no harm to children. That includes anything that is degrading, disrespectful, and potentially emotionally damaging. P-1.2 says that we must not discriminate against any child for a number of listed reasons, including the child's ability and behavior. P-1.3 says that when we make decisions about a child, we must involve all people who have relevant knowledge of that child. Without going any further, the *Code of Ethical Conduct* provided the supervisor with a clear mandate that the child's well-being was more important than any other concern. Clearly, the child's days of closeted time-outs had to end.

Through active listening and nonjudgmental conversation with both the cooperating teacher and the student teacher, the college supervisor helped achieve consensus on the following:

- Child J. should not go back into the closet at all, even for a brief period.
- A team conference with the family and the school support staff should be scheduled as soon as possible.
- Because both the cooperating teacher and the student teacher are in the room, one or the other should focus on child J. if he becomes a distraction so that the other children can continue their activities.
- Positive feedback should be given privately and discreetly because public praise is ineffective. Avoid punishment.
- Guidance talks should be done privately, individually, and discreetly.

Comments

The child's welfare had to come first; this was nonnegotiable. The student teacher was correct in bringing the situation to the attention of the college supervisor. The three-way conference provided an opportunity to brainstorm ideas for the future. It was not a forum to criticize what had already been done. These ideas became a starting point for focusing on the child to help him regulate his own behavior.

As you would expect, this was an ongoing process that continued long after Miss A. finished her student teaching. The good news is that life improved for child J. The team met and recommended further evaluation. Child J. was eventually diagnosed with reactive attachment disorder (RAD) and began receiving therapy. He gradually responded to the teacher's repeated efforts to form an attachment with him. Discreet positive feedback, private guidance talks, and avoidance of punishment all began to pay off.

In such cases, understanding *why* a child behaves in a certain way and participating as a *team* member to solve problems make a big difference. Whenever you are tempted to say, "I just don't *like* that child," stop and tell yourself that the child who is most difficult to love is the one who needs your love the most.

Voices of Reality: Student Teachers Speak

I haven't really run into many discipline issues, beyond the ordinary. No one is really openly defiant. They all seem sorry and apologetic when they do something wrong. To me, that's really important!

Krista U.

My coop said, "Teachers don't smile until January." She explained to me that it is much easier to do it this way, rather than trying to enforce rules after none were set high from the beginning. This made sense for me.

Ruth H.

There have been numerous situations when we would both say the same student's name at the same time. They would just go back to their seat. After a few minutes, then, whichever teacher sent them back will go and talk to the student to make sure that they knew why they were sent back. I am not having any real problems so far.

Nancy F.

❖ THE SUPPORT GROUP MEETS

Behavior management issues were frequently discussed during the support group meetings of the early childhood student teachers. Some centered on how to handle sensitive discipline issues. Some of these students' shared thoughts may sound familiar to you as well.

As a result of student teachers' increasing awareness of the inappropriate behavior children are exposed to in their own homes and in their communities, the group discussions became emotion-filled and reflective.

Do not, however, think for a moment that all students' experiences were negative. For example, other students shared stories that were quite different. Perhaps you can relate to these comments.

❖ FINAL THOUGHTS

Even when you feel a bit tired or discouraged, you may find that the simplest things will make all your efforts seem worthwhile:

One of my girls picked a flower and brought it in to me this morning. It's amazing how a near-weed can brighten a morning when received from a child.

Krista U.

ACTIVITIES FOR REFLECTION AND ACTION

1. What is your cooperating teacher's philosophy of behavior management? List three key elements of her approach to discipline.

2. Write a statement that describes your philosophy of behavior management. Include a plan of action concerning what you will do if a child misbehaves repeatedly. What will you do first, second, third, and so on? At what point will you involve the child's family?

   Portfolio: Your philosophy of behavior management statement is an artifact that you can place in your portfolio. Students report that they are often asked to describe their philosophy of behavior management when they are interviewed for a job.

3. Describe a behavior incident involving one of your children. List two different ways to respond to this incident, depending on your philosophy of behavior management.

4. *Portfolio:* A description of a behavior incident that you handled appropriately is an artifact you can place in your portfolio. Students report that they are often asked to describe how they would respond to a particular behavior incident when they are interviewed for a job. Reflecting upon an actual experience you have had will be good preparation for an interview.

5. As you reflect on your growth as a teacher, what insights have you gained about creating and maintaining a positive learning climate?

6. List the rules you think are most important to have in your classroom. What will be the consequence if these rules are not followed the first time, the second time, and so on?

7. Practice using "I messages" to express your feelings in each of the following scenarios. Refer to the pattern discussed in the chapter for guidance if you need it. You may wish to work with a partner so that you can give and receive feedback. You may also create your own scenarios for further practice.

   a. Mrs. X., your cooperating teacher, has been unusually silent all day. She has not given you any feedback on the lesson you taught this morning.

   b. The paraprofessional in your classroom complains to you about your cooperating teacher.

   c. A parent tells you that the school policy about not having holiday parties is ridiculous.

   d. Your cooperating teacher always seems to give her opinion while you are teaching a lesson.

CHAPTER 5

Classroom Management: Environments and Routines

In searching for the fundamental principles of the science of teaching, I find few axioms as indisputable as are the first principles of mathematics. One of these is this, He is the best teacher who makes the best use of his own time and that of his pupils. For time is all that is given by God in which to do the work of improvement.

Emma Hart Willard

You have a limited amount of time to make a difference in the lives of young children. What you do in the relatively brief period children are with you can have a lasting impact. Therefore, you must carefully plan the classroom routines you implement, the transitions you use to move children from one activity to another, and the overall environment you create. When children enter your room, do they feel safe, respected, accepted, and celebrated for their uniqueness? Is your room a place for dreaming and laughter as well as learning? How well do you use the gift of time to do the work of improving the young lives entrusted to you? The answers to these questions will help you fulfill your commitment to honor the children in your care (Turner, 2000). Perhaps you can relate to the following words of a student teacher in the peer support group.

You too will find your own ways of communicating to children that you care about them. The physical environment will also show children that their emotional needs will be met in this place. Therefore, you need to give careful thought to how you will manage the physical space of your classroom.

❖ PHYSICAL SPACE AND CLASSROOM MANAGEMENT

One important aspect of the physical environment is aesthetic appeal. The ideal early childhood learning environment will have an inviting, homey atmosphere. Color, materials, and furniture are important factors in creating the sense that your room is a wonderful, safe, caring place (Feeney et al., 2001; Hendrick, 2003). As a student teacher, you will be able to affect the aesthetics of the environment as you create learning stations, bulletin boards, and interest centers. At the same time, safety must always be an important concern when planning the physical environment. Consider the following factors as you plan.

Safety and the Classroom Environment

The physical environment of the classroom should be one in which children are safe from harm at all times. The arrangement of items in the room may be predetermined by your cooperating teacher. However, you can still do some troubleshooting. For example, you can closely examine the environment for potential threats to child safety. The following questions for classroom safety assessment may help guide you as you examine the environment:

- Are there any electrical cords that may trip children?
- Are there any electrical cords that children can pull?
- Are all electrical outlets equipped with safety covers?
- Are there any appliances plugged in that may attract the attention of inquisitive children?
- Are there any rough or sharp edges on tables and counters that could hurt a child?
- Are all floor surfaces free from spilled water?
- Do floor coverings have safety grip backings to prevent slipping? (Adapted from Branscombe, Castle, Dorsey, Surbeck, & Taylor, 2003)

You may also find it helpful to get down on the children's level as you make your safety check. There may be potential threats to safety that you cannot see from an adult perspective, such as loose screws or splintered wood underneath furniture.

Add to this list of safety assessment questions as you examine your classroom. The seven questions listed above do not ensure that your environment is safe for young children. They are merely a good beginning to help you monitor children's safety.

Excellent Web sites, as seen in Figure 5.1, are available to help you locate extensive safety checklists and more detailed information regarding health and safety issues.

- **Healthy Kids, Healthy Care: Parents as Partners in Promoting Healthy and Safe Child Care** provides information on health and safety for parents of young children that will be helpful to you. For example, the Web site contains several detailed checklists on various aspects of health and safety including a *Safety Checklist*, an *Emotional Health Checklist*, and others. This Web site also has resources in Spanish.
  http://www.healthykids.us/
  http://www.healthykids.us/checklists/safety_chk.htm
  http://www.healthykids.us/checklists/emotional_chk.htm
- **American Academy of Pediatrics (AAP)** Web site provides up-to-date information on child safety and health matters on topics as varied as immunizations, children and stress, childhood obesity, and public policy. The AAP also sponsors the Healthy Child Care America Campaign.
  http://www.aap.org/
  http://www.healthychildcare.org
  National Resource Center for Health and Safety in Child Care and Early Education (NRC) Web site provides practical, user-friendly information on health and safety matters. For example, tips for preventing injuries include information about playground surfaces and cushioning material, use of helmets, and potential dangers of open windows and window shades. The NRC also posts new or revised state childcare regulations.
  http://nrc.uchsc.edu/
- **Bright Futures** Web site is a national healthcare initiative that provides free information that can be downloaded easily. Topics include information on nutrition, physical activity, child development, and oral health.
  http://www.brightfutures.org/
- **U.S. Consumer Product Safety Commission (CSPC)** Web site provides childcare safety checklists in both English and Spanish. The CSPC also provides updated lists of safety information and recalls of children's toys and products.
  http://www.cpsc.gov/cpscpub/pubs/childcare.pdf
  http://www.cpsc.gov/cpscpub/pubschildcarespanish.pdf

FIGURE 5.1   Sample Health and Safety Web Sites for Resources File

Color and the Classroom Environment

The study of the psychology of color is controversial at best. Even without the benefit of scientific research, some people insist that color can affect the mood and overall tone of a physical space. They suggest the use of bright colors such as red or orange for active play areas and muted colors such as shades of blue or green for quiet activity or rest areas. You may want to experiment with colors as you designate various activity centers of your room and decide for yourself what, if any, effects color has on the psychological climate of the area. Use of colors and decorative artwork is frequently suggested in order to create a sense of beauty and emotional well-being in children's environments (Cruickshank, Jenkins, & Metcalf, 2003; Feeney et al., 2001). Just be sure to display items at the children's eye level, not at yours.

Texture and the Classroom Environment

Some children are sensitive to the feel of materials such as hard, soft, and coarse. For example, in quiet areas such as the book corner, place large, soft pillows and soft carpeting. In the blocks area or painting area, use harder surfaces on flooring. Children enjoy using their senses to explore their environment, so give them the opportunity to play with sand, water, and sandpaper-covered letters and numbers. You can help preschool children make a texture book containing fabrics and materials of various textures. Texture books also offer opportunities to stimulate conversation. You can use any number of items, including material collected on nature walks, to stimulate language development and exploratory activities. See the texture activity in Figure 5.2 for an example.

Figure 5.2 **Example of Texture Activity**

1. Collect a variety of materials cut in approximately the same size and shape so that the only identification clues will be tactile. Suggestions include velvet, vinyl, burlap, silk, corduroy, and fake fur.
2. Blindfold a child, have her close her eyes tightly, or put materials in a bag so that they cannot be identified by sight.
3. Have the child use words to describe how each sample feels. Children may work in pairs or with an adult.

(Based on Schirrmacher, 2002)

Furniture and the Classroom Environment

When possible, you can have an area in your room that contains comfortable home furnishings such as chairs or a sofa with soft pillows. Even a soft rug with big pillows will provide an inviting area for children to enjoy story books. Some teachers set up aquariums with fish or small pets, areas for listening to soothing music, and quiet areas for children who need to take a break from busy group activities (Branscombe et al., 2003). This type of planning leads to a sense of physical security in your classroom (Whitehead & Ginsberg, 1999).

Multicultural Elements and the Classroom Environment

Display nonstereotypical posters, photographs, artwork, and artifacts of people representing various ethnic and racial backgrounds. Integrate displays with picture books and story books that also show children and adults in a positive light. Children will benefit from learning about their own culture and those of others on a continuing basis. This topic will be discussed at greater depth in Chapter 9.

The physical environment of your classroom can help create a climate of safety and emotional security that encourages learning.

Arrangement of the Physical Environment and Program Philosophy

Physical space in early childhood rooms is often arranged in conjunction with the program philosophy. For example, a room arrangement in which your desk is the center of attention and each child has a separate desk or table indicates a teacher-centered approach. Many teaching professionals, including the author, believe that a teacher-centered approach is *not* appropriate for early childhood education. Such a room arrangement discourages the active learning and collaboration that are an integral part of the child-centered, constructivist process of child development.

If you also prefer a child-centered approach, you may choose round tables or clusters of desks to encourage collaboration by cooperative groups of children; your desk may be tucked away in a corner (Brewer, 2001). A project approach, typically seen in the preschool programs of Reggio Emilia, may require spaces for discovery purposes as well as a special space called the *atelier*. The atelier contains materials for children to make visual recordings documenting their learning experiences (Henniger, 2002). Thus, you can sometimes determine the philosophic approach of a particular program by the arrangement of the physical environment. This is something for you to consider carefully. When the time comes for you to go on job interviews, prospective employers often ask how you would arrange your classroom. How you organize the physical space will send a strong message about your philosophy of early childhood teaching and learning.

Common Types of Physical Space

You can expect to see various types of physical space designated in early childhood rooms. Of course, there will be variations, depending on the age and needs of the children and the goals of the program. The following list, suggested by Davis, Kilgo, and Garnel-McCormick (1998), is fairly typical:

- Space for gross motor play activities
- Space for fine motor activities requiring tables
- Space for large-group activities
- Space requiring a water source
- Space for each child's personal belongings
- Space for teacher materials
- Space to store materials and consumable supplies
- Space for parent or family member conferences and information

A number of considerations may guide your decisions about arrangement of space. Some of these considerations may be beyond your control, such as the size and location of your room in the building. Figure 5.3 lists a few guidelines that may be helpful (Dodge & Colker, 2000).

Figure 5.3 **Guidelines for Use of Available Space**

- Use shelves or furniture to define separate areas so that children focus on activities, with few outside distractions.
- Keep noisy areas close together, such as those with blocks and large toys.
- Keep quiet areas close together, such as those with books and puzzles.
- Place interest areas close to resources, such as painting areas near a water source.
- Store children's supplies in a separate area from the teacher's supplies.
- Arrange the traffic pattern to minimize interruptions and to allow access for children with special needs.
- Arrange interest areas so that you can see all children at all times.

You may have only limited opportunities to influence the physical environment of the room during your practicum. However, your cooperating teacher may allow you to decorate an activity center or rearrange some of the furniture for a time. Keep in mind that you should try to create a place that *all* children and their families will feel "is already made for me, both snug and wide open, with a doorway never needing to be closed" (Morrison, 1998, p. 12).

Physical Environment and Inclusion of Children with Special Needs

Children who have special needs are routinely included with their typically developing peers in early childhood centers and classrooms across the country. Successful inclusion requires more than merely placing a child with disabilities in a setting. It requires doing whatever is necessary to ensure that *all* children enjoy meaningful participation and learning (Filler & Xu, 2006).

The physical environment is an important factor to consider as you include children who have many kinds of special needs. You need to be aware of potentially life-threatening allergic reactions that can be triggered by objects in the physical environment. For example, a child who has spina bifida may be included in your program. She should avoid all objects that have latex. If she comes in contact with latex, she is likely to have a serious allergic reaction that may include itching and watery eyes, hives, difficulty breathing, and possibly death. Other children may also have latex allergies. Many common objects (see Figure 5.4) that contain latex could pose a serious health and a safety risk for children (French & Cain, 2006).

A more extensive list of objects containing latex and suggested substitutes can be found on the Web site of the Spina Bifida Association at

---

- **Balloons.** Use Mylar balloons instead.
- **Costumes and masks.** Check labels carefully.
- **Pacifiers.** Use products such as those of Gerber and Binky.
- **Rubber bands.** Use nonrubber products such as plastic bands.
- **Toys such as older Barbie dolls.** Use toys such as Little Tykes and Discovery.
- **Handles on riding toys.** Cover handles with cloth; use vinyl handles.
- **Balls such as Koosh balls.** Use Nerf balls.
- **Art supplies such as paints and erasers.** Use acrylic paints and soap erasers.

(Based on Spina Bifida Association, 2007)

FIGURE 5.4 Common Objects That Contain Latex

www.spinabifidaassociation.org. Information about latex allergy and other common childhood allergies may be found at the Web site of the American College of Allergy, Asthma, and Immunology at *http://www.acaai.org.*

Families may be your best resource for information about their children's environmental health needs, including allergies to latex and/or specific foods. You should talk with your cooperating teacher about any plans that may already be established for prevention or what to do in the event of a crisis.

Another consideration is the arrangement of the physical space in your room. You may need to make some modifications in order to maximize the participation of children with special needs. For example, if you are including a child who uses a wheelchair, a walker, or crutches, you may need to create larger spaces around tables to increase accessibility (French & Cain, 2006). Special furniture such as wheelchair-accessible activity tables will allow all children to participate. You may also need to allow space for more adults in the room who provide support services to children with special needs (Cook et al., 2008). For example, an occupational therapist, an assistive technologist, or a language therapist may work with the child in your room rather than pull her out.

The modifications you make in the physical environment can be quite simple things that benefit all of your children. For example, in order to help a child who has a visual impairment, make sure that the routes from one area of your room to another are as direct as possible. Keep tables free of clutter, and use tactile cues such as soft carpet to indicate a quiet area. Keep your routines consistent and your schedule as predictable as possible. This predictability and structure will help a child who has autism or a more typically developing child who has difficulty with transitions or change (Bender, 2002; Cook et al., 2008; Kostelnik et al., 2002; Salend, 2005).

Classroom arrangements that are child-centered allow children to work and play safely at all times. There are areas designated for specific purposes.

❖ EMOTIONAL CLIMATE AND CLASSROOM MANAGEMENT

You can help create a safe, caring, warm climate in your room by doing several simple things each day (see Figure 5.5). Each child in your care deserves a good beginning to her day. You can be at the door to greet children when they arrive. This may also be an opportunity to encourage positive communication with family members who drop off children in the morning. You may learn if some event in the child's life may impact her behavior during her day with you. Similarly, each child deserves a good ending to her day. Perhaps you can share information with family members who arrive as you say good-bye to each child (Feeney et al., 2001).

Despite your best efforts, there may be events that impact young children's lives in a negative manner. At those times, you may have to ask for assistance from your cooperating teacher and support personnel. Sometimes, you can help children work through their fears as they play.

Young Children and Fear

Young children can be affected by events even though they do not yet have the language to express their fears. In fact, these children tend to

---

Figure 5.5 Ways to Nurture a Positive Emotional Climate

- Give each child some individual attention each day.
- Display children's projects and work products.
- Model the behavior of calling attention to children's achievements and encourage them to praise each other.
- Allow children to make appropriate choices.
- Include elements of children's cultural identity in daily lessons.
- Demonstrate appreciation of children's families by inviting them to participate in activities.
- Remove any objects that might frighten a young child (example: a pet snake in an aquarium).
- Use daily greetings as positive affirmations to reduce fears (example: "We take care of each other here.").
- Listen to children who are fearful even if their fears seem illogical and reassure them that they will be safe at school.

(Based on Gestwicki, 1999; Schiller & Willis, 2008)

---

generalize their fears to other people and situations more readily than do older children. This can lead to increased distress as they believe that the adults in their world can no longer protect them from danger (Jackson, 1997).

Children are often exposed to images of war and terrorist attacks on television. Even if children do not see the news, they are frequently exposed to images in various media that frighten them. This fear may manifest itself in behavioral changes as they play or draw.

Using Play to Develop Emotional Well-Being

In your early childhood environment, you may be able to help children "transform their play from acting out violence into imagining a more comforting and secure resolution" (Levin, 2003, p. 73). You can provide props that will allow them to create safe endings to their play scenarios. Also, do not be afraid to talk with children about disturbing news events. For example, watch their play and ask "why" questions. You can lead them to tell you what they already know about a topic such as war or terrorists. Children may be looking for reassurance that they are safe and protected. They may not ask you for more detailed information than they already have.

If you believe, however, that a child's fears require intervention from a specialist, talk to your cooperating teacher about your concerns. Some schools and centers have play therapists as members of the support staff team. Play therapy is actually derived from the work of Carl Rogers on client-centered therapy in the early 20th century. Often, children engage in unstructured play in a room filled with specially selected toys and materials. A therapist observes, engages the child in conversation, and helps the child discover solutions to problems (Warner & Sower, 2005).

Bloom's Taxonomy and the Affective Domain

As you reflect upon how you will create a positive emotional environment for young children, you may find it helpful to think about how Benjamin Bloom and his colleagues organized a classification structure of affective educational objectives related to areas of emotion, feelings, and attitude. This taxonomy or classification organizes a continuum of behaviors from the simplest to the most complex:

1. *Receiving* (or *attending*).   The learner has awareness, is willing to take notice, selects, or chooses to attend. Examples: The child pays attention to others, listens to information, and remembers it. She points to an object, requests an object by name, or uses an object.
2. *Responding* (or *willingness*).   The learner participates voluntarily or willingly. Examples: The child helps, complies with a request, or answers. She knows the rules, and she practices them.
3. *Valuing* (or *recognizing that something has worth*).   The learner willingly accepts that an object, a phenomenon, or a behavior has worth. Examples: The child joins in play with diverse groups of children. She initiates play with others who vary by individual and cultural background. She selects picture books that show people of various racial and ethnic groups.
4. *Organization* (or *places values into some kind of system*).   The learner recognizes the need to follow prescribed rules of behavior. She takes responsibility for her behavior. Examples: The child adheres to the class rules. She explains what each rule means. She generalizes appropriate behaviors to a variety of settings.
5. *Characterization* (or *internalization of values*).   The learner has developed a set of values that controls her behavior and shapes her worldview. She behaves in a manner that is consistent with her values. Examples: The child displays cooperation and teamwork when interacting with others. She practices self-reliance as she works independently. She modifies her judgments when presented with new evidence.
(Based on Krathwohl, Bloom, & Masia, 1956)

This taxonomy or hierarchy of the affective domain may be useful as you observe young children and try to understand their emotional development. For example, if an infant or toddler is in the *Receiving* category, you can encourage her interest in trying new things and exploring her environment as she attends to you. Talk with her, read to her, and play with her as she learns to associate names with objects; use music and movement to engage her in learning. If a young child is in the *Responding* category, you can encourage her active participation in Circle Time and pretend play with others. Present children with choices and provide opportunities for them to be classroom helpers. You may want to take another look at the behaviors associated with all five categories in the affective domain. What activities can you suggest to encourage the development of children's social nature and emotional well-being in appropriate ways?

You may have children in your program who are functioning at different levels of the affective domain. Therefore, you may interact differently with one child than another in order to meet the individual needs of each child. You must be mindful of each child's uniqueness. One important aspect of mindfulness is acute awareness, which means "being aware of the needs of the infants, toddlers, and families with whom one is working" (McMullen & Dixon, 2006, p. 49). Your knowledge of children's affective development will help you become more mindful as you think about what you are doing.

Classroom Management and Rules

Children's behavior and discipline have been addressed in Chapter 4, but establishment of classroom rules is something you should consider as you plan the overall management of your program. Creating a positive tone with your class rules will contribute to the overall emotional climate of your room.

In general, rules should be few in number. They should be simple. They should be worded positively. They should be clearly defined and displayed somewhere in the room. They should also be applied consistently (Slavin, 2000; Warner & Sower, 2005). For younger children, picture cues may accompany each rule. Many teachers believe that children should participate in the development of the rules so that they are more motivated to live by the rules they helped create (Kyle & Rogien, 2004). Notice the class rules in the classroom that you visit. Do they follow the general guidelines suggested here?

Posting simple, positively stated rules is not enough. You need to have discussions with your children about the meaning of each rule. For example, if a rule says "Respect other people's property," then children need to discuss what that means. Children can provide examples of how they can respect property.

In addition, if you have particular rules of behavior that you want children to follow while you are student teaching, you need to discuss those rules with your cooperating teacher and with the children. For example, you may have a different tolerance for noise levels and movement during play and work time than your cooperating teacher. Children can generally adapt to different expectations of behavior around different people.

❖ CLASSROOM ROUTINES

Management of classroom routines is another important element in creating a positive learning climate. Children feel secure in an environment in which routines are well established. Indeed, for some children, the greatest stability in their volatile lives is the predictability of their daily routines away from home. Research indicates that having a schedule and following it consistently significantly increases children's sense of security and reduces stress, even in young children (Hamner & Turner, 1996). This is not to say that flexibility is harmful but rather that predictability is reassuring (Honig, 1996).

Therefore, while you are observing your cooperating teacher, be extremely aware of the daily routines. Take notes if necessary. Some cooperating teachers do not mind if you make changes. Others prefer routines kept exactly the same way because they do not want to have to reteach procedures to the children after you leave. In any case, check with your cooperating teacher before making any changes. Keep in mind that some schedules are controlled by the school or must be coordinated with other classes and are beyond your control. For example, you must share the playground space and equipment with others on a tightly coordinated schedule.

Daily Routines

Whether you are teaching infants, preschoolers, or children in the primary grades, the arrival and departure routines are important. The arrival period must be handled in such a way as to make a smooth transition from the child's home. This should be a friendly, relaxed time in which each child is greeted and parents may wish to share information with you. Depending on the age of the child, there will be consistent, daily routines of diapering/toileting, circle time, snack/meals, clean-up, learning stations, instructional time, individual and group play, and rest/nap times. Departure routines are equally significant in order to provide a sense of closure. Departure gives you an opportunity to share information with each child's family, either in person or by some other means such as a sharing journal. Sometimes this informal daily communication can be more effective than a formal conference (Warner & Sower, 2005).

Reflect on Routines in Your Life

- What morning routines do you have in your daily life? Evening routines? Exercise routines? Recreation routines? Driving routines?
- What purpose do you think these routines serve?
- How do you feel if something prevents you from carrying out your planned routines?
- What is it about your routines that you like?
- What routines have you implemented in children's lives? Why?

In order for you to appreciate the importance of routines in the children's lives, think about your own life and the routines to which you have become accustomed. The following questions, adapted from Feeney et al. (2001), may be helpful.

Even though routines are important in early childhood programs, you still have the flexibility to make some changes. For example, if children are engaged in an activity that is totally absorbing their attention, you may elect to prolong it. If you must eliminate or shorten another activity, then you should tell the children what the change in routine will be and why.

❖ TIME MANAGEMENT

Time management is an important aspect of classroom management. For some student teachers, adhering to a schedule or monitoring the pace of lessons and activities is difficult at times. For example, you may plan activities that you think will be challenging and take considerable time, only to find that children breeze through them without difficulty. Other activities that you thought would be simple need more time because you did not anticipate misunderstandings. Occasionally, you may forget to watch the clock in order to draw activities to a close at the scheduled time, particularly if you are absorbed in teaching a lesson you have spent hours preparing. Do not despair; **pacing** is something that generally improves with experience.

Pacing refers to time spent on each portion of the lesson such that children feel neither rushed nor bored waiting for others to finish.

Schedule for Managing Classroom Time

During your practicum experience, you will have minimal opportunity to organize a schedule for your children. It is more than likely already organized by your cooperating teacher within certain restrictions set by the school or center regarding meal time or recreation space shared with others.

Even so, pay close attention to how blocks of time are organized for your children's developmental age. Every program may make certain adaptations or accommodations for the interests and needs of its unique children. There are many variations. One sample schedule is provided in Figure 5.6.

Figure 5.6 Sample Schedule for All-Day Kindergarten

8:00–8:45 **Free Choice Center Activity at Centers**

8:45–9:15 **Opening, Daily Calendar, and Morning Messages**
Actively involve children with morning song, calendar and weather, and daily schedule.

9:15–9:45 **Shared Story Time with Teacher**
Teacher reads with a Big Book, a predictive story, or a story reflecting a particular theme.

9:45–10:15 **Emergent Literacy Activity**
Teacher may model thinking aloud, writing some thoughts with a marker, and drawing pictures to illustrate some words.
Children have time to write in their journals while teacher encourages and coaches.

10:15–10:45 **Recess/Snack**
Snack may relate to story read earlier such as theme about apples.

10:45–11:45 **Assigned Centers**
Centers may be designed around a particular theme, such as a recent visit to an apple orchard.

11:45–12:15 **Lunch**

12:15–1:15 **Math**
Math activity can revolve around theme such as making a class graph of favorite apple foods or colors.

1:15–1:45 **Shared Writing: Language Experience Story**
Children talk about a recent field trip to apple orchard while teacher writes simple sentences they say aloud onto chart paper.
Sound-letter relationships and other beginning literacy skills are developed.

1:45–2:15 **Outdoor Physical Activity**
Children explore and use play equipment in kindergarten play area.

2:25–2:45 **Center Activities: Children's Choice**
Children have time to explore activities of their choice in centers that promote learning.

2:45–3:00 **Daily Summary**
Review day's activities and prepare to go home.

Schedules will vary with the developmental levels of different children and the goals of the program. Gestwicki (1999) suggests the following guidelines for the development of good schedules:

- Predictability in the sequence of activities throughout the day
- Flexibility to allow for special events or sudden changes in the weather
- Blocks of time for child-initiated as well as teacher-initiated activities
- Blocks of time for active as well as passive experiences
- Variety of activities to allow for developmental differences in attention span and in abilities

These guidelines also apply to classrooms in the primary grades. Keep in mind that your daily schedule may be structured around certain nonnegotiable blocks of time allocated for lunch, recess, and special subject areas such as art, music, and physical education. These may be predetermined by an administrator. Although there are many variations, a sample primary grade schedule is shown in Figure 5.7.

In the primary grades, there is increasing emphasis on academic subjects. You may receive guidance about how many minutes you should

Figure 5.7 Sample Schedule for a Grade 3 Class

8:30–8:45	**Arrival, Opening, Attendance, Lunch Count**
	Children may also have a quiet, routine activity to complete during the arrival period such as daily oral language exercise.
8:45–9:00	**Class Meeting**
9:00–10:00	**Math**
10:00–11:30	**Reading**
11:30–11:45	**Spelling**
11:45–12:30	**Lunch and Recess**
12:30–12:40	**Read-Aloud, Sustained Silent Reading (SSR)**
	A chapter book may be read aloud to the whole class and/or children and adults may read books silently.
12:40–1:30	**Writing Workshop**
1:30–2:15	**Science/Social Studies/Health**
	Subjects are taught on a three-week rotation cycle.
2:15–2:50	**Specials: Art, Music, Library, Physical Education, Foreign Language**
2:50–3:20	**Centers: Student Choice**
	Interdisciplinary centers may be related to themes being taught in subject areas.
3:20–3:30	**Closing, Homework, Clean-Up, and Dismissal**

allow for daily reading and math instruction, for example. As a student teacher, you should follow the routine established by your cooperating teacher.

Transitions

Transitions are also an important segment of classroom management for you to plan. Anytime you change activities or move children from one area of the room to another, you must consider how to make these transitions as orderly and brief as possible. You may find that many children become excitable and prone to creating disruptions during less structured times. Therefore, plan ahead.

Student teachers sometimes struggle with noninstructional or transition time. Research indicates that as much as one-fourth to one-third of the day can be lost due to transition times between activities (Newcomer, 2003). This unstructured time can be especially difficult for children with special needs, such as those with attention deficit hyperactivity disorder (ADHD).

In order to minimize mistaken behaviors during transition times, you need to do careful planning. Some teacher tips include "using a color wheel to indicate a new activity, playing 'beat the clock,' using transition buddies, and marking the end point of the transition with a fun or rewarding activity" (Newcomer, 2003, p. 255).

Lost time can be a management problem at all levels of early childhood education from nursery school through the primary grades. One surprising study found that as much as 35% of the nursery school day is spent transitioning from one activity to another (Berk, 1976). Consequently, observe how your cooperating teacher handles these activity changes without disruptions. You may discover that her methods work for you or you may want to be creative and try a few of your own. Guessing games or memory games can occupy children's minds and bodies while they are lining up and waiting to go play outside. You may even want to solicit children's ideas as to how to make transitions smoother. They may be more cooperative in putting their coats on quickly if they have developed the solution to the problem themselves (Alger, 1984).

If you find that transition times are not as quick or smooth as you would like, then ask yourself the following questions:

- Have I given the children notice that a transition is coming? What signal(s) have I used?
- Do the children understand what is expected during each transition?
- Are my directions simple, clear, specific, and consistent?

Figure 5.8 Sample Ideas for Transitions

- Use transition buddies for children who have difficulty remembering transition procedures.
- Give a warning 5 minutes before the transition time.
- Use a picture schedule for children as needed.
- Use music as a transition cue.
- Use pretending, such as tiptoeing like a quiet mouse.
- Name a color that children are wearing to indicate who may move to a location.
- Use gestures as a signal. For example, when children see your hand raised, they silently make the gesture until everyone has her hand raised.
- Use riddles or clues as transition cues.

- Have I allowed sufficient time for transitions? Too much time? Too little time?
- Do I need to allow for individual differences in the transition process?

As you gain experience and observe other teachers, you may collect your own bag of tricks or ideas to smooth transitions between activities; see the samples provided in Figure 5.8. Creative ideas can help make transitions pleasant, productive times rather than stressful time wasters.

Outdoor Physical Environment

Another equally important component of management to consider is children's use of outside areas. Regular outdoor experiences are readily acknowledged as an integral component of developmentally appropriate practice for children through age 8. These experiences require careful planning to maximize opportunities for development of gross motor skills as well as exploration of the natural environment (Bredekamp, 1987).

Young children benefit from outdoor play spaces that are created to simulate a home environment (Whitehead & Ginsberg, 1999). For example, gardens, shrubs, flowers, and vegetable gardens expose children to a variety of multisensory experiences. Both the context of the outdoor space and the design of the play facilities "engage and entice children's sense of inquiry, stimulate their imaginations, invite exploration, communicate a sense of belonging and cultural identity, and support their sense of developing competencies" (Debord, Hestenes, Moore, Cosco, & McGinnis, 2002, p. 33). Thus, a child-centered outdoor physical environment can enhance the development of the whole child.

❖ FINAL THOUGHTS

Many of the strategies you learn to apply to classroom management are preventative in nature. The procedures you establish with your children will indicate that "this is how we do things so that everyone can work and play together safely." The positive emotional climate you create as well as the physical arrangement of the room will indicate much about your respect for each child. Preplanning will prevent many difficulties concerning behavior or safety issues.

Watch closely how your cooperating teacher begins and ends each day, how she has children enter and exit the room, and how she gets children's attention and transitions them from one activity or space to another. Notice the routines that she has established for everyday activities such as bathroom use, getting a drink of water, asking for help, cleaning up, and putting things away. These are all decisions you will be making when you are a professional early childhood teacher.

Voices of Reality: Student Teachers Speak

I am using the clapping rhythm to get their attention. For the majority, they all listen and respect me as the "real" teacher. I know I am not the "real" teacher but I sure feel like it!

Jasmine L.

I will be doing full time on Monday. This is going to be a unit on pumpkins. I think I am well planned for it, but I am still worried about transitions or time fillers. I will probably be overplanned, but until I [have] done it, I will probably worry a little. I think it is different when it is not your room.

Nancy F.

Students respond so much better to rules and limits if they're made fun. We made paper airplanes and I immediately set the limits so that airplanes were not just flying through the air. But instead of just telling them to put them away, I told them air traffic control didn't clear them for takeoff so they had to fly over to their airports (a.k.a. backpacks) and stay parked. It seemed to work and I had no problems with them. It was just one of those spur-of-the-moment things but my co-op mentioned to me afterwards that she thought it made such a difference as opposed to simply listing rules.

Krista U.

ACTIVITIES FOR REFLECTION AND ACTION

1. Design a room arrangement for an early childhood grade or age group that you would like to teach. What do you think this room arrangement reveals about your philosophy of teaching?

2. What list of rules would you expect to see displayed in your own classroom? Write a list of five rules, keeping in mind the guidelines listed in this chapter. What do your believe your list reveals about your philosophy of teaching young children?

3. *Portfolio*: Your list of classroom rules and your reflection on what you believe it reveals about your philosophy of teaching young children can be placed in your portfolio as an artifact.

4. What can you see yourself doing to create a learning climate in which children feel safe and cared for?

CHAPTER 6

Observations and Evaluations of Student Teaching

To be a teacher in the right sense is to be a learner. Instruction begins when you, the teacher, learn from the learner, put yourself in his place so that you may understand what he understands and in the way he understands it.

Søren Kierkegaard

Kierkegaard's thoughts on being a teacher in the right sense underscore the importance of learning from your learners, no matter how young they may be. Your student teaching observations and evaluations provide you with unique opportunities for inquiry and collaboration. The feedback you receive will guide you in your process of reflection and self-analysis to maximize your opportunities to become a teacher in the right sense.

❖ MAKING THE MOST OF THE OBSERVATION/ EVALUATION PROCESS

Each student teacher's reactions to observations and evaluations may vary due to individual differences in experiences and temperament. After initial adjustments, however, most people find their own ways of responding positively to these opportunities for personal attention and assessment. A common reaction is for students to desire more rather than less feedback.

You may find that each of you discovers your own way to deal with your feelings during observations and assessments. The more you can focus on your children rather than on your observers, the better off you may be. Some experienced teachers will admit to having a case of the jitters when administrators, parents, or even student teachers watch them.

Voices of Reality: Student Teachers Speak

My supervisor comes in all the time, so it's just normal to have her there. But I really just stay true to myself and be me when I'm observed. Yes, I do have a tendency to check myself and watch more closely what I do, but it doesn't change the way I teach. I guess it helps that I have a theater background, so it's easy for me to stay me!

Keeley N.

I've had a lot of trouble with this! I think student teaching is so hard because you have people [coops/supervisors] watching your every move. Being watched like that has made me nervous, and I tend to make mistakes.

Lauren C.

Just doing what I have planned and not looking at them is a big help. Many times there are other teachers in the classroom. The whole idea of it happening on a daily basis really plays a big role in the comfort level.

Jamal D.

All teachers receive formal written feedback yearly. Although the forms vary, they generally contain information summarizing the lesson content and the teacher-child interactions, comments regarding the strengths observed, and suggestions concerning improvements or things to think about. This observation/evaluation and follow-up discussion process will be ongoing throughout your professional career because there is always room for improvement. As Asa Hilliard (1999) states, "Learning to be a teacher is a long-term process. . . . As teachers mature, experience, study, and reflection help develop their perspective . . . [which] is as necessary for teachers of young children as for teachers at the higher grades" (pp. 58–59). In addition, as a lifelong learner, you will be a role model for your children.

Goals of Observations

The goals of observations and follow-up discussions vary according to the assumptions on which good teaching is based. Generally, you will find that your college supervisor, for example, will be interested in more than whether or not you are doing a good job. She may be inquiring about your concerns and questions as well as your personal reactions to your experiences (Rodgers & Dunn, 2000). In other words, the observation visits may be somewhat holistic in nature, centering on your overall well-being in addition to your teaching proficiency. Try to view these visits as an opportunity:

- To receive specific feedback based on valid assessments of your performance
- To exchange ideas and receive suggestions that will improve your skills
- To develop a positive attitude toward your continuous self-improvement
- To encourage the practice of reflection and self-assessment
- To further develop your practice of the accepted standards of early childhood teaching (Based on Machado & Botnarescue, 2001)

In addition, take a few moments to look carefully at the National Council for Accreditation of Teacher Education's standards for teacher candidates found in Appendix B (NCATE, 2007). These standards provide *unacceptable*, *acceptable*, and *target* descriptors of the knowledge, the skills, and the dispositions you should possess as you complete your preparation to teach children. You may find it helpful to refer to these descriptors as you reflect upon your progress toward your goals.

Climate of Trust

An important goal of student teaching observations is continual improvement in a climate of trust. You will have many opportunities to learn from your cooperating teacher and your college supervisor. They, in turn, will also learn from you as you share your reflections and questions. This mutual learning opportunity is significant because the backgrounds of professionals in many early childhood programs vary widely (Caruso & Fawcett, 1986).

❖ OBSERVATIONS OF TEACHING

When student teachers think of observation, the first mental picture is often that of a cooperating teacher and/or a college supervisor sitting in the back of a room with a clipboard writing notes. This is the most common practice, but it is not the only means of observational data collection.

Direct Observation

The traditional approach to assessing student teacher competence involves some type of direct observation. The assumption here is that good teaching behaviors are objectively identifiable and measurable in multiple contexts (Danielson, 1996; Stodolsky, 1985).

In any event, when you are observed, your college supervisor will utilize a rating form to record observations and make suggestions as a basis for discussion with you and your cooperating teacher. This approach has been criticized as a snapshot of performance on isolated occasions (Gellman, 1992–1993). Therefore, in order to get a better overall picture of your performance, college supervisors generally make an effort to observe you interact with children or teach different types of lessons at various times of the day.

Format

A clinical model of supervision by your college supervisor will generally include five steps:

- **Preobservation conference.** The focus of the observation may be established. Your college supervisor may wish to take a look at your written lesson plan or goals. Because of scheduling concerns, however, this step is not always possible.
- **Observation.** Generally, an activity or a lesson is observed in its entirety so that transitions, introduction, and closure may be viewed.
- **Summary and analysis.** A written record of teacher-child interactions, strengths, areas for improvement, and suggestions may be created.
- **Postobservation conference.** Preferably, this will occur immediately following the observation. If not, then a time is usually arranged as soon as possible. This meeting may be two-way, between you and your college supervisor, or three-way, among you, your cooperating teacher, and your college supervisor.
- **Postobservation conference analysis.** Generally, you will be asked to reflect on what went well and what could be improved, as well as strategies to try in the future. In time, your self-analysis will be confirmed or you will be counseled concerning changes.

Purposes of the Observation

Observations can be a helpful means of receiving professional coaching and increasing your ability to self-assess. A variety of observation strategies may be helpful to you.

- **Tracking your movement.** An observer draws a sketch of the room that includes tables, desks, activity centers, and boards. The room may be roughly sectioned into quarters. Then the observer traces your movement with a pencil for a specified period of time. Later, when you examine the drawing, you will see if you circulate throughout the room or if you have a limited territory or power base from which you operate (Boreen et al., 2000; Henry, Beasley, & Brighton, 2002).

■ **Gender discrimination.** Most student teachers strongly deny having any favoritism toward girls or boys. For example, you may be positive that you respond to the girls as often as to the boys. How sure are you? Have an observer keep a list of each child in the room. Each time you respond to a child or initiate communication with a child, the observer can put a tally mark beside the child's name. At the end of a specified time period, you will see who had more of your attention, boys or girls. You will also notice if a few children monopolized your attention to the exclusion of others (Sadker & Sadker, 1994).

■ **Frequency of interaction.** In a room containing a multicultural mix of children, have an observer sketch a matrix. This matrix may use simple identifiers such as AM—Asian male, AF—Asian female, HM—Hispanic male, and so on. Then the observer may tally the number of interactions that occur between you and various children. After a period of time, you will be able to see clearly if any patterns emerge (Adams, Shea, Liston, & Deever, 1998).

The variety of purposes for observation is virtually endless. For example, you may benefit from having an observer record the types of questions you ask, the positive or negative feedback you give, or the amount of wait time you allow various students after posing questions. The information you receive from these directed observations is extremely helpful in increasing your awareness of teacher behaviors that you may wish to continue or alter.

Informal Observations

In contrast, the observations conducted by your cooperating teacher are often less formal because she is with you on a daily basis. The two of you may share a dialogue journal that is passed back and forth, providing an opportunity to jot down questions, comments, and suggestions during your busy day; other teachers prefer to use their own system of index cards or sticky notes to communicate during the day. In other words, creativity and informality are common practice.

Nevertheless, no matter who conducts your student teaching observations, you may expect a discussion to be part of the follow-up process. Too many times, these discussions tend to be "dominated by cooperating teachers and student teachers take a passive role" (Guyton & McIntyre, 1990, p. 525). An opportunity for growth is also lost when conferences focus solely on specific classroom events, with little analysis of the teaching process in general.

Consequently, in order to maximize your satisfaction with the feedback you receive, you may need to initiate a conversation with your cooperating teacher rather than wait for her to do so. A useful practice is a guided reflection that involves asking four questions. They may be used alone, with a colleague, or, in your case, with your cooperating teacher. These questions, suggested by Hole and McEntee (1999), may be adapted to follow an observation in order to encourage dialogue and analysis:

- Step One: What happened?
- Step Two: Why did it happen?
- Step Three: What might it mean?
- Step Four: What are the implications for my practice? (pp. 34–35)

You can use this four-step process to reflect on events that occur randomly in our daily interactions with children. For example, the author observed Diane L. reading a story to a group of kindergarten children who were seated in a circle around her. Her story time was disrupted by a series of events beyond her control. She expressed displeasure with the way she handled the situation. Here is her use of the four-step process described above:

Step One: Outside, a late spring rainstorm had been brewing for some time. The rain came and all of a sudden there was a loud clap of thunder, and a large streak of lightning appeared. One child jumped up and ran to the window, followed by a few others. Another child burst into tears. Others just sat there. But no one was paying any attention to me. So, I got up and closed the curtains and insisted that everyone come back to our rug so that we could finish the story.

Step Two: I know that they are just naturally curious about everything. I also know that thunder and lightning can be frightening. So, why did I feel I had to ignore their reactions and just get on with business? I knew I was making a mistake even as I closed the curtains and told them to be quiet and come sit back down.

Step Three: I think I felt I had to finish my activity with the children because I was being observed. I was afraid of appearing to lose control. I didn't know how to handle something so unexpected.

Step Four: In the future, I need to take care of children's immediate feelings. We needed to talk about thunder and lightning and answer their immediate questions. We also needed to talk about fears. This would have been a more important lesson than my read-aloud story any day.

Through this type of critical incident reflection, you can cultivate the skills you need not only to survive but also to thrive in the complex world of teaching young children.

Peer Coaching

Another form of direct observation that is gaining notice is peer evaluation during student teaching. This process is sometimes referred to as *peer coaching*. Students have been making observations of each other and giving feedback during early field experiences for years. Many studies have found peer coaching to be a valuable means of increasing collaboration and transforming knowledge from theory into practice (Anderson, 1998; Anderson & Radencich, 2001; Buttery & Weller, 1988; Hatch, 1993; Hudson, Miller, Salzberg, & Morgan, 1994). Rauch and Whittaker (1999) report findings from a study in which students utilized peer coaching during their student teaching semester. Each student chose a partner who was also student teaching. One formal observation with a written evaluation was required of each peer. The results suggest that students generally find coaching from a colearner to be helpful, particularly when a postobservation conference is part of the process. It is suggested that, in order to be successful, this model of peer coaching must be "built on a pre-service program that emphasizes collaborative experiences and reflective teaching in all education courses" (p. 75). If your college does not require peer observation and feedback, this may be an option to consider if you feel comfortable doing so. You may want to discuss this with your college supervisor and cooperating teacher to add another dimension to your experience.

Video Observations

College supervisors and cooperating teachers often suggest that you video-tape yourself. Valuable information can be gleaned from observing yourself teaching formal lessons as well as interacting with children in less formal situations.

Before using this option, check with your administrator to see if there is any policy you need to know about regarding the use of a video camera in your room. Some parents do not want their children's picture taken for any purpose. This is something you need to check on before proceeding.

Often, student teachers feel self-conscious about using this observation tool. You can reduce the anxiety of being on camera by setting up the video camera in the room for several days before turning it on. That way, the children (and you) become used to its presence.

Some student teachers prefer to watch the tape alone. Others want their cooperating teacher's input. Regardless, you may find that observing the tapes gives you an "aha" moment. Tapes provide the distance you need to see mannerisms you may have been unaware of or classroom procedures that can be improved. They also provide a record of exemplary teaching that you can incorporate into an electronic portfolio. Portfolios and their use will be discussed later in this chapter.

❖ EVALUATION

Generally, a discussion and an analysis will follow your observations. You will have the chance to evaluate your own performance and to receive evaluative feedback. This is an opportunity for continual improvement. Probably at no other point in your career will anyone pay so much attention to what you are doing and care enough to provide you with both positive feedback and suggestions for improvement.

Receiving Criticism

Effective teachers recognize that learning about teaching is a lifelong process. Therefore, expect to receive constructive criticism. How you deal with it is of paramount importance. Some observers are even urged to find something to suggest for improvement, no matter how flawless the lesson appears to be.

Receiving constructive criticism is an art. You may be tempted to cry, leave the room, get defensive, or argue. Do none of these things. Denial, anger, and depression are counterproductive reactions. Remember that the person who is giving you feedback genuinely wants you to succeed.

You can take several steps to turn negative feedback into a positive experience. If you do not understand, seek clarification. Try focusing on one thing at a time. The following questions give you the idea of how the process works:

- What is the one thing I can adjust to make my instructions to the children clearer?
- What is the one thing I can change to make my classroom management better?
- What is the one thing I can change to make transitions smoother?

These kinds of questions give you the specific response you may need to make positive changes. They also indicate that you are willing to seek help. Even if you do not agree with the message you hear, thank the evaluator for her suggestion. Try the suggestions to see what happens. Even if a particular suggestion does not work for you, at least you tried it, and you will be perceived as someone who is receptive to new ideas.

Personal Characteristics

Although pedagogical knowledge and technical skill are important, a positive student teaching experience requires effective interpersonal communication skills. Hence, many teacher education programs assess professional potential by evaluating students' personal and professional characteristics, social and emotional characteristics, and interaction and communication skills. Figure 6.1 provides a sample form utilized by cooperating teachers and college supervisors to address these areas; self-evaluation by student teachers is also encouraged. In the opinion of some, these characteristics and skills are important enough to be considered an 11th competency in

---

Code: N–Not Observed **O**–Unsatisfactory **I**–Satisfactory **2**–Superior **3**–Exceptional

N   0   I   2   3   Personal and Professional Skills

        A. Meets obligations and deadlines by appropriate planning
        B. Follows guidelines, procedures, and rules
        C. Exhibits behaviors that reflect high professional standards
        D. Submits work products that reflect high professional standards
        E. Demonstrates effective use of problem-solving techniques
        F. Demonstrates tenacity and self-reliance in pursuit of solutions

N   0   I   2   3   Social and Emotional Characteristics

        A. Demonstrates rapport with students
        B. Demonstrates rapport with school personnel (includes all support staff)
        C. Displays appropriate affect and emotions
        D. Demonstrates awareness of social behaviors and expectations
        E. Demonstrates awareness of professional social behaviors and expectations
        F. Reflects on and takes responsibility for own behavior
        G. Accepts suggestions positively and modifies behavior appropriately
        H. Demonstrates enthusiasm and a positive attitude
        I. Accepts the role of both positive and negative experiences in personal development
        J. Demonstrates the ability to make the best of all experiences

N   0   I   2   3   Interaction and Communication Skills

        A. Demonstrates respect for the feelings, opinions, knowledge, and abilities of others
        B. Is empathetic with others
        C. Uses effective interpersonal skills
        D. Functions effectively in a variety of group roles
        E. Solicits and considers alternative viewpoints
        F. Communicates effectively with diverse audiences

FIGURE 6.1   Evaluation of Personal and Professional Characteristics

addition to those based on the Interstate New Teacher Assessment and Support Consortium (INTASC) 10 core standards (Blue et al., 2001).

Your heightened awareness of these somewhat subjective areas may be helpful in your ongoing reflection on your personal growth as you interact with children, parents, colleagues, and others in the community. You may also want to talk with your college supervisor to find out what observation/evaluation criteria she will use and compare her criteria to those in Figure 6.1.

❖ SELF-EVALUATION

You are already aware that good teaching requires continual and thoughtful deliberation. Throughout your teacher education program, you have been asked to reflect on your learning and its implications for practice. During your student teaching experience, critical reflection provides an opportunity for self-evaluation that may take several forms, including writing journals and developing portfolios.

Reflective Journals

You may have been asked to respond to reflective journal assignments in various education courses. This is a common approach used by professors of education to encourage you to examine the beliefs and assumptions you already possess regarding teaching and learning. These assignments often help students become more receptive to new ideas (Carter, 1998).

Furthermore, reflective journals can be an effective tool for self-evaluation and improvement during student teaching. College supervisors often require you to maintain a daily log, either in a notebook or in electronic form, in which you record daily events as well as your thoughts and reactions to those events. Sometimes this journal is for your eyes only; sometimes it is shared as a basis for dialogue between you and your supervisor or cooperating teacher.

The theoretical basis for a journal requirement is well grounded in the literature. The concepts of *reflective thinking* and *reflective teaching* have been the focus of attention for decades (Zeichner & Liston, 1996). For example, Dewey (1933) promoted reflective thinking as a necessary goal of education. He viewed it as an active process involving the deliberate consideration of beliefs and knowledge and the potential consequences of actions based on those beliefs and knowledge. Equally important, Schon (1983) recommended both formative and summative reflection on the teaching-learning process that he called *reflection-in-action* and *reflection-on-action*.

Figure 6.2 **Sample Personal History Questions**

- What importance did your family place on education? What attitudes were expressed toward education by your family?
- How have your family's attitudes toward education influenced your current attitude and teaching practice?
- What critical incidents stand out in your life as a learner? How have they influenced your teaching practice today?

(Cole & Knowles, 2000)

Forms of Inquiry

More recently, Cole and Knowles (2000) distinguished between two forms of inquiry that have different goals. As they explained, reflective inquiry is the process of examining teaching practices so that they may be improved; reflexive inquiry, on the other hand, is the process of examining personal histories or teaching autobiographies in order to understand the source of one's beliefs and assumptions. An example of personal history questions is shown in Figure 6.2. Both forms are valuable for understanding yourself as a teacher as you write in your journal or teaching log.

As a reflective teacher, you realize that you teach "students who live lives beyond the classroom walls, and schools and classrooms exist in settings that directly affect the type and quality of education that can occur" (Zeichner & Liston, 1996, p. 77). Therefore, your reflection should include a focus on the context as well as the content and manner of children's learning.

Process of Journal Writing

Some students view journal writing as drudgery, whereas others enjoy it as an outlet for personal expression. To facilitate the process, consider the possibility that the only rule in journal writing is that there are no rules. For example, writing lists and drawing sketches are just as acceptable as formal paragraphs. You may want to consider some of the topics suggested by Cole and Knowles (2000) to help you get started:

- Instances in your classroom that you identify as real learning
- Preconceptions or stereotypes that have been challenged or changed as a result of your experiences with students
- Relationships with colleagues
- Students with special needs
- Issues of gender, race, and class

- Working with parents
- Highlights of the day, week, or term
- Your professional development needs
- Your disconnections in teaching: the things that cause you grief, the things you do not understand
- Things about teaching that excite you (p. 60)

Whether you share your journal with anyone or not, you may find that your writing provides a unique opportunity for self-evaluation and growth. Over time, the written reflections may become a vehicle for problem solving and communication that continue throughout your professional career.

Portfolios

Another form of self-evaluation, portfolio development, may be considered an extension of the reflective journaling process (Yoo, 2001). Indeed, the use of reflective portfolios is becoming widespread. Children, even in the early childhood years, are capable of thinking about their work and choosing samples that showcase their progress. You are, in effect, doing the same thing when you select **artifacts** and write reflections to demonstrate your progress in meeting established criteria. Similarly, many schools now expect teachers to develop a portfolio that indicates their professional development as effective educators (Painter, 2001; Wolf, Whinery, & Hagerty, 1995). This self-evaluation tool has even been hailed as the most effective means of improving the teaching-learning process (Zubizarreta, 1994).

Artifacts are concrete evidence of knowledge as well as the ability to demonstrate understanding of the knowledge and apply it in a meaningful way.

Definition of Terms

A portfolio has been defined in various ways. Ryan and Kuhs (1993) define it as a student's collection of work that shows progress toward specific predetermined goals. However, Wolf (1996) cautions that it should be much more than merely "a miscellaneous collection of artifacts or an extended list of professional activities" (p. 34). He warns against portfolios characterized as either a scrapbook of meaningful mementos or a trunk containing large quantities of random artifacts. Shulman (1998) offers a definition that delineates significant steps included in the process of portfolio creation:

> A teaching portfolio is the structured documentary history of a set of coached or mentored acts of teaching substantiated by samples of student work and fully realized only through reflective writing, deliberation, and serious conversation. (p. 37)

Equally important, portfolios are an active and interactive process. They have even been suggested to be a more accurate representation of teacher quality than either a direct observation or a high score on a paper-and-pencil test (Gellman, 1992–1993). Perhaps they do indeed have a more lasting

Your portfolio is a reflection of who you are as a teacher. You will keep it and modify it throughout your career.

impact on both teachers and their children than other assessment options (Lyons, 1999).

Levels of Portfolio Development

As a student teacher, you may need to be concerned about two or three different levels of the portfolio development process: the working portfolio, the exit portfolio, and the interview portfolio (Dietz, 1995; Toro & Newell, 2001).

- The *working portfolio,* as its name implies, is a work in progress. It documents your growth toward the performance standards of your teacher education program; you may receive coaching or mentoring as needed throughout this process.
- The *exit portfolio* is also becoming an accepted rite of passage prior to graduation as you present evidence that you have mastered required teacher education competencies; often, a somewhat formal presentation involving conversations with interested faculty, peers, and others is part of the exit portfolio process.
- Finally, you will, in all likelihood, develop an *interview portfolio* that is a modified form of your exit portfolio. This is the portfolio you will take to your job interviews. It contains a resume and the highlights of your experience and teacher preparation activities that will sell you to a prospective employer.

Electronic Portfolio Development

Many students are developing an electronic version of their paper portfolio to give prospective employers. While completing your student teaching, you may want to keep this approach in mind. Typically, you will be collecting artifacts such as sample lesson plans, photographs of your bulletin boards, and photographs of you and your children engaged in various learning activities. You may also consider making video and audio clips as well as links to your own Web site that you can include in a compact disc. You can use this electronic format to demonstrate your creativity and your technology skill (Heath, 2004; Kilbane & McNergney, 1999; Spencer, 2004).

Electronic portfolios are becoming the norm rather than the exception. Some states and national organizations strongly recommend that all teacher candidates prepare such portfolios as part of the exit criteria for graduation from teacher preparation programs (C. Edwards, personal communication, June 19, 2008). As a result, some colleges and universities require all students to create a digital archive of their work where they save specific artifacts throughout their teacher preparation program. Then they prepare a portfolio in electronic form as a graduation requirement.

The electronic portfolio is quite different from the traditional paper portfolio. It allows you to include digital pictures, video and sound clips of your teaching, drawings, animations, and written artifacts such as lesson plans (Spencer, 2004). You may also include recordings of children if you have permission from their families. Yes, this is a time-consuming process, but many students believe it to be an asset during the all-important job search process.

In panel discussions of the job interview and hiring process, one school superintendent and several principals expressed a preference for electronic portfolios (A. Slamp, personal communication, March 2008). They prefer to interview candidates, narrow down their list, and then view electronic portfolios to make their final hiring selection. Each childcare center and school district may conduct the hiring process in its own way. However, having a copy of your electronic portfolio to leave with a prospective employer indicates that you are knowledgeable about technology. Demonstrating that knowledge is an important plus whether you are working with children of school age or younger ones.

Criteria for Assessment

Many teacher education programs use standardized criteria in order to establish consistency in the assessment of portfolio quality in what may be a somewhat subjective process (Smith et al., 2001). Students generally select performance categories such as those established by Danielson (1996):

- **Planning and preparation:** Design of instruction and organization of content for children's learning
- **Classroom environment:** Noninstructional interactions necessary for effective learning to occur
- **Instruction:** Engaging children in the process of learning
- **Professional responsibilities:** Professionalism and professional development

Then they develop their portfolios to indicate how they meet specific standards in each category.

When you create your own portfolio, you may include materials that showcase your personality as well as your teaching skills. You may assemble a product that contains many of the following:

- One or more examples of your best lesson plans and units
- Instructional materials that you prepared yourself
- Photographs of children playing or working at various centers that you created
- Photographs of bulletin boards that you created
- Photos or diagrams of ways you have organized your classroom
- Written evaluations of your teaching that you are particularly proud of
- Samples of children's work
- Certificates of attendance at a workshop or conference
- Your resume
- A statement of your philosophy of teaching young children

No matter what products or artifacts you gather for your portfolio, the important thing to remember is the written reflection on *why* you have chosen to include each one. What does each item reveal about you as a successful early childhood student teacher who is meeting the standards for entry into this profession?

Regardless of what standards and categories you select, your portfolio should indicate that you are a reflective practitioner. At some point, whether in portfolio conversations with professors or in interviews with prospective employers, you must take ownership of your portfolio as an authentic representation of who you are as both a teacher and a learner. Accordingly, the portfolio documents your willingness to be a lifelong learner who closely observes and understands children, who assesses herself and develops goals for continual improvement, who learns through inquiry, and who collaborates with others (Yoo, 2001).

❖ STATE STANDARDS AND HIGH-STAKES ASSESSMENT

According to a poll conducted in May 2002 for the Educational Testing Service (ETS), 93% of the respondents endorsed testing teachers on their knowledge of both teaching skills and subject matter, and 90% favored teacher training programs to prepare highly qualified teachers (Perkins-Gough, 2002).

Praxis Tests

In order to meet the demand for testing of teacher candidates, the ETS has developed a series of Praxis examinations. These examinations are perhaps the ultimate in high-stakes assessment for future teachers. The consequences of passing these examinations have a direct influence on your ability to obtain the teaching position you desire. According to testimony of Patty McAllister, Executive Director of State and Federal Regulations at ETS, the Praxis Series has a 50-year history of use in the United States. The examinations are now administered in all 50 states, six times a year at 650 test sites. They are continually updated to reflect the current knowledge of technology, pedagogical knowledge, and practice expected of qualified teachers (McAllister, 2003). The results of these tests affect licensure decisions. The specific Praxis test requirements vary from state to state. Therefore, you must investigate the particular requirements not only for the state in which you are completing your teacher education program but also for any states in which you think you might wish to seek employment.

Passing the Praxis Tests

To help you pass the Praxis examinations, you may obtain study guides prepared by the ETS. You may also check your state's Department of Education Web site. For example, Pennsylvania's Department of Education offers samples of various Praxis tests online. Beginning in the fall of 2003, a Diagnostic Preparation Program was made available from ETS to help you plan a course of study to prepare for the examinations. In addition, check out the ETS Web site (*http://www.ets.org*) to explore test preparation options.

ETS will also grant testing accommodations for the Praxis Series if you have appropriate documentation of a disability such as a specific learning disability or a visual impairment. The ETS Web site contains information on the types of documentation necessary as well as the procedure for obtaining accommodations. If you are accustomed to receiving extra time on tests or to being tested in a separate room, for example, you may have these same accommodations for the Praxis Series if you follow the specified procedures for requesting them.

Certification

As you complete your student teaching, start considering where you would like to teach if you have not done so already. In your planning, be aware that many states have reciprocity agreements that accept other states' certification requirements. There is a National Association of State Directors of Teacher Education and Certification (NASDTEC) contract to help educators who move to other states. Approximately 48 jurisdictions, including the District of Columbia, Guam, and Puerto Rico, have signed the current NASDTEC Interstate Contract allowing appropriately trained personnel to transfer their certifications to other locations. Requirements regarding experience may vary; so, to be safe, check with the Department of Education in each location you are considering. Each jurisdiction has its own office of certification and licensure that may impose special requirements to be fulfilled within a reasonable time period (Goethals & Howard, 2000; NASDTEC, 2002).

❖ PEER SUPPORT GROUP

Early in the semester and even during your weeks of full-time teaching, teaching observations and assessment can become issues of concern. Later, as the semester comes to an end, one of the topics of frequent discussion is the often-required portfolio presentation and its ensuing evaluation. The following thoughts shared by the peer support group may give some insights regarding their experiences as well as yours.

Evaluations and the Unexpected

Student teachers quickly realize that flexibility is one of the qualities they must develop if they do not already possess it in abundance. On a daily and sometimes an hourly basis, the unexpected can be expected to occur. Student teachers have been known to remark that one of the few things predictable about children is their unpredictability; occasionally, they find the same to be true of their cooperating teachers and college supervisors.

Time Management

A common complaint of the peer support group seems to be that there is too much to do and not enough time. Student teaching, as you know, becomes all-consuming. Then, as graduation looms, you realize that not only do you have to compete for a professional teaching position, but you also have one or two important tasks to complete before graduation. For many students, the prospect of portfolio presentations and/or portfolio conversations is a stressful reality. Even the preparation of the portfolio itself can get

Voices of Reality: Student Teachers Speak

This whole portfolio thing has me really stressed out! I don't know when I'm supposed to have time to finish it while I'm student teaching. I want to do a CD for my interviews but I just don't have time to prepare everything right now. How are we supposed to student teach, finish a portfolio, and begin filling out applications for teaching positions?

Angie D.

I'm going to concentrate on finishing my paper portfolio right now. And after graduation, I'll have time to burn CDs to hand out. The only thing I'm worried about is making the presentation—the questions I'll get. I'm going to practice ahead of time. I also want to do mine on the last day so I can see what other people's portfolios look like.

Lauren C.

Actually, I'm looking forward to the whole presentation thing. I want to tell everyone what I've been doing, and I'll have a captive audience! I'm not worried. The portfolio is part of who I am.

Keeley N.

out of hand; some students spend excessive money, time, and energy to prepare attractive binders or multimedia presentations (Wheeler, 1996). This is not necessary. Even with limited resources, high-quality, professional-looking portfolios can be produced.

❖ FINAL THOUGHTS

You have learned by now that teaching is an exceedingly complex blend of art and science. Danielson (1996) claims that "a teacher makes over 3,000 nontrivial decisions daily. It is useful then to think of teaching as similar to not one but several other professions, combining the skills of business management, human relations, and theater arts" (p. 2). For this reason, student teaching is a period in which to develop the habits and skills of observation, reflective analysis, and collaboration with peers that will guide your development as a lifelong learner. Throughout your professional career, you will probably participate in direct observation, journal writing, professional conversations, and portfolio development. Becoming a skilled professional takes time and the courage to take risks. As Dewey (1902/1959) wrote, "It involves reaching out of the mind" (p. 95). Accordingly, the ability to think outside the box sometimes requires a transformation, the development of new habits of the mind through connections or mentoring with others (Freidus, 1996).

ACTIVITIES FOR REFLECTION AND ACTION

1. All student teachers are observed and assessed in various ways as a learning experience. In teacher evaluation, there must be some vision of what good teaching is. What is your vision of good teaching? How will you know when you are a good teacher?

2. Observe your cooperating teacher and make notes to review later. Pay attention to her classroom routines. How does she start a lesson or activity? How does she give directions? How does she motivate children? What is the sequence of steps for a lesson? How many minutes does she spend on each step? What questions does she ask? How does she know if the children understand? How does she handle misbehavior? How does she allow for differences in ability? How does she end the lesson? How do the children react to the lesson? Reflect on what you have observed. What would you do the same way or differently? What questions do you have for your cooperating teacher?

3. Locate two artifacts that you have saved during your courses or your practicum. Write a reflection on each artifact that explains why you have chosen it and what it indicates about you as a teacher. Share your artifacts and reflections with a partner.

4. *Portfolio*: If you have not already done so, collect the artifacts that you have produced so far. Consider which ones you want to include in your portfolio, and write a reflection to accompany each one. Save them in your electronic folder or in a binder.

CHAPTER 7

Assessment of Young Children

To teachers, students are the end products.
All else is a means. Hence there is but one
interpretation of high standards in teaching:
standards are highest where the maximum
number of students—slow learners and
fast learners alike—develop to their
maximal capacity.

Joseph Seidlin

These words are particularly relevant in the education of children today. Terms such as *high-stakes testing, assessment,* and *accountability* have become controversial. Debates ensue over the necessity of assessing young children. Parents and teachers question not only the need for assessing young children but also the manner in which results will be reported and used. Educators even disagree over how assessments should be conducted, especially when examining children who have disabilities or children who are not from the majority culture. These concerns represent only the tip of the iceberg.

You are student teaching at a time when the mere mention of National Education Goals and/or No Child Left Behind may elicit strong opinions regarding school readiness, educational performance, and program evaluation. Throughout your student teaching practicum, you will have opportunities to participate in ongoing discussions about these contemporary issues as you interact with early childhood teachers, paraprofessionals, parents, and others who share similar interests. In fact, you may even find yourself questioning what it means to expect all children to reach their highest potential or "maximal capacity" in an educational climate of high-stakes testing and accountability.

As beginning teachers, you want all children in your care to feel that their place of learning is an emotionally safe environment. Therefore, you may find yourself questioning whether or not young children should be

Voices of Reality: Student Teachers Speak

When we do assessment, they are told they are going to play a game and everyone will get a chance to play. . . . I believe the children see the timer that the teacher presses and concentrate on that rather than the task at hand. And this testing is a deciding factor of who goes to EDK [extended day kindergarten].

Jackson L.

The first three days were 20-minute conferences with each student, individually, to evaluate what their ability is. We actually had students cry because they did not know the answers to some of the questions. We had to tell them each time that it is okay, that we don't expect them to know the answers; these are things that they will be able to understand at the end of kindergarten.

Nancy F.

In our multiage room, most of our first and second graders had never seen a test like the math or reading pretests before. That, combined with some of them having a definite need to finish and be successful despite how difficult a test is, made it quite a stressful experience. Each section of the test ended in tears for at least a few. This brings up the question of whether such a test is worth it.

Saul D.

assessed at all. Regardless of your reaction to the topic of assessment, this issue is not going away. Accordingly, you may want to consider how to make the process of evaluation nonstressful for children. No one wants to see children reduced to tears because they feel anxious in an unfamiliar testing situation. Therefore, the topics of assessment, testing, standards, and evaluation are important for you to consider as you prepare to enter the profession of early childhood education.

❖ ASSESSMENT: A BLESSING OR A CURSE?

A review of recent history reminds us that, in 1990, President George H. W. Bush and the nation's governors called for the establishment of National Educational Goals. The first goal was that by the year 2000, all children would enter school ready to learn. In 1994, Congress called for the creation of "clear guidelines regarding the nature, functions, and uses of early childhood assessments" (Shepard, Kagan, & Wurtz, 1998, p. 3). Then in January 2002, President George W. Bush signed the No Child Left Behind Act (NCLB) of 2001. The NCLB calls for the annual assessment of children in Grades 3 through 8, along with the development of content and performance standards for reading, mathematics, and science. Although the regulations focus primarily on school-age children, they have an impact on the development of standards in preschool programs as well (Kagan & Scott-Little, 2004; Kendall, 2003). In fact, the federal government has instituted accountability measures that mandate biannual testing of children in Head Start programs in the areas of language, literacy, and premath. As a result, some critics decry the focus on assessment of cognitive skills rather than an emphasis on the social/behavioral development of young children (Raver & Zigler, 2004). More discussion regarding the national testing and assessment of preschoolers continues as policymakers examine the evidence being collected over time.

The NCLB is currently up for reauthorization. Over 100 bills have been introduced in Congress that propose revisions to improve it. Some of these bills provide funding to increase the number of children served in prekindergarten programs. As part of your ongoing involvement in the profession of early childhood education, you should stay up-to-date with the reauthorization process and how it will impact your work with young children. Suggested Web sites include the following:

- *http://www.nea.org*   You can read the National Education Association's (NEA's) position on NCLB. This Web site also suggests how you can become involved by contacting your members of Congress.
- *http://www.naeyc.org*   You can read the NAEYC's recommendations for the 110th U.S. Congress by going to its Web site. This site also offers suggestions on how you can become involved in advocating for your profession.
- *http://www.ed.gov/nclb/overview/intro/reauth/index.html*   You can go to the Department of Education's various links to read the latest news regarding NCLB. Links include proposed regulations to strengthen NCLB as well as information from the office of the Secretary of Education.

This is an important time for the field of early childhood education. You need to be keenly aware of changing regulations involving funding, requirements for teacher certification, assessment, and accountability. Therefore, even when you complete your teacher preparation program, you must continue your commitment to learning.

What Assessment Is and What It Is Not

Assessment has been defined as "the process of documenting what children do and how they do it in order to make decisions affecting children" (Hyson, 2002, p. 62). Although definitions vary, they generally include several common ideas. For example, the process of assessment may include the following characteristics (Airasian, 2001; Mindes, 2003):

- Decision-making purpose
- Variety of methods

- Application to an individual or to a group
- Creation of one or more products that may be interpreted
- Inherent ethics and responsibilities

Assessment is so important that it is considered a right of all young children. Even the youngest children deserve thoughtful "assessment that is ongoing, appropriate, and developmentally supportive" (Hyson, 2002, p. 63). It is a broad topic that includes observations, family interviews, testing, and alternative approaches to assessment, such as authentic assessment. An overview of these forms of evaluation will be discussed in this chapter as well as the appropriate uses of each in the context of early childhood education.

❖ ASSESSMENT-RELATED TERMINOLOGY

High-stakes testing refers to the administration of tests the results of which are used to make important decisions affecting the future of children, teachers, schools, and educational programs.

Unfortunately, some people mistake testing for assessment. This is not surprising because the media continually report test results and nationwide *test targets* as the focus of school improvement efforts. Testing, however, is not the same as assessment. Therefore, a brief overview of a few terms associated with assessment may be helpful at this point.

Several terms frequently mentioned in discussions of assessment include *testing, measurement,* and *standards.* These words are value laden in that they often evoke preconceived ideas in the minds of those who hear them. This is particularly true in an educational climate in which **high-stakes testing** is common (Salvia & Ysseldyke, 2004; Venn, 2004). ·

Testing

Testing may be defined as one form of assessment used to collect data. The data are usually reported numerically in the form of test scores. Tests are generally administered in a prescribed manner for a specific purpose. They may include many types of formal standardized tests and less formal teacher-made tests (Mindes, 2003).

When thinking about administering tests to children in early childhood programs, you should discuss the following questions with your cooperating teacher and your college supervisor:

- How will this test benefit children?
- What decisions will be made as a result of the test?
- What training is necessary in order to administer the test appropriately?
- Has this test been evaluated for developmental and linguistic appropriateness?
- How will families be informed of the test results?

Reflection on these questions will help you be prepared when families and policymakers want to know if a particular child is making progress or if a particular early childhood program is successful.

The testing of young children must proceed cautiously and responsibly (NAEYC & NAECS/SDE, 2003). In fact, both NAEYC and the Association for Childhood Education International (ACEI) urge caution regarding the standardized testing of young children. They believe that no decisions should be made regarding any child based on the results of one test (Crosser, 2005).

Measurement

Measurement is a broader term than testing. It refers to "the process of determining the ability or performance level of students" (Venn, 2004, p. 5). Although a test is one kind of measurement, it is not the only kind. For example, you can collect data from the careful observation of children that will help you not only understand children's behavior but also optimize their opportunities for growth and development (Nicholson & Shipstead, 2002). Observational methods such as running records, checklists, and time sampling will be discussed later in this chapter.

Standards

Standards may be defined as shared expectations for learning and development. In other words, standards in early childhood "specify what young children should know and be able to do" (Kagan & Scott-Little, 2004, p. 390). Standards have been a fact of life in K–12 education for years. Now, with increased state investment in early childhood education, early learning guidelines or standards that specify outcomes have become the norm. In fact, all 50 states plus the District of Columbia and three territories (i.e., Guam, Puerto Rico, and the Commonwealth of the Northern Mariana Islands) have developed early learning guidelines (Drew, Christie, Johnson, Meckley, & Nell, 2008; NCCIC, 2007). The ages of young children specified in these guidelines vary somewhat from state to state. For example, Minnesota and Pennsylvania developed early childhood guidelines for children of ages 3 to 5 several years ago and then more recently developed guidelines for children from birth to age 3. Other states specify guidelines for children of ages 4 to 5 or ages 3 to 4. In order to see what guidelines your state has developed, you may go to the Web site for the National Child Care Information and Technical Assistance Center at *http://www.nccic.org/pubs/goodstart/elgwebsites.html.* There you can find comparative data among states as well as links to your particular state's early learning standards.

Care must be taken to ensure that standards are developed to benefit children rather than to harm them. For example, stimulating discussion and creating a consensus about what should be included in an early childhood program is beneficial for all. In contrast, placing negative consequences on children who do not meet prescribed standards is harmful.

NAEYC and NAECS/SDE (2002) recommend that standards contain four essential features that promote positive outcomes for children, as shown in the Figure 7.1. The development of early childhood standards

Essential Features	Characteristics
1. Developmentally appropriate content and outcomes	All domains of development and learning outcomes included Expectations meaningful to well-being and learning Expectations based on developmental research Expectations linked to age and/or developmental periods Expectations accommodate variations such as cultural, linguistic, and individual ones
2. Process for appropriate evaluation, review, and revision	Expectations validated through examination of effectiveness Wide range of participants such as families, early childhood educators, and professional groups included in examination of standards Information regarding standards and their implications shared openly for discussion Process established for ongoing examination and revision as needed to ensure continued relevancy
3. Implementation and assessment practices considered ethical and appropriate	Curriculum and its implementation promote positive learning and development Assessment connected to standards and yields information considered useful and valid Assessment information used to make decisions that benefit children
4. Support for early childhood programs, families, and professionals	Use of research findings and resources to create environments for effective implementation of standards Systematic, ongoing professional development for early childhood teachers and administrators Collaborative, cooperative approach to communicating with children's families

Source: Essential features adapted from the *NAEYC and NAECS/SDE Joint Statement on Early Learning Standards* by the NAEYC and NAECS/SDE (National Association of Early Childhood Specialists in State Departments of Education), 2003.

FIGURE 7.1   Essential Features of Beneficial Early Childhood Standards

has been called "the true litmus test of the future direction of the field" (Kagan & Scott-Little, 2004, p. 395). Reaching agreement concerning appropriate standards and appropriate curricula for young children is not an easy task. This is due, in part, to the fact that early childhood education has been relatively unstructured in comparison with public education K–12. Consequently, you are entering the field during a significant period of transition.

Teachers with many years of experience are grappling with these issues. Assessment is truly one of education's "hot topics." When you have the opportunity, ask your colleagues for their opinions.

❖ PURPOSES OF ASSESSMENT

Four general purposes of early childhood assessment are generally acknowledged (Bowman, Donovan, & Burns, 2001; Jones, 2004; Shepard et al., 1998):

- To support children's learning
- To identify those children in need of special services
- To evaluate programs and to monitor trends
- To instill accountability

All four of these purposes should be occurring continually (Mindes, 2003). Because young children are the focus of everything you do, your ongoing assessment of their learning and development guides each decision you make. As you monitor the effectiveness of instructional activities, you gather information that will enable you to answer parents' questions concerning how their children are doing. In addition, legislators and program administrators are focusing more attention on the funding of early childhood programs. They want evidence concerning program quality and effectiveness. Assessment data also provide the information that enables you to answer their questions.

Assessment to Monitor Understanding

Assessment should benefit children. It should be related to the goals established for a particular program, and the results should be used to plan appropriate experiences for your children. You may do a *preassessment* to determine children's level of functioning before instruction, a *formative assessment* during instruction to check progress and understanding, and then a *summative assessment* at the end of instruction to determine if your goals have been met. For example, if you are having young children follow directions to make paper bag puppets for a dramatization, you may

Voice of Reality: A Cooperating Teacher Speaks

I understand the importance of standards but not all "square pegs" will fit into a "round hole"—all children will never master the state standards. I tell my student teacher not to get bogged down with meeting all the standards—NO ONE has the solution to that one! Besides, don't lose those "teachable moments" because they are important also. . . . Reality is [that] no matter what you do, some children are going to have a very hard time meeting the standards. Legislators don't have a clue—it's that simple.

Barbara L.

preassess to make sure that they understand what a paper bag puppet is. You may show them some sample puppets. During construction of the puppets, you may do a formative assessment to see how well the children are following directions by walking around and observing their progress. If you find that children are getting confused, then you will need to rephrase and/or clarify your instructions. You may need to make adaptations, such as assigning children to work with partners. Then summative assessment of the ability to follow directions will be the final product: a paper bag puppet ready for use.

Assessment as a Screening Tool

Screening is a commonly used term that refers to the process of collecting information to decide if more extensive assessment is needed. The parents of children being screened must be notified about the purpose of the intended screening and later given the results. They must also be notified if further in-depth assessment is recommended. You may expect to work closely with them because they have the right to be continually involved in any decisions made regarding their children.

Children are screened at many points in their early years. For example, childcare facilities, preschools, and school districts commonly conduct vision, hearing, and cognitive screening to determine which children have difficulties that warrant further testing. Screening cannot identify children as eligible to receive special services, but it can indicate which ones need in-depth evaluation (Maxwell & Clifford, 2004; Mindes, 2003; Salvia & Ysseldyke, 2004). Therefore, screening is assessment that benefits children.

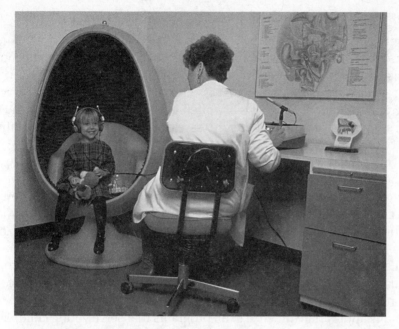

Routine screening benefits children by identifying those who have difficulties that warrant further in-depth evaluation.

You can do informal screening in your classroom in the form of a functional assessment. For example, if you are concerned that a particular child may have difficulty meeting the behavioral expectations of first grade, you can create your own rating scale to use as a referral tool (see Figure 7.2). This informal rating tool can at least provide you with a basis for discussion if you believe that the child could benefit from behavioral support.

Figure 7.2 Sample Informal Rating Scale

Classroom Behaviors	1 (never) to 5 (always)				
Sits in the circle at story time	1	2	3	4	5
Raises a hand to be called on	1	2	3	4	5
Follows directions	1	2	3	4	5
Walks in line in the hallway	1	2	3	4	5

(Based on Mindes, 2003)

Assessment to Evaluate Programs

Parents and the public in general want to know if children are making progress as a result of instruction. As a teacher, you are accountable, or responsible, for providing appropriate education for all the children in your care. *Accountability* is a word that is often heard these days in relation to program evaluation. Programs are often evaluated on the basis of the children's reported progress. Therefore, assessment is critical to the continuation of funding for specific programs.

This assessment can and should take many forms. For example, as a teacher, you may collect data by making observations of children. You may assemble representative samples of children's work in portfolios. You may also give tests before and after instruction based on the curriculum you are teaching. Accordingly, you can demonstrate children's progress in many ways (Rosenberg, O'Shea, & O'Shea, 1998; Salvia & Ysseldyke, 2004).

Early learning guidelines or standards are an integral part of program evaluation. The NAEYC Early Childhood Program Standards and Accreditation Criteria (NAEYC, 2005b) have set high expectations for developmentally appropriate practice in all programs that serve young children and their families. Some critics hail them as "the gold standard for parent selections, state standards, and reimbursement rates for child care services" (Bowman, 2006, p. 44). The expectation is that programs evaluated as having met these criteria of appropriate practice are doing the right things the right way.

For example, the Pennsylvania Department of Education's Office of Child Development and Early Learning (PDE/OCDEL) used assessments to evaluate the effectiveness of its state-funded initiative called *Pre-K Counts*. The purpose of *Pre-K Counts* is to increase the number of children who benefit from high-quality pre-K education. Classes are kept small, teacher qualifications are specified, and the curriculum is aligned with the state's standards for early learning. Program effectiveness is judged by various means, including electronic portfolios of each child's progress, narrative reports, site visits by early childhood specialists, and rating scales administered by independent evaluators (PDE/OCDEL, 2008).

Assessment for Accountability Purposes

Accountability assessments hold people accountable for outcomes. For example, in order to ensure the quality of *Pre-K Counts*, Pennsylvania's Office of Child Development and Early Learning "created a comprehensive system of reporting, site monitoring, and Early Childhood Environment Rating Scales Assessments . . . (as well as monitoring) child outcomes, fiscal, enrollment, and narrative reports" (PDE/OCDEL, 2008, p. 15). The outcome data measured children's progress in meeting specific early learning standards. The fiscal data allowed the state to monitor expenditures. The enrollment data monitored information such as each child's enrollment date, attendance record, and risk factors such as being an English-language learner or having an IEP. The Early Childhood Environment Rating Scales Assessment evaluated interactions that occurred in the room between adults, between children and adults, between children and the materials in their physical environment, and so on.

In *Pre-K Counts,* first-year assessments indicate that nearly 70% of the 11,000 3- and 4-year-olds who participated in the program during its first year achieved the desired age-appropriate outcomes in various domains. Assessment data also indicate that 21% of the children who entered the program with no age-appropriate skills demonstrated emerging age-appropriate skills after 1 year. In order to ensure continued success of *Pre-K Counts,* Pennsylvania plans to increase its investment in early childhood education.

❖ FORMAL ASSESSMENT

Assessment can also be in the form of formal standardized tests in which children's performance is compared to that of a representative sample of children of the same age or developmental level (Airasian, 2005; Salvia & Ysseldyke, 2004).

There are special concerns when evaluating programs based on the outcomes of tests administered to young children. Experience tells us that young children typically demonstrate extreme variability in development across domains. They also have limited ability to understand the abstract nature of testing in general. The entire concept of administering formal tests to young children has been called technically indefensible by some critics (Shepard et al., 1998). Nevertheless, the federal government has mandated "a new set of accountability measures that will be used to test Head Start children twice a year on language, literacy, and pre-math skills" (Raver & Zigler, 2004, p. 58). You may have the opportunity to formulate your own opinions as you observe and participate in the assessment process.

❖ INFORMAL ASSESSMENT

Informal assessments may take several forms. They should be as unobtrusive as possible to avoid interfering with children's typical behavior. Generally, the use of paper and pencil is less obtrusive than the use of a camera or video recorder, for example.

Observation

You will find that you can learn quite a bit just from observing children and paying close attention to details. Observation is a skill that will improve with practice (Mindes, 2003). Figure 7.3 presents several techniques that you can use effectively.

At the end of this chapter, Figures 7.5, 7.6, 7.7, and 7.8 are samples of various formats that may be used to collect data. These sample formats, based on Alberto and Troutman (2003), may be adjusted in many ways to meet your particular needs.

No matter which observation techniques you use, there are several tips to help you make informed decisions. Dichtelmiller (2004) recommends

---

Figure 7.3 **Examples of Observation Techniques**

- **Event sampling:** You may wish to observe children's behavior when specific events occur. For example, you may select one or two children to observe during outside recess, particularly if you have concerns about inappropriately rough play. You may observe the kinds of social interactions that occur.
- **Time sampling:** If you wish to monitor the frequency of occurrence of particular behaviors, you may use a technique called *time sampling*. You observe a child for a period of time, such as 10 minutes. You have a checklist of behaviors such as "calling out" or "touching others." Each time the child exhibits a behavior on the checklist, you record a tally mark on the chart. You can tailor a chart for a particular child and record on-task and off-task behaviors, for example. An advantage of this technique is that it is an objective measure of the frequency of occurrence of observable behaviors.
- **Anecdotal records:** You may use anecdotal records to record quick impressions of an event right after its occurrence. The difficulty with anecdotal records is that they are somewhat subjective. The observer can decide that a behavior is irrelevant and leave it out of the record. Nevertheless, anecdotal records can be useful in providing documentation to support a teacher's actions (Salvia & Ysseldyke, 2004).
- **Running records:** You may use running records to write a narrative of a child's behaviors to in order to provide a sequential description of an event. Generally, a running record focuses on one child. You limit yourself to a period of time, such as 15 minutes. Then you can review your notes and analyze evidence of particular competencies or behaviors. When two children's behaviors are described in the same narrative, the accuracy of the record declines.

(Adapted from Daniels, Beaumont, & Doolin, 2002)

that you make a point of observing children daily at varying times. You can compare your notes with observations made by your cooperating teacher. When appropriate, share information with children's families in order to encourage two-way communication. For example, if you observe changes in a child's behavior, ask family members if they have noticed similar changes at home. Teacher-family partnerships benefit everyone, especially the children.

❖ AUTHENTIC ASSESSMENTS

Many advocates for young children support the use of authentic assessment as a preferred means of evaluation. Authentic assessment is an alternative to the more traditional paper-and-pencil tests. It involves activities like those commonly used in the real world, such as building a model, illustrating a story, performing a dramatization, or contributing to a class newspaper.

Some students are more motivated to do well on assessments if they perceive that you are asking them to do something worthwhile (Kyle & Rogien, 2004). Therefore, it makes sense to assess learners who have a wide range of interests and strengths in a variety of ways.

Children's Portfolios

Portfolios are one form of authentic assessment that provides tangible evidence of a child's progress. Often even young children can help select the work products to be included in their portfolios. They can attend the parent-teacher conferences and perform a show-and-tell about each item.

Children's portfolios do not have to be limited to paper-and-pencil evidence of work. You can be creative about what items to include. Some suggestions include the following (Bender, 2002; Gestwicki, 1999; Kostelnik, Soderman, & Whiren, 2007):

- Tape recording of a child speaking about a story as you ask questions to evaluate understanding
- Photograph of an art project
- Video recording of a dramatization
- Anecdotal records of observations
- Child's choices of good work

You may want to collaborate with your children in deciding what items to include in their portfolios so that they feel a sense of ownership. Portfolios are most effective when they are a vehicle for active learning and the children have a "voice in the process" (Hill & Ruptic, 1994, p. 35). You can

Children play an active role as they show and tell about the work chosen for inclusion in their portfolios.

stimulate children's active involvement by encouraging them to engage in reflection.

Although portfolios represent a valuable collection of children's work, they should have a purpose, such as assessing a child's improvement over a period of time. Scoring portfolios is an issue that deserves careful attention. Scoring systems can be flawed by subjectivity, so grading or scoring of portfolios has limited value (Salvia & Ysseldyke, 2004). Rubrics (shown in Figure 7.4), rating scales, and checklists based on specific criteria need to be carefully considered. If you choose to use portfolio assessment, then work with your cooperating teacher to develop procedures that function best for you and the children.

Suggested Prompts for Reflection

- Why did you choose these pieces of work?
- What is your favorite sample of work? Why?
- What does this sample say about you?
- What did you learn from doing this sample of work?

Figure 7.4 Format for Sample Rubric

Category	3 points	2 points	1 point
Readiness	Completely prepared and rehearsed	Somewhat prepared; rehearsal lacking	Not prepared
Stays on topic	On topic 100%	On topic most of the time (75% or more)	Hard to tell what the topic was
Listens to other presentations	Listens carefully, no distracting noises	Sometimes does not appear to listen but is not distracting	Sometimes does not appear to listen and makes distracting noises

Performance Assessment

There may be times when you have the opportunity to use *performance assessment* with young children. This is assessment of behaviors that occur in simulated situations. For example, if you are teaching social skills to children who are having difficulty giving and receiving compliments, you can talk about appropriate behavior, model the desired behavior, and then set up a role-play so that children can practice giving and receiving compliments. The role-play is a contrived or simulated situation. Nevertheless, you can assess the children's behavior during this activity. In order to be effective, you should establish performance criteria before the simulation begins, explain these criteria to the children, and give feedback afterward (Kostelnik et al., 2007; Rosenberg et al., 1998).

❖ ALTERNATE ASSESSMENT

Ever since the passage of the Individuals with Disabilities Education Act (IDEA, 1997) and NCLB (2001), alternative assessment has been a focus of attention. All children must be included in formal state and district assessments. Children who have severe disabilities may have an alternate assessment instead of a paper-and-pencil test. Each state may determine which children are eligible for an alternate assessment. Each state may determine what that alternate assessment will look like. You can visit the Web site for the National Center on Educational Outcomes to find out your state's current policy on alternate assessment at *http://education .umn.edu/NCEO/TopicAreas/AlternativeAssessments/StatesAltAssess.htm*. Some states require a scripted test that is video recorded. Others allow observation checklists and portfolios. Because formal assessment of young children occurs in the primary grades and now extends to some preschool programs, you should be aware of your state's policies regarding alternate assessment.

❖ ASSESSMENT CONSIDERATIONS FOR SPECIAL POPULATIONS

English-language learners refers to individuals who speak a home language other than English.

As already discussed, assessment is extremely important for improving program quality and for monitoring effective practices to meet children's needs. However, appropriate assessment can be a challenge when dealing with special populations of young children. Children who are **English-language learners** and children who have been diagnosed with special needs require particular consideration.

English-Language Learners

According to NAEYC (2005c), appropriate assessment must be "culturally and linguistically responsive." Too often, children have been wrongly diagnosed as developmentally delayed because observers have not had access to culturally and linguistically appropriate assessment instruments. Young children who have limited English proficiency should be assessed in their native language and in English. This is difficult when you consider that over 460 languages are spoken by English-language learners in this country (NAEYC, 2005c). Finding appropriate means to assess them is a challenge. Even if assessment instruments can be translated, the cultural bias inherent in the instruments may remain. For example, the author has observed the use of a standardized test that contains the question "How many seasons are there?" Depending upon the child's cultural heritage or life experience, she may answer that question in several ways. Both formal and informal assessments should ideally be conducted by someone who is bilingual or multilingual and familiar with the child's culture. Observations should be conducted in the child's natural environment and should include interviews with the family in order to reduce the risk of cultural bias (Cook et al., 2008; NAEYC, 2005c). Further information is available from the Web sites of the following organizations:

- **Culturally and Linguistically Appropriate Services Early Childhood Research Institute.** Many articles can be downloaded for free; some

technical reports must be purchased. The resources on this site include materials on culture and language, disabilities and early intervention. The site has information available in both English and Spanish.
http://CLAS.uiuc.edu/

- **The National Center for Culturally Responsive Educational Systems.**   Some materials, such as articles, power points, and workbooks, may be downloaded for free; others must be purchased. Resources include information on culturally appropriate responses to intervention, screening, and progress monitoring.
http://www.nccrest.org/

Children Who Have Special Needs

In addition, you are likely to work with young children who have special needs in early childhood programs. New IDEA regulations were issued in August 2006. They contain provisions for early intervention services for infants and toddlers and their families (Mandlawitz, 2007). The National Early Intervention Longitudinal Study (NEILS) indicates that "there is no such thing as a typical child in early intervention" (Scarborough et al., 2004, p. 480). Some of the children who receive early intervention (EI) are considered healthy and typically developing. They may still be eligible for EI because they are considered at risk due to family circumstances. Other children may have speech or communication delays, motor delays, or birth-related abnormalities. You will be expected to work as a member of a team of professionals to provide these children and their families with the support and services they need. Keep in mind that, just as all children who receive EI are unique, "there also can be no standard intervention, curriculum, or approach that would be appropriate for all children" (Scarborough et al., 2004, p. 480). Ask your cooperating teacher to talk with you about the IFSP for these children. These plans may specify learning outcomes and specific types of informal and formal assessment that monitor progress.

The IDEA regulations issued in 2006 include a new category of disability called *developmentally delayed* that states may apply "to any subset of the age range of 3 through 9, including ages 3 through 5" (Mandlawitz, 2007, p. 2). Inclusion of this new category makes it even more likely that you will have children with diagnosed special needs in your early childhood program. Beginning at age 3, young children who have been diagnosed with a disability, as defined by IDEA, will generally have an IEP. Children between the ages of 3 and 5 may, at the discretion of the **Local Education Agency**, have an IFSP rather than an IEP. Some families prefer the IFSP because of the family support it provides. If this is the case, then IDEA specifies that the IFSP for 3- to

Local Education Agency generally refers to the local school districts or reporting agencies accountable for following the regulations of the IDEA.

5-year-olds must contain "an educational component that promotes school readiness and incorporates pre-literacy, language, and numeracy skills" (Mandlawitz, 2007, p. 87). Ask your cooperating teacher to share and discuss information about any IEPs or IFSPs that your children may have. They will contain important information about learning outcomes, behavior support, and assessment. The assessment component of these documents will tell you, among other things, if the child needs assessment in her native language or in another form of communication such as Braille or sign language. You may find the following Web sites helpful:

- **IDEA Data**　Web site provides updated information about children with disabilities who are served by IDEA. Information is separated into IDEA Part B (ages 3 through 21) and IDEA Part C (birth through age 2). *http://www.IDEAdata.org*
- **National Early Childhood Technical Assistance Center (NECTAC)** Web site provides information about federal policies and regulations such as those related to IDEA and Head Start. It also includes free, downloadable research on preschool inclusion and state policies related to children from birth to age 6. There are also links to resources related to the IFSP process and family-centered services in the natural environment. *http://www.nectac.org/*
- **Wrightslaw**　provides up-to-date information on IDEA. It also highlights advocacy issues on a variety of topics, such as how to advocate for a child who has a communication problem and what to do when a school does not protect a child from life-threatening allergies. *http://www.wrightslaw.com/*

Voices of Reality: Student Teachers Speak

Some teachers do the testing because they have to and others do it because they believe in results, and getting results is a way of helping a child in need.

Jackson L.

Today was an early dismissal day. The afternoon was for report cards. I couldn't believe how subjective they are! Most of it is on a scale from 1 to 3, and we don't base it on grades because we don't have any! It is all backed by anecdotal records, but it is definitely subjective!

Krista U.

❖ FINAL THOUGHTS

Assessments can be challenging for all teachers, which is one reason that the purposes for assessment must be carefully considered. It is important to remember that our assessment should benefit children, not harm them. Airasian (2005) reminds us that assessment "is more than a technical activity; it is a human activity that influences and affects many people" (p. 20). As the *NAEYC Code of Ethical Conduct* reminds us, the special vulnerability of young children must be kept in mind as well as respect for each young child's uniqueness. Therefore, we must refrain from making hasty judgments because what we do during the important process of evaluation and assessment does indeed affect many people.

ACTIVITIES FOR REFLECTION AND ACTION

1. How will you know if your children have learned as a result of your teaching?
2. Observe your cooperating teacher. What informal strategies does she use to assess student learning? What formal strategies?
3. Create a checklist that can be used to observe the behavior of a child in your class who concerns you. Use it for a brief period, such as 15 minutes. Share the results with your cooperating teacher.
4. *Portfolio*: Make a copy of your behavior checklist (without the child's name) to place in your portfolio in order to demonstrate your use of assessment. If you have the opportunity to complete event recording, time sampling, anecdotal records, or running records, you may place samples in your portfolio. Just remember to remove the names of the children or teachers to protect confidentiality.
5. Locate the early childhood standards for your state. See the text for suggestions about where to look for them. Choose three or four standards that you think are appropriate for the children with whom you work. Talk with your cooperating teacher about how you can use these standards as you work with children in your practicum.

Figure 7.5 Sample Format for Event Recording

Child:
Observer:
Objective: Child will demonstrate appropriate social interaction during recess.
Criterion: 100% appropriate social behavior during recess for 5 consecutive days.

Dates

Behaviors							Comments
Takes turns							
Plays with others							
Refrains from name-calling							
Refrains from physical aggression							
Total observed							

Figure 7.6 Sample Format for Time Sampling

Child:
Observer:
Objective: Child will remain on task during seatwork.
Date:
Time Start:
Code: X = occurrence

5-Minute Interval Time Sampling

	5	10	15	20	25	30
On task						
Verbally off task						
Physically off task						
Passively off task						

Figure 7.7 Sample Format for Anecdotal Records

Child:
Others present:
Observer:
Date:
Time:
Setting:
Purpose of Observation:
Anecdote: (Include context of event, action observed, and conclusion of event.)
Reflection: (Include interpretation and significance of event.)

Figure 7.8 Sample Format for Running Record

Child:
Observer:
Date:
Context of Observation: (Include relevant background information.)
Observation:
Reflective Comments:

CHAPTER 8

Supportive Instruction

It is a general insight, which merits more attention than it receives, that teaching should not be compared to filling a bottle with water but rather to helping a flower to grow in its own way. As any good teacher knows, the methods of instruction and the range of material covered are matters of small importance as compared with the success in arousing the natural curiosity of the students and stimulating their interest in exploring on their own.

Noam Chomsky

Noam Chomsky's words are particularly relevant as you assume more and more responsibility for planning lessons and implementing developmentally appropriate curriculum. By now, you have already seen the joy and excitement young children bring to your class each day. You notice the sparkle in their eyes as they take pleasure in the community of mutual respect and meaningful interaction that you help create. As you begin your student teaching practicum, you may be focusing on the details of writing lesson plans that follow curriculum guides written by practicing teachers or state Departments of Education.

Remember that good teaching is not so much about beautifully written plans as about children. You want to nurture each child's natural curiosity and joy of learning. As you focus on your children's interests and individual needs, you will become more adept at implementing a variety of teaching strategies and an integrated curriculum that engage the whole child in meaningful learning. Accordingly, you will play a significant role in helping each one of your young flowers grow.

❖ RECOGNIZING CHILDREN'S UNIQUE WAYS OF KNOWING

Research indicates that young children have unique ways of constructing meaning. As you may recall from your child development classes, young children rely heavily on sensorimotor interaction with their physical

Voices of Reality: Student Teachers Speak

My first lesson on oceans—I was so nervous. I was afraid I would forget something. It wasn't until later that I realized I forgot to put the Arctic Ocean on the board. The students had no problem switching over to the fact that I was the one teaching. They participated fully—it was funny to see their reaction when tasting regular and salt water. One boy flipped because he is allergic to salt, but he calmed down when his mom said it was okay to try it. All in all it was a good day and a great lesson!

Paula M.

I taught my math lesson. When I told them to get in their groups from yesterday and do their worksheets, this is where it all went downhill—they didn't understand. I didn't know how to explain, and it was "HELL." My Egyptian girl was crying in frustration/ confusion. This made me want to cry, but I just sat with her and helped her through. Now I have to think about what went wrong and how to re-teach tomorrow.

Rosa K.

Today was a big planning day. I'm a little nervous about the things that I am being put in charge of only because I feel like I'm not being given a lot of direction. She [the cooperating teacher] told me that she will only give me limited direction because she wants to see what I come up with. . . . . [I]t makes me a little uneasy. I am used to being told.

Ruth H.

environment in order to learn. They benefit from active exploration in a social setting with other children and caring adults (Berk, 2002; Santrock, 2003; Slavin, 2003; Wilson, 2000). The challenge for you is to decide *what* to teach based on your knowledge of children's interests, experiences, and developmental levels. In addition, you must decide *how* to teach based on your knowledge of effective techniques and available technologies.

As you read the student teachers' comments, you may have a pretty good idea why Rosa's lesson did not turn out the way she hoped. You may be able to appreciate Paula's case of nerves or Ruth's uneasiness. Think about your own feelings the first few times you planned lessons and taught a new group of learners.

As beginning teachers, you want all children to continue feeling excited to be in school. Your heart breaks as you see a child cry in frustration; your spirit lifts when you observe children making inquiries and discovering truths about their environment. As you proceed through student teaching, you will understand the meaning of supportive instruction as a result of your own hands-on experiences. With the help of your cooperating teacher and college supervisor, you will become more confident about your ability to plan, implement, and evaluate developmentally appropriate practices in an integrated, child-centered curriculum. Then you will enable your children to experience less frustration and more joy.

❖ RELATING INSTRUCTION TO YOUNG CHILDREN'S WAYS OF KNOWING

You have likely already completed one or more courses in child development. Therefore, a repeat of basic principles is not necessary. Nevertheless, you may benefit from a brief reflection on the particular ways in which young children make sense of their world. After all, as Rousseau (1762/1969) wrote centuries ago, "Nature provides for the child's growth in her own fashion, and this should never be thwarted" (p. 50). Unfortunately, in misguided efforts to provide the best possible educational opportunities for young children, adults are accused of hurrying the growing-up process. According to Elkind (2001), today's child is, in fact, "the unwilling, unintended victim of overwhelming stress—the stress born of rapid, bewildering social change and constantly rising expectations" (p. 3). Even well-intended efforts to hurry children's development may be in vain. Consider the words of the noted child development specialist Arnold Gesell, who wrote that "enriching the child's environment and providing him with the fullest opportunities possible permits him to express himself at his very best, but it does not make him 'better' or smarter or speedier than he was born to be" (Gesell, Ilg, Ames, & Rodell, 1974, p. 15). Keep the words of these influential theorists in mind as you think about how you can create a learning environment that allows young children to maximize their biologically determined potential.

Children's Ways of Knowing

Research indicates that young children have a unique way of knowing and processing information. For example, preschool children construct meaning through direct sensory interaction with their environment. They also ask many "Why?" questions as they try to make sense of their world. This can be frustrating and humorous at the same time as you try to give an answer and move on. For example, a 4-year-old may ask to play outside and you say, "Not today." She asks, "Why?" You answer that it is raining hard outside. She asks, "Why?" This dialogue can go on and on until you get tired or run out of answers. Your challenge may be to redirect the child to another activity and perhaps pull out a story book about a rainy day.

You may also find that your children's perceptions lead them to inaccurate interpretations of physical events (Palmer, 1995). They may even attribute human qualities to the inanimate objects in their environment, such as the animal-like movement of clouds or the eyeball-like headlights of a car (Piaget, 1963; Richards & Siegler, 1986). These inaccuracies may stem from incomplete knowledge rather than magical thinking because they disappear as children become exposed to new information over time (Woolley, 1997).

Accordingly, you may benefit from being a student of the young child's world. In other words, you observe, assist, listen intently to what children say, ask them questions, and support each child as she explores her environment and discovers her interests and strengths. Then you can make planning developmentally appropriate activities for young children; this is an excellent opportunity to demonstrate your creativity.

As you plan opportunities for learning, keep in mind Piaget's view that children learn most effectively through active participation in their learning. In other words, they benefit from interacting with other children and with their environment (Piaget, 1971). If you want children to learn about animals, for example, take them to a zoo or an aquarium, preferably one that has a supervised "Please Touch" area for children. Your follow-up classroom activities will be more meaningful when children can relate what they have seen and experienced to what they are learning.

Scaffolding is providing a helpful structure or support for the developing child.

As you may recall from your child development coursework, your active involvement in **scaffolding** children's play is strongly recommended by the work of the late developmental psychologist Lev Vygotsky. He maintained that encouragement of social interactions and make-believe activities promote children's development (Berk, 1994; Vygotsky, 1978). In fact, he said that you can help children progress toward abstract thought through make-believe play. For example, a child may begin using a toy telephone to pretend that she is talking on the phone. Later in her development, she may pick up a wooden block that represents a telephone and pretend to talk. You can interact with the child and show her an array of objects that can be renamed and substituted in fantasy play. For example, a carrot wrapped in a blanket becomes a baby. Follow the child's lead. You will have many opportunities to encourage communication and language acquisition as well as social skills development through play.

Utilizing Children's Sensitive Periods

Young children have "sensitive periods" in which their minds are particularly receptive to learning certain types of information. They may display enthusiasm for particular activities during these periods (Humphryes, 1998;

Montessori, 1967). Your recognition of these sensitive periods is critical. Once they pass, they may never return with equal intensity, and opportunities for learning may be lost (Morrison, 2000). Knowing this, you can capitalize on these sensibilities to engage children in developmentally appropriate activities related to their interests.

As an illustration, research seems to indicate that young children's brains are particularly receptive to primary language development as well as acquisition of a second language (Berk, 2002; Bredekamp & Copple, 1997). If you have children for whom English is their second language (ESL), then they need support in maintaining the language spoken at home while acquiring new language skills at school (Wong, 1992). The issues involving ESL will be discussed later in the text.

This sensitive period for language acquisition also applies to children who have special needs. For example, young children who are deaf or hearing impaired are generally able to learn American Sign Language with greater ease than their adolescent or adult counterparts (Mayberry, 1994).

In addition, young children will generally experience other sensitive periods. For example, between the ages of 3 and 6, they may be particularly receptive to the concept of order in their environment. They may enjoy arranging tiny objects and noticing where items belong. Beginning at about age 6, they may experience a sensitive period characterized by a noticeable development in their imagination (Chattin-McNichols, 1992). They may enjoy so-called open-ended materials such as play dough, fabric scraps of different textures, and blocks that can have many uses. Again, the challenge for you is to create a classroom environment in which fantasy, social interactions, and hands-on exploration play a role in a child-centered, developmentally appropriate curriculum.

Applying Gardner's Theory of Multiple Intelligences

Another approach to creating a child-centered curriculum is to apply Gardner's theory of multiple intelligences (MIs). The MI theory examines eight different abilities that are reflected in individuals' learning styles (Gardner, 1999). They are as follows:

1. *Bodily/kinesthetic:* Ability to use one's body and to use movement to solve problems
2. *Interpersonal:* Ability to understand and respond appropriately to other people
3. *Intrapersonal:* Ability to understand oneself and to use that knowledge to guide behavior
4. *Linguistic:* Ability to understand words and use language effectively

5. *Logical/mathematical:* Ability to understand logic, patterns, and numerical reasoning
6. *Musical:* Ability to create rhythm and musical sounds
7. *Naturalist:* Ability to discriminate between natural objects and understanding of the natural world
8. *Spatial:* Ability to perceive visual-spatial relationships accurately

The implication of the MI theory is that children should be taught in multiple ways. Therefore, as you plan instruction, you need to provide experiences in a variety of disciplines.

Because children differ in their individual strengths, you should plan lessons that involve as many of the MIs as possible. For example, if you are teaching a unit on music, you can readily incorporate a variety of activities, such as the following:

- Read a story about a band (linguistic intelligence).
- Collect materials from nature to use in the creation of musical instruments (naturalistic, spatial, and logical/mathematical intelligence).
- Listen to a piece of music and describe the feelings it evokes (intrapersonal intelligence).
- Move to the rhythm of the music (bodily/kinesthetic intelligence).
- Work with others to form a band and put on a musical performance (interpersonal and musical intelligence).

(Adapted from Driscoll & Nagel, 2005)

You do not have to incorporate every one of the MIs in each lesson you teach in order to be effective. However, your children will benefit from your efforts to include experiences that utilize their diverse abilities as much as possible. The inclusion of MIs in your lessons is an effective way to differentiate in order to meet your children's unique interests and abilities (Campbell, 2008). You may find the following Web sites helpful:

- *http://surfaquariou.com/MI/* contains useful information related to MIs, including an easy-to-use lesson plan template, a teaching unit template, profiles of the MIs, and an MI inventory.
- *http://www.nea.org/* contains helpful ideas for developing lessons related to various domains focused on specific ages beginning with pre-K.
- *http://www.thinkfinity.org/* contains suggestions for age-appropriate lessons linked to national education standards.

Developmentally Appropriate Practice and Curriculum

As a student of early childhood education, you have already been exposed to basic concepts of developmentally appropriate practice (DAP). These concepts have been the subject of much discussion and debate since

NAEYC published position statements addressing DAP in 1986, 1987, and 1996. If you have not read NAEYC's *Developmentally Appropriate Practice in Early Childhood Programs* (Bredekamp & Copple, 1997), put this on your professional development must-read list. In fact, it would be a wise purchase to keep in your personal library as you begin your professional career. You may order it online through the NAEYC Web site at *http://www.naeyc .org*. As an added bonus, it is relatively inexpensive compared to many other professional resources.

Developmentally Appropriate Practice

A clarification of terms is important before discussing implementation of practices. *Developmentally appropriate practice* (DAP) has been characterized as "a philosophy (not a curriculum) based upon decades of developmental research and practical experience and is widely held to define best practices in the field of early childhood education" (McMullen, 1999, p. 70). It is the result of decisions teachers make based on knowledge of typical child development in all domains, knowledge of each child's unique needs and interests, and knowledge of the social/cultural context of the particular learning environment (Bredekamp & Copple, 1997; Kostelnik et al., 2007).

If we consider DAP to be a philosophy that results in certain decisions, then we must consider guidelines supported by NAEYC as critical factors in determining best practices. According to Lerner, Lowenthal, and Egan (1998), these factors include the following:

- Integration of multiple developmental domains in planning children's activities
- Encouragement of children's inquiry and exploration by arranging the environment to facilitate active learning
- Progression of children's experiences from the simple and concrete to the increasingly complex and abstract
- Observation of children's individual interests and progress by a variety of means, including **authentic assessment**

Authentic assessment refers to demonstration of the ability to perform tasks in the context of real-life situations.

DAP versus DIP

In order to fully appreciate what DAP is, we must understand what it is not. Bredecamp and Copple (1997) provide examples of appropriate practice compared with inappropriate practice for young children in the following age brackets: infants and toddlers from birth through age 3, children ages 3 through 5, and children ages 6 through 8. That is, developmentally inappropriate practice (DIP) may be considered the extreme opposite of DAP or the absence of appropriate practice (Charlesworth, 1998). Figure 8.1 contains

---

DAP: Infants and Toddlers

Adults recognize that infants have their own patterns for eating and resting, so they set their own schedule.
Toddlers' environment has small, defined areas for individual work/play so children don't crowd together.

DIP: Infants and Toddlers

Adults follow a predictable, unchanging schedule for infant feeding and nap times.
Toddlers' environment includes a large group area for formal group activities.

DAP: Ages 3–5

An open classroom environment that allows for play in a variety of ways, such as sand/water tables. Children are given choices of activities.

DIP: Ages 3–5

A closed classroom environment with a physical arrangement that primarily allows sitting and passive experiences.

DAP: Ages 6–8

Teachers use a variety of strategies to build a sense of the group as a democratic community, such as regular class meetings and group decision making.

DIP: Ages 6–8

Teachers' behaviors and techniques undermine the sense of community, as children often work independently or in competition with others.

(Adapted from Bredecamp & Copple, 1997)

FIGURE 8.1   Examples of Appropriate versus Inappropriate Practice

examples of DAP versus DIP for each age bracket. Adapted from Bredecamp & Copple (1997).

Curriculum

The term *curriculum* means different things to different people. For example, Hendrick (2003) defines curriculum as the "design of experiences and activities developed by teachers to help children increase their competence" (p. 4). This definition is all inclusive and holistic; everything that happens in the child's day at the children's center, day-care facility, or school is curriculum. Other definitions consider the curriculum to be the foundation of learning that focuses on both what and how to teach (Catron & Allen, 2003). Regardless of the definition, appropriate curriculum has eight guidelines, according to Bredekamp and Copple (1997):

- Addresses all developmental areas
- Contains relevant, engaging, and meaningful cross-disciplinary content
- Builds on prerequisite skills and knowledge
- Focuses on one subject at a time or integrates subjects to form connections
- Promotes acquisition and application of knowledge

- Encourages inquiry and active participation
- Supports the family's culture and language while developing the ability to participate in the shared culture and language of the general community
- Sets realistically attainable goals for children's developmental age and ability

With experience, you will become more and more comfortable with integrating these guidelines into your lesson planning.

❖ SUPPORTIVE INSTRUCTION IN COMMUNICATION

Because the development of communication skills is vital for the young child to interact with others and to understand the world, this area of instruction will be addressed separately. Language, literacy, and literature are three focus areas to consider when creating activities and facilitating opportunities for children to communicate their thoughts and feelings (Feeney et al., 2001). As a professional, you are entering into a partnership with each child's parents and other family members to make decisions that affect the communication curriculum. Language skills, emergent reading and writing skills, and appreciation of literature are all areas where a home–school partnership can be an asset.

Student Teacher's Role in Language Development

As a student teacher, your role in children's acquisition of language skills is vital at all stages of child development. Research indicates that what happens to children during the first 3 years of life has a significant impact on their brain development (Shore, 1997). The implication is that as more and more young children receive care in facilities other than their homes, your role as a professional early childhood caregiver becomes increasingly significant. Therefore, your use of developmentally appropriate practices in the infant and toddler years is vital. You can encourage children's language development through your interactions with them (Charlesworth, 2004; Kratcoski & Katz, 1998; Soundy & Stout, 2002). Figure 8.2 offers strategies for encouraging language development.

Accordingly, during your student teaching practicum with young children, you need to create an environment that supports and encourages the sensitive periods for growth in all children. To show one example of how you can encourage this growth, the author will focus on language learning. Your daily conversations with children, even the youngest in your care, will encourage the development of language.

Because you have successfully completed some if not all of your child development coursework, the age-linked stages of language development

---

Figure 8.2 Strategies to Encourage Language Development

1. Expand on what the child has said to make a complete thought or sentence.
   - Child says, "Puppy sad."
   - You say, "Yes, the puppy is sad."
2. Use extensions of the child's words by responding to her comments.
   - Child says, "Puppy sad."
   - You say, "The puppy is feeling sad because he wants a friend to play with."
3. Use repetitions of all or part of the child's words.
   - Child says, "Puppy sad."
   - You say, "Puppy feels sad. Time to find a friend."
4. Use self-talk about your own actions to model vocabulary and sentence structure.
   - Child says, "Puppy sad."
   - You say, "Puppy is feeling sad. Puppy is going to play with a friend."
5. Employ vertical structuring using questions to encourage conversation.
   - Child says, "Puppy sad."
   - You say, "Where is puppy's friend?" Puppy wants to play with a friend."
6. Use fill-ins allowing the child to add words to complete statements in conversation.
   - Child says, "Puppy sad."
   - You say, "Puppy wants to go play. She feels_____."
   - Child says, "Sad!"

(Based on Kratcoski & Katz, 1998)

---

will not be reviewed here. Instead, we will focus on what you can do to create an interactive, language–rich environment for learning. Figure 8.3 gives examples of ways you can encourage the development of skills in a purposeful, social context (Beaty, 2004; Bredekamp & Copple, 1997; Catron & Allen, 2003; Dickinson & Tabors, 2002).

Supporting a Language-Rich Environment for Bilingual Children

In a joint position statement issued in 1998, the International Reading Association and the NAEYC stress that children's primary language and home culture will influence their literacy development. Furthermore, they caution us that a language and cultural *difference* is not the same as a *deficit*. Therefore, as you plan activities to promote language development, you should encourage and support bilingual children's learning of *both* languages (Catron & Allen, 2003). You can obtain storybooks in children's primary language whenever possible. For example, you can request information on good-quality books for children written in Spanish by visiting the Barahona Center Web site at *http://www.csusm.edu/csb*.

Infancy to toddler (ages 1–3)	Repetitive jingles Interactive games such as pat-a-cake Storybook reading Alphabet blocks and puzzles Sing-alongs Dramatization activities Predictive storybooks Reading poster-sized "big books" Exposure to a literacy-rich environment
Preschool (ages 3–5)	Dramatization activities Predictive storybooks Reading big books Exposure to a literacy-rich environment that includes books in many centers, not just the library corner Action songs and rhymes Taped stories to accompany books Printed labels for names and objects
Kindergarten (ages 5–6)	Repeated readings of familiar stories Children's retelling of stories Teacher dictations of language experience stories Story reenactments and dramatic play Big book activities Games involving directions like Simon Says Exploration of sound-symbol relationships Exploration of reading and writing as a means of social communication Exploration of a literacy-rich environment
Primary grades K–3 (ages 5–8)	Daily opportunities to be read to as well as independent or teacher-supported reading Opportunities to communicate in writing for varied purposes Introduction of spelling strategies and word identification strategies Exposure to varied types of text in a literacy-rich environment Opportunities to collaborate in small groups

FIGURE 8.3   Activities to Encourage Literacy Development

Creative play, field trips, and social experiences with bilingual peers and adults, for example, will provide opportunities for communication in both languages. You may wish to choose topics of study with your multicultural students and their families in mind. For example, if you study foods, families can share their unique recipes and foods for the children to taste.

Another aspect of language development that is often overlooked is children's dialectical speech. Children may speak nonstandard English, using a dialect such as ebonics. According to Frederick Erikson (2001) and Carlos Ovando (2001), this speech indicates differences in culture reflected in language rather than differences in social class. As a student teacher, you may model standard English, for example, but allow children to communicate "without correction or domination of conversations" (Catron & Allen, 2003, p. 228).

Antibias Curriculum

As classrooms for children of all ages are becoming more multicultural, you must be aware of the important role that the curriculum can play in confronting bias. Pictures decorating your room, signs written in English and other languages, and thematic units you teach, for example, can all have a positive effect on children's acceptance of diversity. Even children of 2 or 3 are not too young for an antibias curricular approach as they explore human differences and similarities (Derman-Sparks & Phillips, 1997; Hendrick, 2003).

Antibias curriculum refers to a model that recognizes, accepts, and respects human differences while seeking to eliminate stereotypes and bias.

In fact, toddlers may show signs of "pre-prejudices toward others based on gender or race or being differently abled" (Hunt, 1999, p. 39). Therefore, an **antibias curriculum** is an essential component of early childhood education in the 21st century (Henniger, 2002; Machado & Botnarescue, 2001).

According to Louise Derman-Sparks (1999), several quality markers indicate where you are on the journey to creating an effective multicultural antibias program. Recommendations suggest that the daily curriculum in your classroom

- Reflect children's daily life experiences, such as helping to prepare meals.
- Reflect children's cultural and individual needs with input from parents and caregivers.
- Incorporate diversity and social justice issues related to race, ethnicity, gender, disability, elders, socioeconomic status, and different definitions of family.
- Involve families, including those not fluent in English.
- Develop problem-solving strategies for resisting unfair stereotypical behaviors and improving the quality of life of the community.
- Include staff representative of the community's cultural diversity.
- Engage staff in ongoing intentional reflection of personal cultural influences on behavior and attitudes.

As a student teacher, you may be expected to follow the preestablished curriculum, which may or may not include explicitly antibias elements. Even so, you may certainly incorporate many of these quality markers in your own interactions with young children.

In addition, as you plan lessons and activities, look for materials such as storybooks, toys, and prompts that are "diversity-friendly" (Hendrick, 2003; Henniger, 2002). For example, ask yourself the following questions as you preview children's literature:

- Do the illustrations promote stereotypical behavior in regard to gender, race, ethnicity, or disability?
- In the story, who has the power to solve problems or make decisions?
- Can you determine the perspective and/or cultural background of the author and/or the illustrator?
- Does the narrative contain loaded adjectives such as *lazy* or *primitive*? Does the author avoid the use of sexist language?

Your choice of teaching materials can send a message to young children just as clearly as your words and behaviors.

❖ SUPPORTIVE INSTRUCTION USING AN INTEGRATED CURRICULUM

Instruction in the curriculum as well as in other areas is often provided in an interdisciplinary manner rather than as individual subjects. In fact, young children's "development and learning are interconnected across and within domains" (Bredekamp & Copple, 1997, p. 98). Therefore, a curriculum that is interconnected or integrated is a commonsense way to teach the whole child.

During your practicum, you may be asked to develop themes or projects that allow children to explore several disciplines at once. For example, many children's books, such as *Lunch* by Denise Fleming and *Peter's Chair* by Ezra Jack Keats, lend themselves to the development of children's math games (Cutler, Gilkerson, Parrott, & Browne, 2003). You may incorporate opportunities for social development, cognitive development, and fine and gross motor development as you provide hands-on opportunities for children to explore a variety of concepts. As you plan your lessons and activities for an integrated curriculum, you may wish to use a webbing process to create a visual map that shows the curricular areas represented (see Figure 8.4). In this manner, you can see where you need to add or delete items to create balance (Henniger, 2002; Krogh, 1995; Machado & Botnarescue, 2001; Workman & Anziano, 1993; Worsley, Beneke, & Helm, 2003).

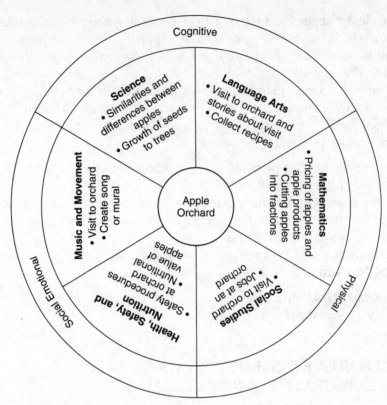

FIGURE 8.4   Sample Planning Web for Integrated Curriculum

Figure 8.5 provides extremely varied examples of activities that may be incorporated into an integrated curriculum (Catron & Allen, 2003; Clements & Sarama, 2003; Dodge & Colker, 2000; Feeney et al., 2001; Hesse & Lane, 2003; Murphy, DePasquale, & McNamara, 2003).

The integrated or balanced curriculum approach is generally considered to be responsive to children's needs and interests. It is somewhat fluid in that it "comes from the children, from their interests, activities, family backgrounds, and community" (Litman et al., 1999, p. 5). A few curriculum models have been discussed in this chapter, but many more exist. Therefore, ongoing communication with your cooperating teacher is essential so that your planning coincides with the prevailing curricular approach used in your facility or school program.

Several generally accepted guidelines may help you as you begin planning appropriate curriculum for young children (see Figure 8.6).

As you begin the planning process, listen carefully to your children. What are their questions and interests? What events are taking place in their lives? Focus on your children, and they will guide the curriculum that you plan. Also,

Study of Foods

Language Arts	Mathematics	Social Studies	Science
Storybook read-aloud	Use measuring cups and spoons to cook	Visit to grocery store	Food drying for snacks
Children's cookbook	Add ingredients	Workers who prepare foods	Seeds
Puppet drama	Sequencing in cooking activities	Use blocks to create a grocery store play area	Edible plant parts (stems, fruits)
Child-authored books	Graph of favorite foods		Kitchen map and community map
Books such as *Stone Soup* or *The Very Hungry Caterpillar*	Sorting food pictures by color and shape, etc.		
Books with pictures by famous illustrators			

FIGURE 8.5 Sample of Integrated Curricular Activities

Figure 8.6 Curriculum Planning Guidelines

1. Provide for multiple areas of development including cognitive, physical, emotional, linguistic, and aesthetic.
   - For example, include materials that children can physically manipulate and enjoy.
2. Plan integrated curricular content including several disciplines.
   - For example, provide opportunities for linguistic development and social interaction.
3. Content is accessible so that children can actively participate in learning.
   - For example, conduct experiments and collect data.
4. Create opportunities for supporting children's home culture and primary language.
   - For example, use family participation and/or leadership in activities as appropriate, such as sharing the cultural heritage and stories of childhood.
5. Develop realistic outcomes or attainable goals.
   - Provide scaffolding as needed to help children master skills, such as the use of scissors or access to age-appropriate computer software.
6. When using technology, integrate it into the curriculum plan and the teaching process.
   - Provide for technology that enriches the learning environment, such as supervised use of a microscope to examine veins in leaves.

(Based on Gestwicki, 1999, p. 53)

consider your own particular interests. Even if you must incorporate state-mandated topics into the curriculum, you can do it within the framework of children's interests, your interests, and their immediate needs (Branscombe et al., 2003; Gestwicki, 1999; Goethals & Howard, 2000; Wortham, 2002).

After you select a topic for your curriculum unit, brainstorm ideas using a web. For example, if you are teaching in the fall in an area where apples are harvested, then you can easily have an apple theme, as shown in Figure 8.4. You may include types of apples, taste different kinds of apples, cook foods that contain apples, create a graph of children's apple preferences, visit an apple orchard or a grocery store, create a classroom grocery store, make a book of apple recipes, and read books about apples and apple products. The list can go on and on. After you complete your web, consider which activities best meet your children's needs. What skills do you want your children to develop from each activity? You can then develop your outcomes or objectives. For example, as a result of visiting an apple orchard, children will understand that workers in an orchard have different responsibilities.

The Project Approach and the Integrated Curriculum

The project approach stems from information about the use of projects in the preschools of Reggio Emilia, Italy. In the United States, early childhood teachers incorporate projects into the curriculum as an "in-depth investigation of a topic worth learning more about . . . as a research effort focused on finding answers to questions about a topic posed either by the children, the teacher, or the teacher working with the children" (Katz, 1994, p. 1). A project is a child-centered inquiry that may incorporate activities involving MIs as well as a variety of disciplines. Project ideas often emerge from children's interests or from particular events in their lives. The projects themselves generally have three sequential phases:

- **Planning phase:** Children share information about what they know and what they want to learn. They collect materials and plan experiences.
- **Activity phase:** This phase may include field trips, guest speakers, investigation, building, reading, writing, drawing, and creating.
- **Concluding phase:** Children demonstrate what they have learned in a variety of ways, such as plays, reports, stories, displays, and exhibits.

(Adapted from Driscoll & Nagel, 2005)

The project approach focuses on children's needs and interests as they make choices about their learning. It allows you to accommodate children with a wide range of abilities and special needs. For example, children who have attention deficit hyperactivity disorder (ADHD) often benefit from active, hands-on learning activities that allow them to move in the classroom.

Project work provides children with opportunities to pursue their interests and make choices as they are actively engaged in learning.

Children who are considered gifted may prefer to work independently or to take leadership roles in group activities. Children with cognitive impairments may benefit from working with a peer helper or a circle of friends (Choate, 2003). The project approach allows you to guide children with special needs who require assistance and to serve as a resource for others who benefit from the freedom to pursue inquiry on their own.

Content Areas and Standards

There are national and state standards for each content area, such as mathematics, social studies, and science, at each grade level (Eggan & Kauchak, 2006). You may be required to specify which standards you are including in each of your lesson plans. The following Web sites contain links to both national and state standards in all content areas:

http://www.educationworld.com
http://edStandards.org/Standards.html

When you check online, you will find links to national educational organizations such as the National Council of Teachers of Mathematics and the National Council of Teachers of English. Professional organizations have created national standards that are organized by grade levels. You will also find links to the standards by topic and grade level developed by each state.

In best practices, teachers integrate these content areas. As you develop lessons, note that you should also integrate content standards. Take the time to examine the standards listed in the areas of fine arts, language arts, mathematics, physical education and health, science, social science, and technology.

Lesson Planning

In order to demonstrate that you have a positive impact on your children's learning, you will need to plan effectively. Structured and sequenced planning is necessary for good teaching because "learning should be intentional, not incidental" (Schoenfeldt & Salsbury, 2009, p. 8). A *lesson plan* is a blueprint of learning with a clear beginning, middle, and end (Serdyukov & Ryan, 2008).

A number of lesson plan models exist. Some schools or early childhood programs may require you to use a particular format. However, two models of lesson planning will be discussed in this section: planning for direct instruction and planning for an inquiry lesson. Both plans have a beginning, a middle, and an end.

In direct instruction, the *beginning* is where you "grab" the children's attention, create or heighten motivation, communicate the purpose (i.e., goals) you establish, and tap into children's prior knowledge. The *middle* is where you provide sequential direct instruction of content. You may model behaviors yourself, guide the practice of a new skill, allow time for independent practice, and check for understanding. The *end* of the lesson provides closure. This is your opportunity to clear up any misunderstandings as you provide a strategy for reviewing the main points of the lesson. Direct instruction tends to focus on you as the teacher and the choices you make to deliver knowledge (Jarolimek, Foster, & Kellough, 2005; Schoenfeldt & Salsbury, 2009). The knowledge you deliver is often based "on prescribed curricular content" (Gray, 2006, p. 227).

In contrast, an inquiry model of teaching tends to focus on the children. You serve as the facilitator of children's learning as they discover or construct meaning. You still need to plan your lesson carefully with a beginning, a middle, and an end. In the beginning, you choose the topic. Often this topic results from children's interests and curious questions. You select the standards and determine the objectives. Children often take an active role in developing questions for their exploration; they make observations and develop explanations; they test their understandings and construct meaning. Assessment is often based on evaluation of a product or a project that demonstrates learning. Throughout the inquiry process, you will be guiding children and modeling behaviors. You will also be learning because "each new inquiry enhances a teacher's understanding of how children learn and what strategies make that learning meaningful" (Fischer, 2002, p. 14).

Helpful Web sites include the following:

- *http://www.readwritethink.org/* provides links to sites that contain inquiry lessons involving a variety of content areas. Numerous age-appropriate lessons are available to give you ideas.
- *http://illuminations.nctm.org/* provides lessons that promote inquiry beginning at pre-K. The lessons are linked to the principles and standards for school mathematics.
- *http://www.AAAS.org/* is sponsored by the American Association for the Advancement of Science. It provides ideas for science inquiry lessons with links to the national science standards.

Before you write a lesson plan, you need to determine the topic or focus of your lesson. Sometimes your topic comes from your state's curriculum guide or from one of the Web sites mentioned earlier in the chapter. Sometimes it comes from the specific interests and needs of your children. Your cooperating teacher may suggest a topic and ask you to prepare one or more related lessons. Once you know your topic, check your state's standards. Which specific standards apply to your topic?

States use different terminology when referring to their standards. For example, the Pennsylvania Department of Education (PDE) and the Department of Public Welfare (DPW) consider the early childhood learning standards to be a framework along a continuum from infancy to Grade 3 from which teachers can plan their lessons. Each early childhood pre-K standard, for example, lists *Standards* in specific learning areas, *Indicators* that define each standard, *Examples* that suggest ways children can demonstrate their mastery of each standard, and *Supportive Practices* that describe materials and teaching practices (PDE/DPW, 2007). Examples include the following:

- *Standard AL 5:*   Demonstrate imagination, creativity, and invention.

  Indicator: Use or combine materials/strategies in novel ways to explore and solve problems.
  Example: Use and create props during dramatic play activities.
  Supportive Practices: Provide and rotate new materials and props in all centers and aspects of the environment to stimulate and extend learning, exploration, imagination, and creativity.

- *Standard CA 9.2A:*   Express self through movement and music.

  Indicator: Express self through movement.
  Example: Participate in teacher-guided movement activities.
  Supportive Practices: Provide large- and small-group activities that focus on movement and music participation.

Other states may refer to *Indicators* as *Benchmarks* (Schoenfeldt & Salsbury, 2009). When you look up your own state's standards, you should familiarize yourself with the particular terminology used in your location.

Next, decide *why* you are teaching this lesson. In other words, what are your goals and objectives? What do you want the children to do/discover/know? This is your beginning point. In the examples given above, the standard may be viewed as a goal and the indicator as an objective. You can see from the examples that goals are broad statements, whereas objectives are more specific. If you are teaching a new skill and have little time, you may choose to use direct instruction. If you want children to problem-solve and apply knowledge, you may choose to use inquiry. You should talk with your cooperating teacher to receive her input as you consider your choice of options.

Keeping the end in mind, think about how you will know if children have achieved the goals and objectives you select for your lesson. Decide how you will evaluate children's learning before, during, and after your lesson. A *preassessment* will give you information about the knowledge children already possess. For example, a K-W-L chart will let you know what your children already *know* prior to the lesson, what they *want* to learn about a topic, and afterward, what they *learned*. A *formative assessment* will provide information about how well children are learning during the lesson. For example, through your observation and questioning during the lesson, you can determine the children's level of understanding. You may decide that you need to change the pace of the lesson (e.g., slow down to provide coaching and practice or quicken the pace if mastery of a new concept has been achieved). A *summative assessment* occurs at the closure of the lesson. Summative knowledge can be demonstrated in many forms, such as a drawing, a play, shared conversation, or a "ticket out the door" in which each child says something she learned (Petersen, 1996; Serdyukov & Ryan, 2008). Determining how you will evaluate children's performance is an important part of your planning process (Petersen, 1996; Serdyukov & Ryan, 2008). Remember that children can also be an effective part of the evaluation process as they think about their own learning and share their thoughts with you, other children, and their families (Pataray-Ching & Roberson, 2002).

Once you have decided what topic to teach, why you will teach it, and how you will know that learning has taken place, select the materials and resources to achieve your goals and objectives (Schoenfeldt & Salsbury, 2009). Support your children's interests and be responsive to their needs as you plan your lesson. Remember that your enthusiasm and interest are contagious and will increase their motivation to learn (Bartholomew, 2008; Sullo, 2007). A sample lesson plan is provided in Figure 8.7.

Lesson Topic

Classification/Sorting

Grade Level

Kindergarten

Rationale

Classification is an essential tool scientists use to make order of large groups, including animals, plants, rocks and minerals, and chemicals. Developing an understanding of how to classify objects and organisms by traits or characteristics is an important ability to develop beginning in the early years.

Standards

NSE Physical Science Content Standard B—Properties of objects and materials

Cross-Curricular Connections

IRA/NCTE Standard 1—Children read a wide range of print and nonprint texts to build an understanding of texts, of themselves, and of the cultures of the United States and the world; to acquire new information; to respond to the needs and demands of society and the workplace; and for personal fulfillment.
NCTM Data Analysis and Probability Standard—Sort and classify objects according to their attributes and organize data about the objects

Objective

To classify/sort objects by specific attributes

Cross-Curricular Connection

Science, language arts, mathematics

Assessment

Teacher observation

Essential Question

Allow children to develop their own essential questions. They must be approved by the teacher and must have something to do with classification or sorting of shoes.

Materials/Instructional Technology

Shoes from Grandpa by Mem Fox
Collection of shoes
Chart paper and markers
Hula hoops

Accommodation for Children with Special Needs

Individualized as needed. Examples include extra wait time to answer questions, special seating, partner with a big buddy.

(Continued)

Guidance and Behavior

Review expectations of positive behaviors when in a circle at story time and during an activity.

Procedure

Beginning

- Have the children sit in a semicircle on the carpet in the story time area of the room.
- Take off your shoes and place them in front of you. State that the children may also take off their shoes, if they wish to do so, and place them in front of their feet on the carpet.
- Introduce the book *Shoes from Grandpa* by Mem Fox and show the pictures.
- Ask the children what they are curious about. Allow them to make predictions about the characters and the story.

Middle

- Read *Shoes from Grandpa*. Allow the children to determine if their predictions were correct and encourage them to talk about their own experiences that relate to the story.
- Ask the children to look at all the shoes on the floor. What more would they like to know about the shoes? Record children's comments in the form of *questions*. (These questions can also be the basis for future lessons.)
- Ask how the children can group the shoes. Record their suggestions.
- Choose one type of grouping or attribute for today's activity.
- Place the hula hoops on the floor. Label each one. If you want to extend this activity to a Venn diagram, then overlap the hoops.
- Children may work with a partner to place one of their shoes in the hoop they think is appropriate. Encourage discussion about why they chose a particular hoop.
- Ask the children to count (as a group) the number of shoes in each hoop.
- Record the number of shoes by attribute on the chart paper graph you have prepared.

End

- Review the attributes recorded on the graph.
- Ask the children to tell what they think the graph indicates about the shoes they like to wear.
- Ask the children to share what they liked best about the story *Shoes from Grandpa*.

Extensions

Continue exploration of shoes related to the list of questions generated by the children during the middle of the lesson. This may lead to another sorting activity, another story about shoes such as *The Elves and the Shoemaker*, and an almost endless number of art, language arts, creative play, science and math activities, and so on. Let the children's inquiry be your planning guide.

Source: Selected statements adapted from Jones (2008). Used with permission of Dr. Marla Jones.

FIGURE 8.7   Example of a Teacher-Guided Inquiry Lesson Plan

❖ TECHNOLOGY AND SUPPORTIVE INSTRUCTION

You can use technology effectively to support your instruction with young children. It is, however, somewhat controversial. Some critics decry technology as a potentially harmful means of denying children key developmental experiences. Others support technology as a means to extend learning opportunities. The author believes that technology can be a valuable learning tool if used appropriately.

Technology in Preschool

Technology applications can be introduced in preschool and then expanded in the primary grades. Preschoolers may benefit from opportunities to explore open-ended interactive software such as CD-ROM storybooks that allow them to have some control over the pace and content of the presentation. Children develop a sense of cause and effect as they learn that they cause animation, for example, on the screen. They may progress to developmentally appropriate software that allows them to create and illustrate their own stories (Robinson, 2003).

As a beginning teacher, you will have increasing opportunities to connect technology with your curriculum in meaningful and creative ways. In addition, you will have many decisions to make. For example, some proponents of technology discuss criteria for selecting interactive computer software for children as young as 18 months (Robinson, 2003). Others caution against using computer technology with children younger than age 3 years (Haughland, 1999). Some critics warn that young children's exposure to computer technology may lead to social isolation. Others report that computers lead to increased social interaction and collaboration with peers (Male, 2003; Sandholtz, Ringstaff, & Dwyer, 1997). Regardless of these opinions, one thing remains certain: Technology is here to stay. In 1997, the U.S. Department of Education declared children's use of technology to be a national research priority (Fischer & Gillespie, 2003; Haughland & Wright, 1997). Ultimately, you will have to make decisions based on your knowledge of each child and the technology and resources available to you.

Developmentally Appropriate Software

Certain guidelines can help you select developmentally appropriate software (Dodge & Colker, 2000). For example, you may ask questions such as the following:

- Is the content free of stereotypes and bias?
- Can levels of difficulty be varied as needed?
- Can the child alter the pace of the program?

- Is the program open-ended to allow for exploration?
- Is the content age appropriate?
- Does the program appeal to children with various learning styles?
- Can the child operate the program independently?
- Does the program meet curricular goals and objectives?

Regardless of the software selected, you will want to engage the children in dialogue. By doing so, you will encourage them to reflect upon not only what they are doing but also why.

Assistive and Adaptive Technology

Because children with special needs are often included in early childhood programs with their typically developing peers, **assistive** and **adaptive technology** can be a powerful tool to encourage communication and learning. This technology is considered part of the early intervention services available under IDEA regulations, and its use is becoming more common in inclusive educational settings.

Assistive technology refers to any tool, such as a switch or a specialized keyboard, that improves an individual's functional capabilities.

Adaptive technology refers to modifications of traditional tools such as voice-activated software.

Today's inclusive classrooms often include children with special needs. Assistive technology allows children who have communication disabilities to interact with their more typically developing peers.

Voices of Reality: Student Teachers Speak

I feel that I am being an effective teacher when my students are excited about what they are learning and when they are able to make connections to other things. I know that a student is "getting" what I am teaching when they run up to me in the morning to tell me that they saw the moon (after we had talked about the moon) or when they bring in a map to show me (after we had talked about maps).

Ruth H.

I think it is harder to teach in early childhood not because of the curriculum but because of the children's needs at those ages. Anyone can stand in front of a twelfth-grade class and teach a math class. But it is a lot harder teaching a math class in the younger early childhood years.

Lauren C.

During your student teaching practicum, you may have the opportunity to collaborate with early intervention special educators and support staff. You may also find yourself working closely with your cooperating teacher, families of children with special needs, and technology specialists to find tools that allow each child to take part in daily routines and activities. These tools may be high-tech devices such as electronic communication boards or low-tech devices such as weighted pencils and markers. A goal of technology is to help a child with special needs participate to the maximum extent possible in developmentally appropriate activities with same-age peers who may or may not have disabilities (Belson, 2003; Male, 2003; Mulligan, 2003). You may also assist children with special needs by doing something relatively simple, such as pairing a child who has developmental delays with a typically developing child. Cooperative/collaborative learning opportunities utilizing computer software, for example, can be beneficial to both children (Dodge & Colker, 2000).

❖ FINAL THOUGHTS

Finding the right balance of supportive instruction can be a challenge as you consider children's unique ways of knowing. You plan developmentally appropriate instruction within the framework of curriculum guidelines. You are mindful of desired outcomes and accountability while providing a supportive environment for *all* children. You interconnect themes between and across domains while incorporating developmentally appropriate technology for typically developing children and for those with special needs. It is no wonder that these challenges can seem overwhelming at times! As you read the rest of the chapters in this book, keep in mind that you will be improving your skills in these areas throughout your professional career. Perhaps you can relate to the comments made by the student teachers in the support group.

ACTIVITIES FOR REFLECTION AND ACTION

1. Develop of list of educational materials you would include in your own classroom that promote a multicultural, antibias curriculum. Include specific examples of children's literature, toys, games, electronic media, and any other materials you deem appropriate. Reflect on why you add each item to your list.

2. Think of a topic theme that you want to teach. It may be any theme that is timely and interesting to your children. Create a chart or web that shows how you will integrate this theme across several disciplines.

3. Develop a lesson plan that is appropriate for the children in your practicum. If you choose a lesson that incorporates all of the MIs, then state how each MI is incorporated into your plan.

4. *Portfolio:* Place a copy of your lesson plan in your portfolio. If you have the opportunity to teach your lesson during your practicum, write a reflection of what you think was good about it and why. Also write about what, if anything, you would change next time you teach the lesson and why.

5. Interview two teachers about the types of software they use with their students. What percentage of these programs are drill-and-practice? What creative ways can you think of to incorporate technology into your lessons?

CHAPTER 9

Understanding Diverse Communities and Interacting with Children's Families

It is that openness and awareness and innocence of sorts that I try to cultivate in my dancers. Although, as the Latin verb to educate, *educere*, indicates, it is not a question of putting something in but drawing it out, if it is there to begin with. . . . I want all of my students and all of my dancers to be aware of the poignancy of life at that moment. I would like to feel that I had, in some way, given them the gift of themselves.

Martha Graham

As a student teacher of young children, you are in the special position of working with children who possess a refreshing openness and a unique awareness of the world. Your challenge is to draw out the abilities they possess and provide them with opportunities to develop their individual potential. Giving them the gift of themselves is perhaps your greatest undertaking and your greatest joy.

This challenge is particularly notable today, as the children and their families who come to you represent greater cultural diversity than ever before in our nation's history (Marshall, 2002). Your skill in working with culturally different children and their families is critical not only to your career as a teacher but also to the people whose lives you touch.

We cannot assume that successful completion of child development courses, teaching methodology courses, and a practicum prepares anyone for teaching in today's changing schools. Teaching competence now requires an understanding of the many social and psychological factors required to teach children from culturally diverse backgrounds. Therefore, a focused effort is necessary in order to develop their potential in a culturally responsive manner.

Voices of Reality: Student Teachers Speak

The music teacher had been teaching the kids a song that she wrote. The whole school had been reading The Quiltmaker's Gift *last week and talking about quilting. The song is about all the squares coming together to make a quilt, loving and unity. We all sang that song together. It was very moving, watching 600+ innocent kids who looked so different all singing this song about caring and togetherness. I couldn't help but tear up, and I noticed as I looked around that many of the teachers were.*

Krista U.

I asked the chief on the Rez [reservation] for advice. He told me, "You have to make sure your heart is pure before you go there. If you think you're going there to save them, you're no better than the missionaries." I quickly came to believe that if I fail in my job, I do more than fail these kids. I destroy their future . . . scared me but I saw the truth in that.

LuAnne A.

❖ CHANGING CULTURAL DEMOGRAPHICS

Changing demographic trends have been noted for years as the nonwhite population in the United States has increased (Healey, 1995). In fact, predictions based on the 2000 census suggest that by the year 2020, "the relative percentages will be non-Hispanic White 64 percent, Hispanic 17 percent, African American 13 percent, and Asian 6 percent . . . and by 2020, four states—New Mexico, Hawaii, California, and Texas—and Washington, D.C., will have 'minority majority' populations" (Diller & Moule, 2005, p. 11).

Results of the 2000 census indicate that other dramatic changes are also occurring in the United States. This census attempted, for the first time, to determine the number of people who consider themselves to be multiracial or biracial. Accordingly, 2.4% of the population, or 6.8 million people, listed themselves as multiracial. Then 93% of this group listed themselves as biracial as follows: 32% White and another group not specified, 16% White and American Indian or Alaska Native, 13% White and Asian, and 11% White and Black or African American (Grieco & Cassidy, 2001).

These changes have caused much speculation about the reasons. The increasing number of immigrants and changes in the birth rate among some groups are generally considered to be major factors. Yearly numbers of immigrants have risen to nearly 1 million. Data from the 2000 census indicate that the birth rates of Whites are declining in comparison with those of Hispanic and Asian American populations (Diller & Moule, 2005).

Demographic Changes and Teachers

What does this dramatic increase in the nonmajority population of the United States mean for teachers? The vast majority of teachers are still White females from middle-class family backgrounds. To make matters worse, "many Teachers of Color have been retiring, and expanding occupational options for People of Color has meant few replacements" (Diller & Moule, 2005, p. 156). If you take a look at the entering classes of colleges with teacher education programs, you will see comparatively few minorities. Speculation abounds as to the reasons, but the bottom line is that the population entering the teaching profession is "becoming increasingly White" (Hodgkinson, 2002, p. 104).

Accordingly, teachers at all levels are finding that they must interact with increasingly diverse communities of children and their families. As an early childhood teacher, you can expect to teach children whose cultural identity is different from your own. This has definite implications for you as you consider what it means to be *culturally competent.*

Terminology

You are culturally competent, according to Diller and Moule (2005), if you have the ability to teach children from cultures that differ from yours. This requires you to have not only knowledge of other cultures but also the ability to demonstrate sensitivity, awareness, and acceptance in your interactions with others. *Culture* includes identifying factors such as shared language, beliefs, values, and family traditions, to name a few. The terms *ethnic group* and *racial group* are sometimes confused. Throughout discussions in this book, the author generally uses *ethnic/racial diversity* for the purpose of convenience. However, they are not the same. An ethnic group refers to people who are distinguished from others by their cultural heritage, whereas a racial group refers to people who are distinguished from others by their genetic heritage. It is important to note that racial identity is no longer considered a purely biological construct. It must be considered within the social context in which people construct identity (Martin & Nakayama, 2005).

Student Teaching and Becoming Culturally Competent

To interact effectively with culturally diverse children and their families, you should understand the impact that their culture has on their lives. Some researchers believe that you cannot do this effectively until you understand the impact that culture has had on your own life (Diller & Moule, 2005; Martin & Nakayama, 2005). You can begin this process of reflection by asking yourself a

---

Figure 9.1 **Reflection on Your Cultural Experiences**

1. What is your earliest memory of realizing that people differed racially or ethnically?
2. With what racial or ethnic group do you identify? When did you first realize that this group had a name?
3. What is your first memory of you or anyone else being treated differently because of race or ethnicity?
4. Is there a time when you remember being especially proud of your racial or ethnic heritage?
5. Is there a time when you felt least proud of your racial or ethnic heritage?
6. How much contact have you had with racially or ethnically diverse groups of people? Has this situation changed over the course of your life?

(Based on Diller & Moule, 2005, pp. 46–47)

---

few questions about your own experiences. Suggested questions may be found in Figure 9.1.

You may want to share your responses to these questions. They can be the beginning of reflective discussions with other student teachers or with your cooperating teacher.

❖ BREAKING DOWN CULTURAL BARRIERS

Children as young as 3 years of age have a superficial awareness of racial and ethnic differences (Grant & Haynes, 1995; Marshall, 2002). Even children of kindergarten age have, in some cases, become socialized to indicate signs of racial preferences in playmates and toy selection (Diller & Moule, 2005). Therefore, you can have an important role in creating a learning climate in which diversity is not only accepted but also celebrated.

Awareness of Diversity Within Minority Cultures

As a teacher who will be communicating with children and families of various heritages, it is important to recognize the variety within the major categories of racial/ethnic groups. For example, the U.S. census category of Native American Indians and Alaska Natives includes roughly 0.9% of the population. Within that category, however, are many cultural differences. Native Americans alone include over 500 different tribes and over 300 reservations. About half of this population lives in urban areas and half lives on reservations in rural areas throughout the United States (Diller & Moule, 2005).

Another example is the 2000 census category of Asians. It consists of roughly 3.9% of the population. Asian Americans represent at least 43 ethnic groups: 28 in the Asian category and 15 in the Pacific Islander category (Diller & Moule, 2005).

The point of this information is that even within a specific category, there is significant diversity among groups. Therefore, instead of accepting what the literature says about a particular racial/ethnic group, you may be better off seeking information from family members of the children in your class. If that is not possible, then information from local cultural or community centers may help you understand each culture more realistically.

Family Involvement and Cultural Diversity

The *NAEYC Code of Ethical Conduct* provides guidance for our dealings with all families. It tells us that we must develop positive relationships with families to ensure each child's success. Part of this obligation is to respect each family's culture, which includes its own particular language, beliefs, values, and customs. You also have an ethical obligation to involve families in all decisions regarding their children and to encourage their access to your classroom. The following questions may give you some guidelines for family involvement:

- Do you invite family members to your classroom?
- Do you consider family members to be resources?
- Do you consider families' cultural events when you plan class activities?
- Do you send home notes and class newsletters in the family's primary language?
- Do you invite extended family members to participate in your activities?
- When meetings are held to discuss plans for a child whose parent is not fluent in English, do you make sure that someone is present who can translate?

Differences in Parent-Child Communication

Since you will have open and frequent communication with families of different cultures, it may be helpful to consider differences in parent-child communication. This is important, particularly if a family's child-rearing practices are different from those of your own culture. You must be careful to suspend judgment unless you have reason to believe that a child's well-being is at risk.

Research indicates that there are some similarities as well as differences between cultures in child-rearing practices. Parents in all cultures tend to adapt their speech and use exaggerated intonations and simple language structure when they talk to young children (Bornstein, Haynes, Pascual, Painter, & Galperin, 2002; Fernald, 1993). However, there are differences in the amount of talkativeness observed. Euro-American and Cuban American parents have been described as extremely verbal, whereas Native American Navajo and Hopi parents have been described as extremely quiet with their children (Chisholm, 1989; Field & Widmayer, 1981). Therefore, the criticism has been made that programs that emphasize language use with young children do not respect the cultural diversity of language patterns in the home. This is a controversial issue with no clear-cut answer.

Cultural differences have also been reported with regard to parents' responses to their children's crying as well as parents' holding practices (Trawick-Smith, 2003). Accordingly, parents may also have different ideas about how you should respond to their children based on their own cultural practice. Therefore, frequent communication is imperative to increase understanding and to build positive relationships.

❖ DIVERSE FAMILY STRUCTURES IN TODAY'S CLASSROOMS

We have focused on the racial/ethnic diversity of families and of the children you will teach as an early childhood professional. However, it is important to remember that there is no such thing as a typical American family. It simply does not exist. Family structure has changed. Indeed, the definition of what constitutes a family has changed. You are likely to have children from married-couple families, blended families of married couples with children from previous relationships, single-parent families, military families with one or both parents deployed, families headed by grandparents, gay and lesbian families, and foster families. Family types are as varied and unique as the individuals they include. In addition, you will need to communicate with children and families who face special challenges such as poverty and homelessness. As you work to create positive relationships with children and their families, you have a fascinating challenge indeed!

Collaboration with Diverse Families

Understanding a particular family's unique characteristics is central to developing an effective collaborative relationship with that family. It is important that you "learn from families how they define themselves within the context of observable characteristics in order to understand more clearly the attitudes and values operating within that family" (Olsen & Fuller, 1998, p. 55). You may find that your own values and ideas of what constitutes a family may be challenged. If so, then you must adapt to make your program an inviting, caring environment for each child.

Grandparent-Headed Families

You may have children in your care who are being raised by grandparents instead of a biological parent. The grandparent-headed family is becoming far more common in the United States. According to the American Association of Retired Persons, over 6 million children under the age of 18 are growing up in homes headed by grandparents; in over 2.5 million of those homes, there is no parent present (AARP, 2007). In some cases, this arrangement is permanent due, for example, to the death or long-term incarceration of parents; in other cases, it is temporary for reasons such as parents' military service or illness (Doucette-Dudman & LaCure, 1996). This phenomenon has been termed "skipped generation families (grandparents raising grandchildren)" (Birchmayer, Cohen, Jensen, & Variano, 2005, p. 101). You may be interested going to AARP's Web site, *http://www.aarp.org/grandparents*, to look at your particular state's data on grandparents raising children. This Web site also contains helpful links to organizations that offer support and information to grandparents raising grandchildren. Many of them have helpful information sheets that can be downloaded for free. You can start your own file of resources to share with grandparents if the need arises. Look for ways to include grandparents in your class activities. Remember that not all grandparents are elderly. Many are not much older than the parents of most of your young children. They may be still raising their own children along with their grandchildren (Hanson & Lynch, 2004).

Families with One or More LGBT Parents

You may also have children in your program who are growing up in families with one or more lesbian, gay, bisexual, and/or transexual (LGBT) parents. According to the Family Equality Council (2007), approximately "27% of same sex couples identified in Census 2000, over 600,000 couples, have a child under the age of eighteen living in the home with them . . . (and) gay and lesbian parents are raising 4% of all adopted children in the United States, approximately 65,000 children" (p. 1). Keep in mind that, as with any family type, great diversity exists among LGBT families. Some gay and lesbian parents are raising their biological children; others have custody or visitation rights; still others have adopted their children or are raising foster children (Couchenour & Chrisman, 2008). According to Clay (2007), many gay and lesbian parents indicate that "adoption issues are more important to them and their children than issues about having a parent who is lesbian or gay" (p. 26). Therefore, open and ongoing communication with families is essential so that you can meet the needs of their children.

Military Families

Deployment refers to an assignment of active military duty that generally requires temporary relocation.

Military deployments are a fact of life. You will likely have children in your program who have one or both parents in the active military or National Guard. These parents may be facing pending or current **deployment**. Their children will be coping with sigificant changes in their lives that often result in stress and/or anxiety (Atova, 2007).

As an early childhood teacher, you play an important role in creating an environment in which children feel safe, loved, and secure. This is "essential for children affected by deployment as it can help them build coping skills" (Allen & Staley, 2007, p. 83). Preschool children may not understand the concept of deployment. They may believe that they have done something wrong to cause the parent's departure (Atova, 2007). You will need to collaborate with the child's family to provide reassurance as well as a routine and predictable environment.

Young children may exhibit signs of distress such as bedwetting, irritability, withdrawal from friends and family, difficulty maintaining attention, and physical symptoms such as headache or stomachache (Atova, 2007). Talk with your cooperating teacher about any behavioral changes you observe, particularly those that persist over time. She can help you discover family support services that are available through nearby military installations, through the school, and/or through community health professionals (National Child Traumatic Stress Network, 2008). Ongoing collaboration between school and home is essential for the child's well-being.

Numerous Web sites provide links related to deployment and family resources. A few helpful sites are included for you to explore and share with families.

- **The Military Family Network** Information for parents and children coping with deployment *http://www.emilitary.org*
- **Moms Over Miles** Activities and publications to help children stay connected with deployed parents *http://www.momsovermiles.com*
- **Talk, Listen, Connect: Helping Families During Military Deployment** Bilingual resources including *Sesame Street* characters *http://www.sesameworkshop.org/initiatives/emotion/tlc*
- **ZERO TO THREE (Military Families)** Support for the youngest children of military families; focuses on family strengths and family stress. *http://www.zerotothree.org/site/PageServer?pagename=key_military*
- **Educator's Guide to the Military Child During Deployment** Practical information about phases of deployment, children's reactions, and teacher interventions. *http://www.eustis.army.mil/7grp/grp7/familyreadiness/FAMILY_READINESS_04/FRWebsite/CHAPTER10/Deployment*

Voice of Reality: A Cooperating Teacher Speaks

When Maddie's father was deployed to Iraq, I noticed that she became withdrawn. I never knew what would set her off. One day we were doing a unit on cities. We talked about tall buildings and skyscrapers. Maddie became very agitated. She finally shared: "Big buildings fall down. That's why my daddy has to fight." Although she did not understand about 9/11, she knew her daddy was gone because skyscrapers fell. I had to be flexible and deal with her feelings rather than just go on with the lesson.

Barbara L.

As an early childhood professional, you can help create a supportive environment for children whose loved ones are deployed. For example, be a good listener. Encourage children to talk about their feelings and validate their experiences. When children hear from their relative who is deployed, allow them to share the photographs and news they receive (Opong-Brown, 2008). Recognize that holidays and special occasions such as birthdays may be especially difficult for these children and their families. Some teachers invite all children in the class to make holiday cards or prepare "care packages" for a classmate's deployed family member. Other teachers include class newsletters and digital pictures of children's activities on a school Web site.

You may want to include age-appropriate children's books in your classroom that pertain to military deployment, bravery, and feelings of loss. The Web sites *http://www.bookforbrats.net* and *http://www.nmfa.org/site/Page Server?pagename=books_for_children* suggest books you may find helpful. Examples of recommended books include:

- *Daddy, You're My Hero!* and *Mommy, You're My Hero!* written and illustrated by Michelle Ferguson-Cohen
- *Daddy's In Iraq But I Want Him Back!* written and illustrated by Carmen R. Hoyt
- *The Bravest of the Brave* written by Shutta Crum and illustrated by Tim Bowers
- *Daddy, Will You Miss Me?* writeen by Wendy McCormick and Jennifer Eachus
- *The Hero in My Pocket* written by Marlene Lee

Check with local libraries, bookstores, and Web sites to create your own file of children's books on specialized topics such as these. Some teacher materials are available for free from the military Web sites previously mentioned.

Voice of Reality: A Cooperating Teacher Speaks ❖

As a teacher and a single parent who has joint custody, I know how difficult it can be to keep the information flowing between the school and both parents. When I have children in my room whose parents have joint custody, I prepare a "Mom Folder" and a "Dad Folder" of all school-home communications. I also make sure that each folder contains a copy of progress reports and report cards. That way, no parent is kept in the dark.

Barbara L.

Single-Parent Families

According to the KIDS COUNT Data Center (2006), 32% of all children under the age of 18 in the United States live with their own single parent. Data from the Children's Defense Fund (2002) indicate that the number of single-parent fathers raising children has increased from less than 1% to 3.4% since the previous decade. Clearly, the lives of families and their children are changing. These changes are important for you to consider as you collaborate with families in your role as an early childhood teacher.

Some of the children in your program may be from single-parent homes as a result of divorce. They may experience many feelings including loss, denial, anger, and depression (Olsen & Fuller, 2003). They may not have words to express these feelings. However, you may see changes in behavior that concern you, such as withdrawal or aggression. Discuss your concerns with your cooperating teacher. She will have suggestions regarding school-to-home communication as well as possible resources for offering assistance to the child and her family.

Resiliency is the ability to bounce back from misfortune, the behaviors that allow a person to make positive adjustments in response to change.

As an early childhood teacher, you can help young children develop the **resiliency** they need to deal with significant life stresses such as separation, divorce, loss, and poverty. Children who are viewed as resilient share certain commonalities. They may have a greater than expected sensory awareness of their environment, a positive view of their abilities, a set of goals or expectations based on their perceived strengths, and a sense of humor (Breslin, 2005). Resiliency may also be connected to the child's ability to take initiative in meeting her own needs, the ability to express feelings with appropriate words and/or actions, and the ability to form relationships with others (Goldstein & Brooks, 2005). You can help children develop resiliency by creating a caring environment in which children receive encouragement, develop trusting relationships, and experience structure in their lives; you can also help children by modeling appropriate words and behaviors to express feelings (Kersey & Malley, 2005). Other suggestions for guiding young children and creating a positive emotional climate are presented in Chapters 4 and 5.

Families Experiencing Poverty

According to the Children's Defense Fund, "every 35 seconds a child is born into poverty in America" (2007, p. 8). Approximately 21% of children under the age of 6 live in poverty (i.e., a family of four with an income of less than $21,200; a family of three with an income of less than $17,600; a family of two with an income of less than $14,000); in addition, 32% of single-parent families with related children live below the poverty threshold (KIDS COUNT Data Center, 2007; *U.S. Federal Register*, January 23, 2008). The term *poverty* has been called a political designation established by politicians that "can arbitrarily be raised, creating fewer poor people, or it can be lowered, creating more poor people. Many people who are living above the arbitrary poverty [threshold] are still not well off" (Frieman, 2001, p. 126).

Although the definition of poverty is somewhat controversial, you are likely to have a significant number of children in your program whose families are struggling financially, particularly in the current economic climate. The term *working poor* may apply to many of the families you see regularly who struggle to provide their children with the basic needs of food, shelter, and safety. Money for health care, field trips, clothing, and school supplies may be limited or nonexistent.

You may be surprised to learn that some of the children in your program are homeless, even if one or both parents are working. One cooperating teacher shared her reaction to learning about her kindergartener's temporary living arrangement.

As the cooperating teacher's story indicates, homelessness can happen to families in any community, whether or not parents are employed . In fact, "families with children are by most accounts among the fastest growing segments of the homeless population" (National Coalition for the Homeless, 2008). Over 131,000 families with children in the United States are living in shelters or transitional forms of housing; the majority of these children are

Voice of Reality: A Cooperating Teacher Speaks

I was horrified to learn that one of my children has been living in a car with his mother and father and three brothers for more that two weeks. His father is on disability. His mother works at [a fast food restaurant]. They could no longer afford their apartment, so they were living in their car. All four kids have been coming to school every day and bringing their school papers, so no one knew. Finally, one of the older children told his teacher. The director called community services, so now the family has a place to live. I couldn't believe that something like that could happen here.

Barbara L.

under the age of 6 and living with their mothers (Culhane, Khadduri, Cortes, Buron, & Poulin, 2008).

Homeless children have certain rights that are protected by the McKinney-Vento Homeless Assistance Act, passed in 1987. For example, homeless children are entitled to liaisons who ensure that they have access to preschool programs, transportation, and special services (National Law Center on Homelessness & Poverty, 2007). Information about who the law defines as homeless and what teachers and support service personnel should know can be found at several helpful Web sites. Many of these sites have booklets and information for teachers that can be downloaded for free.

- **The National Law Center on Homelessness and Poverty**

  http://www.nlchp.org

- **The National Center on Family Homelessness**

  http://www.familyhomelessness.org

- **The National Center for Homeless Education**

  http://www.serve.org/nche

- **National Center for Children in Poverty**

  http://www.nccp.org/

As an early childhood teacher, you can play an important role in helping children whose families are experiencing poverty. These children may come to school hungry and/or tired. Consistent daily routines regarding arrival, eating, napping, toileting, and departure add structure to their lives. Your ability to establish a relationship with children will help them feel secure. For example, you can increase your personal contact with a child who becomes frantic or disorganized by having her touch base with you at times of transition or at the completion of each activity (Frieman, 2001; Koplow, 2007).

According to the National Center on Family Homelessness (NCFH), children who experience poverty and homelessness may have been exposed to acts of violence, may get sick more frequently than other children, may have serious emotional and behavioral needs, and may show delay in meeting developmental milestones (2008). Therefore, as you observe children and pay close attention to details, you may find it helpful to complete assessments such as those discussed in Chapter 7 (e.g., event sampling, time sampling, anecdotal records, and running records). This information will be helpful to you and your cooperating teacher, as well as to support service personnel who provide assistance to children with special needs of all kinds.

Families of Children with Special Needs

Families of children who have special needs may have their own unique challenges. These families face issues that families with typically developing children do not have to consider (Kaczmarek, 2006). They may have been working with Early Intervention Teams since their child's birth or they may have a child who is newly diagnosed with a disability. They may have had both positive and negative experiences before their child becomes part of your program. Keep in mind that they, like all families, know their child better than anyone else. Your ongoing communication with them is essential. Observe your cooperating teacher's interactions with families and follow her lead. Some teachers communicate with families using a daily teacher-family communication notebook to record the child's progress, concerns, and important events. Other ways to communicate include e-mail, phone calls, and home visits. Ask families what they prefer. You may also find it helpful to begin collecting your own resource file of information related to various disabilities and support services for families. Many Web sites have brochures, fact lists, and booklets that can be downloaded for free. Several are included below for you to check out. Follow the links to add other Web sites to your resource file.

> The Web site *http://www.parentednet.org/* provides links to disability information and parent support groups.
> The Web site *http://www.familyvillage.wisc.edu* has links to disability resources and parent-to-parent links.
> The Web site *http://www.eparent.com* has links to a magazine for exceptional parents and parent resource links.

❖ HOW TO DEVELOP POSITIVE HOME–SCHOOL RELATIONSHIPS

As a teacher of young children, you need to be acutely aware that you set the tone and create a positive emotional climate in your room for *all* children. Some suggestions to consider include the following:

- Show your support for *all* families by displaying pictures, posters, toys, and children's books that show diverse families.
- Instead of a *parent* information bulletin board, have a *family* information bulletin board. Address newsletters to *Dear Family* rather than to *Dear Parent.*
- If you have children draw pictures of their families or write about their families, respect their use of gender pronouns.
- Ask parents or guardians to tell you the names they use to refer to family members and follow their lead.

- Insist that your room be a safe place where bullying or derogatory language will not be tolerated.
- Take the initiative to learn more about *all* families and include them in your classroom activities. Web sites you may find helpful include the following:

  The Web site *http://www.colage.org/resources* provides support for children with parents who are lesbian, gay, bisexual, transgender, queer, or questioning (LGBTQ).

  The Web site *http://www.familieslikemine.com* provides support for LGBTQ families and friends.

  The Web site *http://www.familyequity.org* supports social justice and equality for families.

Building Effective Interaction with Children's Families

Communication with families should be an ongoing process. Family bulletin boards can be placed near your doorway so that they are easily accessible as adults drop off and pick up their children. Notices on the board should be written in more than just the majority language whenever possible. You can set aside a small section on the board for families to bring in notices that they believe will be of interest to others. Even a small gesture such as placing a welcome sign written in several languages on your door sends the message that all visitors are welcome.

School Visits and Interaction with Children's Families

Observe how your cooperating teacher involves families in her class activities. You will get some ideas that you want to remember when you have your own class. Families are often invited for special programs, but you can include them in many other ways as well. If you ask parents, guardians, or extended family members to volunteer regularly, you will find that they have a better understanding of what you do and what their child's day is really like. You will develop a better understanding of them as well. Volunteers can also share their cultural heritage in many ways.

In addition, you can invite families to make suggestions about ways in which they would like to contribute. When they volunteer in your room, remember to send a thank-you note and acknowledge their contribution in your class newsletter.

A Culture-Friendly Room for Children and Families

The manner in which you prepare your room sends a message about how readily you celebrate diversity of all kinds. For example, your learning and activity centers should include dolls and toys that every child can relate to,

Figure 9.2 Families Sharing Their Cultural Heritage

- Invite parents to share pictures, drawings, family stories, traditions, and the language of their cultural heritage.
- Encourage parents to share books and other print material or tapes that will help maintain their child's primary language.
- Have parents and children teach the class songs, dances, and crafts characteristic of their culture.
- Invite parents to participate in a school translation center, either to give or to receive assistance.
- Learn to pronounce each child's name and each parent's name correctly.

such as dolls of different racial/ethnic groups and both genders. The art materials, the music, and the imaginative play prompts should all reflect the children's diversity. Labels on objects around the classroom should reflect children's home languages as well as English. Figure 9.2 lists a few ways to include family culture in the classroom. Books of all types should be available that are culturally relevant and free of stereotypes. Figure 9.3 provides a few examples of multicultural books recommended for young children on a variety of subjects (Valdez, 1999).

Creating a classroom climate that respects children's cultural heritage is an important goal for every early childhood professional.

Figure 9.3 Representative Examples of Multicultural Children's Books

Topic	Books for Young Children
African American history	*On the Day I was Born*, D. Chocolate
	Follow the Drinking Gourd, J. Winter
Asian American culture	*Cleversticks*, B. Ashley
	Sam and the Lucky Money, K. Chin
Columbus—different perspectives	*A Picture Book of Christopher Columbus*, D. A. Adler
	Pedro's Journal, P. Conrad
Hispanic culture	*Poets of Puerto Rico: Don Luis Munoz Marin*, C. T. Bernier-Grand
	Saturday Market, P. Grossman
Jewish history	*A Picture Book of Anne Frank*, D. A. Adler
	Matzah Ball, M. A. Portnay
Migrant workers	*A Day's Work*, E. Bunting
	Radio Man, A. Dorros
Native American culture	*Shannon: An Ojibway Dancer*, S. King
	The Gift of the Changing Women, T. V. N. Seymour
Stereotyping and special needs	*Amazing Grace*, M. Hoffman and C. Binch
	The Girl-Son, A. E. Neuberger
	My Friend Isabelle, E. Woloson
	All Kinds of Friends, Even Green!, E. B. Senisi
Vietnamese culture	*The Lotus Seed*, S. Garland
	Grandfather's Dream, H. Keller

Many of these stories can be included in thematic activities related to history, cultural similarities and differences, dramatizations, language, and self-concept, to name just a few. For example, the book *Cleversticks* by B. Ashley is included in Figure 9.3 as a choice in the category of Asian American culture. Primary school children will enjoy listening to the story to find out what the boy is good at doing. They can follow up with a variety of activities, such as retelling the story to a partner, writing and/or drawing what they think they themselves do best, and making a class book or bulletin board on what the class does best. Further enrichment activities can include other storybooks about Asian American culture, foods, and use of chopsticks (Valdez, 1999).

Selection of Culturally Appropriate Books and Stories

As you teach the children in your practicum, you will have the opportunity to select stories or chapter books for them to enjoy. Later, when you are a professional teacher, you may be on a team to select books for your school to purchase. What guidelines will you use to choose material that is relevant and culturally appropriate? The following questions may be helpful:

- Look at the pictures in the book. Do they show people from minority cultures in non-stereotypical roles?
- Are any references to real people or events historically accurate?
- If there is a preface, does it make any reference to multiculturalism or cultural diversity?
- Does the story depict people and events in an unbiased manner with regard to race, ethnicity, gender, age, and ability?

You may even be able to list other questions that could be added to heighten awareness of cultural sensitivity. The important thing is to be cautious as you select materials that will influence young children's understanding of diverse people.

Home Visits and Interaction with Children's Families

Regular home visits are expected in programs such as Head Start, whose clients just happen to include many people with culturally diverse heritages. Some private childcare facilities and school districts encourage teachers to make home visits, but this practice is less common in these settings. If your practicum site recommends home visits, your cooperating teacher may allow you to accompany her. Generally accepted benefits of these visits include opportunities to promote home-school collaboration and opportunities to better understand the environment in which children live. However, despite your good intentions, some families may not be comfortable having you or any other teacher make a home visit; their feelings must be respected (Olsen & Fuller, 1998).

Parent Conferences and Interaction with Children's Families

During your practicum, you are likely to have the chance to observe and/or participate in parent conferences. Even though you are working to build positive relationships with families, keep in mind that some adults may be uncomfortable about coming to their child's classroom. Although you may not feel particularly intimidating or powerful, parents still view you as an authority figure. Perhaps they had negative school experiences; just walking into a school building may evoke unpleasant memories.

Therefore, for communication to be positive, you should take steps to make sure that families feel comfortable in your room. Have a pleasant area for quiet conversation. Sit with them at a round table or alongside them in chairs of equal height. This may seem simplistic, but sitting behind a desk or seating parents in children's chairs can place an emotional barrier between you and them. Engage in active listening, as discussed previously in the book. Encourage sharing of information.

If the family's primary language is not English, ask that someone be present who can translate if necessary. Also, any notes, letters, or report cards must be translated into the parents' primary language. Schools that have large numbers of children from homes where English is not spoken may find it helpful to contact businesses that translate regularly used documents into families' native languages (TransAct, 2003). Many of these services are now available through Internet sites.

Cultural differences may lead to misinterpretation on your part, so be careful to remain nonjudgmental when interacting with families from cultures other than your own. For example, some parents may show up for conferences and bring the entire extended family as a show of support for their child. Others may be reluctant to show up at all because they feel that educational concerns should be left entirely up to you as the expert. You may mistakenly interpret one family as being overly protective and the other family as being unconcerned (Parette & Petch-Hogan, 2000).

Frequent communication with parents builds a partnership that benefits everyone. Teachers and parents can learn from each other.

Because families know their child better than anyone else, this is a good opportunity for you to learn from them. A common piece of advice that you may hear is to always begin and end conferences on a positive note. If parents have many concerns, then you may want to schedule a follow-up meeting so that you and they are not rushed (Olsen & Fuller, 1998; Seplocha, 2004; Warner & Sower, 2005).

A suggested format for conferencing is presented in Figure 9.4 (Olsen & Fuller, 2008; Seplocha, 2004; Wright and Steglin, 2003).

As previously mentioned, you are likely to be communicating with families whose cultural heritage is different from your own; therefore, a brief discussion of cultural differences in communication may be helpful.

Figure 9.4 Sample Format for Family Conferences

1. Before the conference
- Send a reminder note home verifying the time, place, and length of the conference.
- Review items from the child's portfolio and choose those that you would like to share.
- If the family's home language is not English, you may need to arrange for an interpreter to be present during the conference.
- Arrange the conference area to be comfortable, welcoming, and free from distractions.

2. During the conference
- Welcome the family and establish rapport.
- Begin positively by describing the child's strengths and interests. Share an interesting story about something the child did recently, and show samples from the child's portfolio. Avoid jargon, acronyms, or "teacher talk" as you speak.
- Ask the family what information they would like to share about their child. Use this as an opportunity to learn from them.
- Discuss any concerns regarding the child's progress. Encourage the family to offer suggestions and to work with you to address their needs or concerns. Listen as families express worries or ask questions. Use your active listening skills (see Chapter 3). You may want to jot down brief notes for reference later.
- If you think that more time is needed, then schedule another conference at a time convenient for the family.
- End positively. You may want to provide a handout of simple activities that families can do with their child to encourage learning. Keep the list simple and low-cost or no-cost. Thank the family for coming and say something positive about the child to conclude.

3. After the conference
- Write down a few notes to document what took place during the conference.
- Note information you learned that will help you work with the child and her family.
- Note any follow-up that should take place.

❖ NONVERBAL CULTURAL CODES

Much has been written about differences in nonverbal communication or codes between racial/ethnic groups. The danger is that these variations can become generalized and form cultural stereotypes and prejudices. Therefore, we must be careful to remember that generalizations are only tentative at best. That said, certain nonverbal behaviors or codes are often associated with particular cultural groups.

Voices of Reality: Student Teachers Speak

Last night was my first night of conferences. I had so much fun! I expected it to be a good night because of the conferences scheduled, and I was right. Each conference is twenty minutes. That seemed like a long time, until I sat through one. It flies! If the parents have questions or concerns (which is nice if they do!) it's rushing things. My coop led them all but I gave my input also, and the parents seemed to value it and look at me as one of their child's teachers.

Krista U.

When I have my own conferences someday, I plan to keep little notes on each child. That way I can refer back to the personal notes and tell the parents about these. Since these would be personal, it would allow each conference to be different and break things up.

Nancy F.

One family came right before dinner time. While they were waiting they ate the entire bag of Hershey kisses we had put in a bowl in the hallway by the door. They just dropped the wrappers on the floor! Maybe that was their dinner!

Ruth H.

Being a part of parent-teacher conferences was definitely a good experience for me. As I have never been a part of conferences before. I was anxious to see how questions and comments were handled and how topics were addressed. Most of our conferences went very well and were positive. Plus, we had a good number of parents that are in the classroom helping out on a regular basis, so they are comfortable talking with my coop and me already.

Jackson L.

There were also a handful of conferences during which the child's family issues were discussed more than their school performance. But, this was more pressing and significant to discuss at the time. It is so important to know the child from the parent's point of view.

Saul D.

Physical Proximity, Eye Contact, and Touch

People from countries in South America and southern Europe have been described as *contact cultures* because they tend to stand close together, make frequent eye contact, and touch each other while communicating. People from countries in North America, northern Europe, and East Asia have been described as *noncontact countries* because they tend to stand farther apart, make less eye contact, and touch each other less frequently while communicating (Martin & Nakayama, 2005). So, if you are a teacher whose cultural heritage is that of a noncontact country, then, in theory, you are likely to feel some discomfort when communicating with families from contact countries. These are broad generalizations. However, they indicate that we should be aware of cultural differences in behavior and be flexible in dealing with people whose cultural behaviors are different from our own.

❖ FINAL THOUGHTS

Your heightened awareness of cultural sensitivities will help you become a culturally competent teacher. This ability is no longer optional in this time of rapid demographic change. Children's families can be your best allies in learning about other cultures and incorporating them into your overall curriculum. Therefore, your sincere desire to collaborate with the families of your children will go a long way toward building the trust necessary to make that happen.

ACTIVITIES FOR REFLECTION AND ACTION

1. If you have not already done so, answer the questions for cultural reflection included in this chapter.
2. Think of how you can incorporate elements of cultural diversity into a lesson(s) for children in your practicum. Develop your thoughts in a written plan.
3. How does your cooperating teacher prepare for parent-teacher conferences? What have you observed that you believe contributes to effective conferences?
4. Portfolio: Describe a good parent-teacher conference you observed. What made this conference particularly effective? What did you learn that you can apply to your own parent-teacher conferences in the future? Your narrative and reflection is an appropriate artifact for your portfolio.
5. Add to the list of multicultural book choices suggested in this chapter. Include books and stories about all forms of human diversity, such as those about people

who differ by race, ethnicity, and sexual orientation, as well as those who have special needs and abilities. You may find it helpful to write a brief description of each selection, along with the reason why each is a good choice for your classroom library.

6. Design a bulletin board or display for your classroom that reflects the diversity of your children and their families. Write a reflection about why your bulletin board is particularly appropriate and culturally sensitive.

7. *Portfolio:* Take a picture of your bulletin board or display. Include the picture and your reflection in your portfolio.

CHAPTER 10

Completion of Student Teaching: Looking Ahead

To teach is to touch the lives of many
and to help us learn life's lessons.
But to teach *well* is to make a difference
In all the lives you touch.

To teach is to be a parent, nurse, friend,
    and confidant;
To be a supporter, a leader, and a motivator.
But to teach *well*
    is to be all of these things,
yet not lose sight of who you are.
You share a part of yourself
with all whose lives
you have touched.

To teach is to be tender,
loving, strong, an giving to all who rely
upon you;
to encourage and praise.
But to teach *well*
is to believe in what
and whom you teach.

A teacher comes to master these many jobs
throughout the years.
But those who teach *well*
Recognize that there
Will always be more
To learn in life's journey,
And they never hesitate
To strive to learn it.

Source: Reprinted by permission of
Donna Bulger.

You are nearing the completion of your student teaching practicum with excitement and anticipation of what lies ahead. Some of you will go on to enjoy other placements with cooperating teachers as you get closer to fulfilling the requirements of your teacher education program. For some of you, this is it . . . for now. You will be leaving your practicum site and looking ahead to graduation and the prospects of finding that professional teaching position you have wanted for so long. Others are already teaching in early childhood facilities; with graduation, you will have the certification status that labels you as a teacher in the profession of early childhood education. Regardless of your current status, you are approaching a transition point in your life and in the lives of the children with whom you have spent many weeks.

Donna Bulger's words are worth keeping in mind as you approach this transition. You know that you will be a lifelong learner. You will always strive to improve your teaching and keep up with new information in a field that is never stagnant. The challenge for you, then, is not to teach, but to teach *well*.

Voices of Reality: Student Teachers Speak

Well, I just want you to know that my full time in the classroom went very well, and I feel prepared and ready to set out and find my own classroom! After my week was done, it is now twice as hard to give the subjects back to my coop. I am getting more sad as each day passes. I can't believe it is time to do my last calendar until I have my own classroom.

Jackson L.

I have started doing observations in other classrooms. The teachers I've been to so far have apologized for not having something more exciting for me to observe but it really doesn't matter. I love just sitting there and looking around the room, how it's set up, bulletin boards, etc. You can learn so much just from that! It's also interesting to see different teachers' styles, which usually come out no matter what they're doing at the time. This isn't an opportunity I'll have again. Real teachers can't just leave their classroom to spy on their friends, so I want to take full advantage of this while I can!

Krista U.

The time is drawing near for you to leave your practicum site. You need to consider how that transition should occur.

❖ LEAVING YOUR STUDENT TEACHING PRACTICUM

As your final official day in your student teaching practicum approaches, you may be feeling a well-deserved sense of satisfaction. You have worked hard and learned more than you probably realize right now. You have formed relationships with your cooperating teacher and other colleagues in the building. Perhaps, even more important, you have formed relationships with young children and their families. How you leave is as important as how you began.

Leaving Your Cooperating Teacher and Your Colleagues

A sincere note of thanks is appropriate. The author's personal preference is a hand-written note rather than a computer-generated one. The extra time it takes for you to write a note by hand is appreciated. It is neither necessary nor expected for you to buy a gift for your cooperating teacher. If you have formed collegial relationships with coworkers, administrators, support staff, and volunteers, you should make a point of visiting them to say good-bye during your last week of placement. You never know when you may be working with these people once again during your career, and you want to leave on the best possible terms.

Leaving the Children in Your Placement

Leaving the children is another issue altogether. You should prepare the children for your departure well in advance. They may have questions about why you are leaving and why you cannot stay with them. Some children who have formed an attachment with you may cry at the thought of your leaving. If it is realistic for you to return to visit them after your last day of placement, then telling them about your return visit will help make the adjustment easier.

Although it is not required, some student teachers make a simple, inexpensive gift for each of their children. For example, a card with a picture of you and each child makes a special remembrance. Some student teachers choose to give a gift to the whole class. It does not have to be anything expensive. It could be a plant for the classroom that everyone can enjoy or a new fish for the class aquarium. In some practicum settings, it is customary for the cooperating teacher and the children to have a going-away party for the student teacher who is leaving. This is certainly not a universal practice, but it happens frequently. It is somewhat of a ritual that signifies endings and new beginnings.

Saying good-bye is an important part of bringing closure to your student teaching experience. Children may not understand why you have to leave, so this can be a difficult transition for them and for you.

Final Evaluation of the Student Teaching Practicum

Some teacher education programs require a meeting at the end of the practicum among you, your cooperating teacher, and your college supervisor in order to evaluate your performance. At the very least, you will receive a written evaluation at the end of the semester from your cooperating teacher noting your strengths and areas of needed improvement. The evaluation forms vary from state to state and, to some degree, from college to college. Grading requirements also vary; some programs assign a pass/no pass grade, whereas others assign letter grades to student teachers.

If this is your final practicum before graduation, forms will be submitted by your college certification officer according to your state's procedures for certification. Your college supervisor is often the person who makes sure that all paperwork is in order and ready for the certification officer to process immediately following graduation.

In addition, some colleges routinely give each student teacher the opportunity to evaluate her cooperating teacher and, in some cases, her college supervisor. If this is the case in your program, you may be able to recommend that a particular cooperating teacher be used again as a role model for student teachers—or not. You may comment on the helpfulness and frequency of suggestions you received for improvement.

You may also have an opportunity to do a self-evaluation at the end of your experience. Some colleges require self-evaluation in the form of an exit portfolio presentation. Others require a written self-analysis to present to your college supervisor.

The following questions will begin to prepare you for the kinds of questions you will be asked in job interviews:

- How have you grown as a person as a result of your practicum experience? As a teacher?
- What do you want other people to know about your teaching?
- If you have a portfolio, what does it reveal about you as a teacher?
- How are you a different person as a result of your practicum experience?
- What do you see as your strengths as a teacher? Your areas of needed improvement?
- What evidence can you provide that indicates your skill level in the competencies required by your program?

❖ PLANNING AHEAD AFTER GRADUATION

A few weeks after graduation, you will receive your teacher certificate. However, many early childhood centers and school districts will offer you a contract as a certified early childhood teacher with oral or written verification from your college that you have met the criteria for certification and your paperwork is being processed. Unless you already have a position, you need to think about the job application/interview process before graduation day.

Networking

Think about where you would like to teach. You may be limited to certain areas because of family obligations or other concerns. Perhaps you want to take a risk and move to a completely new area. These are all decisions you must consider. How do you decide what to do?

Networking, or talking with people in your field of study, is one option. Teachers at your practicum site may also have information about positions that will be available in the near future. In addition, most colleges have career and counseling centers that are helpful. They usually keep a file of your resume, letters of recommendation, and transcripts for prospective employers. They also notify students when job recruiters are coming on campus and serve as a good resource of information about job opportunities in various locations (Goethals & Howard, 2000; Pelletier, 2004).

Resume Writing

If you are uncertain about how to write an effective resume and cover letter, then check with your career and counseling center. They may have helpful software programs on their computers that you can use free of charge. They may offer workshops on resume writing and interview skills.

You can also find helpful information about resume writing by going online. Suggestions include the following:

- *http://www.resume.monster.com*
- *http://www.studentcenter.com*
- *http://www.careerlab.com*
- *http://www.1.umn.edu/ohr/ecep/resume/*

These sites include hints about writing good resumes as well as databases of resumes for varied purposes that you may examine (Goethals & Howard, 2000). Even when you have your resume written, ask someone such as one of your professors or an advisor to review it. Objective feedback is always helpful. A sample resume is included at the end of the chapter in Figure 10.4 to give you some ideas about format and content.

Job Fairs

Your teacher education program and your career and counseling center will receive notices about job fairs being held in your area. Independent child development centers, religiously affiliated schools, and international schools rarely participate in these events. These are usually attended by representatives from public school districts. They often have administrators and teachers in attendance who are looking for people in specific areas such as early childhood education or special education.

The fairs are usually held in a location that is convenient to a number of teacher education programs. School districts from near and far will set up tables from which to hand out literature about their districts, their geographic area, and applications. If you arrive at the fair early, before the lines get long, you can often get an interview on the spot. Even if you are not sure where you want to teach, this is a good chance to learn about opportunities you had not even considered.

When you attend a job fair, be sure to take multiple copies of your resume and dress professionally. Some students prepare packets that include a resume, copies of recommendation letters, and copies of Praxis test scores to hand out to districts of particular interest. Because you may have the opportunity to be interviewed, you should wear the same type of attire you would wear to a more formal interview. Therefore, leave the jeans and sneakers at home. Your college supervisor or your career and counseling center can give you guidance about appropriate interview clothing in your area if you are unsure about what to wear.

Applications

Some states now use a common application form for all teaching positions in the public school districts. You can go to the Department of Education Web site for your state and find out if that is the case in your location. Rather than contact each district, you can download the common application and duplicate it for all districts. If you prefer private schools or child development centers, you will have to write to each facility individually. You can even locate available positions in early childhood education by going online at *http://www.early.childhood.teacher.jobs.monster.com*.

When you send an application, always include a cover letter (see Figure 10.1) in which you give a brief introduction and indicate why you are applying to that facility. You can personalize your cover letter by sending it to a specific administrator. Your teacher education department and/or your career and counseling center can help you obtain the names of the appropriate people who should receive your application. A good cover letter can get your application the attention it deserves.

A sample cover letter is included at the end of the chapter in Figure 10.3.

- Address your letter to a particular person who is involved in hiring rather than to a generic "To whom it may concern."
- Limit your letter to one page.
- Make sure that your spelling and grammar are perfect. Have someone else proofread your letter as well.
- Use your permanent address rather than a temporary school address.
- If you learned about the position in the newspaper or somewhere else, say so. If you are merely exploring the possibility that a position may be available in the near future, state that.
- State why you think that this school, center, or district is a good match for you.
- State your qualifications, such as your graduation date with a degree and/or certification in early childhood education.
- Request an interview. Mention your enclosed resume and the portfolio you will have available at the interview.
- Close with a polite statement of thanks.

(Adapted from Pelletier, 2004)

FIGURE 10.1   Suggestions for Effective Cover Letters

❖ INTERVIEWS

When your college's career and counseling center announces that recruiters are coming to the campus for interviews, check the list carefully. Some recruiters may specify early childhood positions. Others may just indicate elementary education. You can interview with either. Remember, the elementary education recruiter may have positions available in a range of grades, including K–3.

Even if you are not particularly interested in the programs or the districts represented by certain recruiters, you should have the interview. The more experience you have with the interview process, the more relaxed you will be and the better you will do in the interviews you really care about.

Preparation for the Interview

If the campus career and counseling center offers a workshop, you may benefit from hearing their interview tips. Also, ask your college instructors, other students, and teachers you know for sample interview questions to think about. Then practice role-playing the interview and your answers to various questions.

When you have an interview scheduled, do a little background preparation. For example, check to see if the program or district has an Internet site. If it does, then review it carefully. It may provide interesting information, such as the program's philosophy, mission, curriculum, student population, and demographics. You will make a better impression at the interview if you are informed.

If you have the opportunity, ask ahead of time who will be conducting the interview. You do not want to go in expecting to be interviewed by one person and then find out when you get there that five administrators from various buildings will all be interviewing you at the same time. If you know what to expect, you will be less nervous.

Make sure that you know what clothing you plan to wear at the interview so that you do not have to be concerned about your appearance.

Sample Interview Questions

Every interview will be unique because of the nature of the particular program and the people who are hiring. It is common practice, however, for schools to conduct screening interviews either in person or by phone. These interviews may be relatively brief, 20 or 30 minutes. Some schools then call a few people back for a second interview or to teach a demonstration lesson.

Interviews generally begin with a few minutes of small talk to make you relax a little before the interview gets underway. A number of questions turn up on interviews frequently enough that a few of them are listed in Figure 10.2 for you to think about.

Some of these questions refer to topics you may have discussed throughout your teacher education program, such as your philosophy of education and the qualities of a good teacher. Other questions may surprise

Voices of Reality: Student Teachers Speak

The only thing I was missing was a pin to put on my jacket. The afternoon before my first interview, I spent an hour at the mall looking for a shiny pin that went with my suit jacket. I finally found one I liked. I knew if they asked me a question I didn't know the answer to, they might be distracted by my pin. That way they might not see the look on my face. I figured I would have time to come up with something to say and I know it sounds crazy but it worked! Oh well, go figure.

Jasmine L.

Figure 10.2 Frequently Asked Interview Questions

1. Why did you decide to apply for this position?
2. What is your philosophy of teaching?
3. Why did you decide to become a teacher?
4. How do other people describe you?
5. What are the qualities of a good teacher?
6. Why should we hire you?
7. What does your classroom look like?
8. What is your greatest strength? Greatest weakness?
9. What procedures do you use for discipline?
10. How would you handle an angry parent?
11. Where do you see yourself in 5 years?
12. Do you have any questions you would like to ask us?

you. They are intended to catch you off guard. For example, the question asking you to name your greatest weakness is a trick question. You should answer carefully by turning your so-called weakness into a strength. You might say, "I tend to think about my work when I am at home, and I spend much of my free time planning activities for my class. I know I really should work on balancing my time a little better." This response makes you seem to be someone who is dedicated to being a good teacher. On the other hand, if you say that "my weakness is that I tend to procrastinate," then your weakness sounds like a weakness. Therefore, when in doubt, take your time, pause, think a moment, and then answer the question. You will appear to be giving careful consideration to your answer.

In spite of your best preparation, you may be asked questions you did not expect. Perhaps you will be asked questions that you thought were very good. Several student teachers have been collecting some of their favorite interview questions.

Additional Interview Tips

Have a couple of questions in mind that you can ask the interviewers. Do not ask what the starting salary is, even if you really want to know. Instead, ask questions that will cause the interviewers to think. For example, you might ask what opportunities for professional growth they offer their teachers. What is their philosophy regarding inclusion? What changes do they foresee for their school or district in the next 5 years?

Try to keep in mind a few general guidelines for nonverbal communication during your interview. For example, make eye contact, refrain from

Voices of Reality: Student Teachers Speak

I took a few minutes to collect some of my BEST and WORST interview questions:

Best Questions

1. **In one minute, sell yourself.**   I was shocked when I heard this question because I honestly never thought I'd hear this one. This question allowed me to highlight those qualities that I have that would set me apart from someone else.
2. **How do you know when a child has been successful?**   It also demonstrates to the interviewer how this teacher perceives himself in the classroom. Whether success is determined from what the students have achieved or what the teacher has done.
3. **Do you know a good listener? Describe them to me.**   MY FAVORITE QUESTION BY FAR (because I really liked my answer too)! Listening requires one to go beyond listening to the words that come from that child's mouth. It's about allowing the person to talk and figure things out for themselves before one would even consider offering any advice.
4. **What do you think a child's definition of FAIR is?**   I liked this because I never thought about it being asked in an interview. It's something to ponder. What is your definition of FAIR? But more importantly, working with children, what is their definition of FAIR?

Worst Questions

1. **What is your weakness?**   It's about rephrasing the question. Don't say this is my weakness. I remember what I said. I said, I don't know whether or not this is my fault, but if you're looking for something that I lack, I don't have professional experience.
2. **What's your position on assessment?**   This question was very tough. I had to take a side without being wishy washy and explain why I thought exactly what I did.
3. **What types of assessment methods have you used?**   This was also extremely difficult. I talked about what I thought would be best and what I would attempt to use in my classroom such as portfolios and rubrics.

Destiny M.

crossing your arms or legs, and keep your jacket unbuttoned and your hands out of your pockets. Try not to "talk with your hands," but leave them open and relaxed. These tips will help you send the nonverbal message that you are a confident, cooperative, and open person (Fuller & Olsen, 1998).

Follow-Up to Your Interview

After your interview is over, reflect on your experience. If possible, write down as many of the interview questions as you can remember. Each

Try to relax and enjoy the interview process. Remember that you are also deciding if the position is a good fit for you.

time you go through this process, you will become more confident and self-assured.

Within the next day or two, send a thank-you note. You can call the school secretary to verify the names and correct spellings of the people who interviewed you. The school will contact you concerning the next steps; either a second interview or a demonstration lesson is common practice. If you hear nothing or if you receive a rejection letter, then move on and pre-pare for your next interview. You may have several interviews in a row and then be in the fortunate position of having more than one offer. In that case, do not feel pressured to sign a contract quickly. It is acceptable to say that you need to think it over because you have another offer pending.

❖ FINAL THOUGHTS

As you complete your student teaching practicum, you will have many decisions to make. This is an exciting period of your life. If you do not already have a professional teaching position, the process of finding one can be nerve-wracking as well as rewarding. Keep in mind that you have many helpful resources at your disposal, and do not hesitate to ask for assistance. The time will come when you will be a mentor for others who follow the path you have chosen. This is indeed a lifelong journey: to teach *well* and to learn life's lessons as you make a difference in the lives you touch.

Voices of Reality: Student Teachers Speak

In another couple of months I will be looking for a job! I am wondering and concerned how the children will do when I am not here. I did not know if that is something I should think about, but I do...I am really going to miss these kids!! One mom said "I pray to God every night for teachers like you." I was so amazed and flattered. More and more I can teach kindergarten, and I will be determined to get a job in this class/age level.

Jasmine L.

You may choose from among several acceptable formats to write your cover letter and resume. Suggestions are provided in Figure 10.3 and Figure 10.4. Remember to check for spelling and grammar errors and to personalize each cover letter for the particular position you are seeking.

Figure 10.3 **Sample Format for a Cover Letter**

Permanent Address
City, State
April 25, 2005

Dr. Jane Doe
Superintendent
Good School District
City, State

Dear Dr. Doe:
I am applying for the early childhood teaching position that is posted on the Good School District Web page. I will be graduating from Good College this May with certification in Early Childhood Education.

Your school district has an excellent reputation for its strong instructional programs designed for a diverse population of students. My course of study included field experiences in multicultural settings with children of mixed abilities, and I have experience working collaboratively with others. I believe my background would be a good fit for your district.

Enclosed please find my resume. I will be available at your convenience for an interview. I look forward to meeting you. Thank you for your consideration.

Sincerely,
Grade A. Applicant

Figure 10.4 **Sample Format for a Resume**

GRADE A. APPLICANT
Permanent Address
City, State
Phone:
E-mail:

OBJECTIVE   **Teacher: Early Childhood Education**
EDUCATION   **Good College**
                 City, State
                 Degree—Date
                 Major:

STUDENT   **Early Childhood Center**
TEACHING   **Pre-K Teacher**
                 City, State
                 Dates

                 Responsibilities:
                 * (Briefly list activities as bulleted items.)
                 *
                 *
                 *

                 Local School District
                 Grade 2 Teacher
                 City, State
                 Dates

                 Responsibilities:
                 *
                 *
                 *
                 *

RELATED   Counselor, Good Summer Camp, Dates
ACTIVITIES   Volunteer Tutor, After-School Program, Dates
                 Art Instructor, Good Community Center, Dates
CREDENTIALS   Good College Career Planning Center
                 City, State
                 Phone:

❖   ❖   ❖

ACTIVITIES FOR REFLECTION AND ACTION

1. How will you leave the children in your practicum? What will you do for a good-bye activity?
2. Review the interview questions in this chapter. Plan your answer to each question.
3. Write your resume and a sample cover letter. Ask someone at your career center to read them and provide feedback. Your college supervisor and your cooperating teacher may also be willing to provide feedback.
4. *Portfolio:* Include your resume in your portfolio.

NAEYC Code of Ethical Conduct and Statement of Commitment
A position statement of the National Association for the Education of Young Children

❖ PREAMBLE

NAEYC recognizes that those who work with young children face many daily decisions that have moral and ethical implications. The **NAEYC Code of Ethical Conduct** offers guidelines for responsible behavior and sets forth a common basis for resolving the principal ethical dilemmas encountered in early childhood care and education. The **Statement of Commitment** is not part of the Code but is a personal acknowledgement of an individual's willingness to embrace the distinctive values and moral obligations of the field of early childhood care and education.

The primary focus of the Code is on daily practice with children and their families in programs for children from birth through 8 years of age, such as infant/toddler programs, preschool and prekindergarten programs, child care centers, hospital and child life settings, family child care homes, kindergartens, and primary classrooms. When the issues involve young children, then these provisions also apply to specialists who do not work directly with children, including program administrators, parent educators, early childhood adult educators, and officials with responsibility for program monitoring and licensing. (Note: See also the "Code of Ethical Conduct: Supplement for Early Childhood Adult Educators," online at www.naeyc.org/about/positions/pdf/ethics04.pdf.)

❖ CORE VALUES

Standards of ethical behavior in early childhood care and education are based on commitment to the following core values that are deeply rooted in the history of the field of early childhood care and education. We have made a commitment to

- Appreciate childhood as a unique and valuable stage of the human life cycle
- Base our work on knowledge of how children develop and learn
- Appreciate and support the bond between the child and family
- Recognize that children are best understood and supported in the context of family, culture,* community, and society
- Respect the dignity, worth, and uniqueness of each individual (child, family member, and colleague)
- Respect diversity in children, families, and colleagues
- Recognize that children and adults achieve their full potential in the context of relationships that are based on trust and respect

* The term *culture* includes ethnicity, racial identity, economic level, family structure, language, and religious and political beliefs, which profoundly influence each child's development and relationship to the world.

❖ CONCEPTUAL FRAMEWORK

The Code sets forth a framework of professional responsibilities in four sections. Each section addresses an area of professional relationships: (1) with children, (2) with families, (3) among colleagues, and (4) with the community and society. Each section includes an introduction to the primary responsibilities of the early childhood practitioner in that context. The introduction is followed by a set of ideals (I) that reflect exemplary professional practice and by a set of principles (P) describing practices that are required, prohibited, or permitted.

The **ideals** reflect the aspirations of practitioners. The **principles** guide conduct and assist practitioners in resolving ethical dilemmas. Both ideals and principles are intended to direct practitioners to those questions which, when responsibly answered, can provide the basis for conscientious decision making. While the Code provides specific direction for addressing some ethical dilemmas, many others will require the practitioner to combine the guidance of the Code with professional judgment.

The ideals and principles in this Code present a shared framework of professional responsibility that affirms our commitment to the core values of our field. The Code publicly acknowledges the responsibilities that we in the field have assumed, and in so doing supports ethical behavior in our work. Practitioners who face situations with ethical dimensions are urged to seek guidance in the applicable parts of this Code and in the spirit that informs the whole.

Often "the right answer"—the best ethical course of action to take—is not obvious. There may be no readily apparent, positive way to handle a situation. When one important value contradicts another, we face an ethical dilemma. When we face a dilemma, it is our professional responsibility to consult the Code and all relevant parties to find the most ethical resolution.

❖ SECTION I: ETHICAL RESPONSIBILITIES TO CHILDREN

Childhood is a unique and valuable stage in the human life cycle. Our paramount responsibility is to provide care and education in settings that are safe, healthy, nurturing, and responsive for each child. We are committed to supporting children's development and learning; respecting individual differences; and helping children learn to live, play, and work cooperatively. We are also committed to promoting children's self-awareness, competence, self-worth, resiliency, and physical well-being.

Ideals

I-1.1 To be familiar with the knowledge base of early childhood care and education and to stay informed through continuing education and training.

I-1.2 To base program practices upon current knowledge and research in the field of early childhood education, child development, and related disciplines, as well as on particular knowledge of each child.

I-1.3 To recognize and respect the unique qualities, abilities, and potential of each child.

I-1.4 To appreciate the vulnerability of children and their dependence on adults.

I-1.5 To create and maintain safe and healthy settings that foster children's social, emotional, cognitive, and physical development and that respect their dignity and their contributions.

I-1.6 To use assessment instruments and strategies that are appropriate for the children to be assessed, that are used only for the purposes for which they were designed, and that have the potential to benefit children.

I-1.7 To use assessment information to understand and support children's development and learning, to support instruction, and to identify children who may need additional services.

I-1.8 To support the right of each child to play and learn in an inclusive environment that meets the needs of children with and without disabilities.

I-1.9   To advocate for and ensure that all children, including those with special needs, have access to the support services needed to be successful.

I-1.10   To ensure that each child's culture, language, ethnicity, and family structure are recognized and valued in the program.

I-1.11   To provide all children with experiences in a language that they know, as well as support children in maintaining the use of their home language and in learning English.

I-1.12   To work with families to provide a safe and smooth transition as children and families move from one program to the next.

Principles

P-1.1   Above all, we shall not harm children. We shall not participate in practices that are emotionally damaging, physically harmful, disrespectful, degrading, dangerous, exploitative, or intimidating to children. *This principle has precedence over all others in this Code.*

P-1.2   We shall care for and educate children in positive emotional and social environments that are cognitively stimulating and that support each child's culture, language, ethnicity, and family structure.

P-1.3   We shall not participate in practices that discriminate against children by denying benefits, giving special advantages, or excluding them from programs or activities on the basis of their sex, race, national origin, religious beliefs, medical condition, disability, or the marital status/family structure, sexual orientation, or religious beliefs or other affiliations of their families. (Aspects of this principle do not apply in programs that have a lawful mandate to provide services to a particular population of children.)

P-1.4   We shall involve all those with relevant knowledge (including families and staff) in decisions concerning a child, as appropriate, ensuring confidentiality of sensitive information.

P-1.5   We shall use appropriate assessment systems, which include multiple sources of information, to provide information on children's learning and development.

P-1.6   We shall strive to ensure that decisions such as those related to enrollment, retention, or assignment to special education services, will be based on multiple sources of information and will never be based on a single assessment, such as a test score or a single observation.

P-1.7   We shall strive to build individual relationships with each child; make individualized adaptations in teaching strategies, learning environments, and curricula; and consult with the family so that each child benefits from the program. If, after such efforts have been exhausted, the current placement does not meet a child's needs, or the child is seriously jeopardizing the ability of other children to benefit from the program, we shall collaborate with the child's family and appropriate specialists to determine the additional services needed and/or the placement option(s) most likely to ensure the child's success. (Aspects of this principle may not apply in programs that have a lawful mandate to provide services to a particular population of children.)

P-1.8   We shall be familiar with the risk factors for and symptoms of child abuse and neglect, including physical, sexual, verbal, and emotional abuse and physical, emotional, educational, and medical neglect. We shall know and follow state laws and community procedures that protect children against abuse and neglect.

P-1.9   When we have reasonable cause to suspect child abuse or neglect, we shall report it to the appropriate community agency and follow up to ensure that appropriate action has been taken. When appropriate, parents or guardians will be informed that the referral will be or has been made.

P-1.10 When another person tells us of his or her suspicion that a child is being abused or neglected, we shall assist that person in taking appropriate action in order to protect the child.

P-1.11 When we become aware of a practice or situation that endangers the health, safety, or well-being of children, we have an ethical responsibility to protect children or inform parents and/or others who can.

❖ SECTION II: ETHICAL RESPONSIBILITIES TO FAMILIES

Families* are of primary importance in children's development. Because the family and the early childhood practitioner have a common interest in the child's well-being, we acknowledge a primary responsibility to bring about communication, cooperation, and collaboration between the home and early childhood program in ways that enhance the child's development.

Ideals

I-2.1   To be familiar with the knowledge base related to working effectively with families and to stay informed through continuing education and training.

I-2.2   To develop relationships of mutual trust and create partnerships with the families we serve.

I-2.3   To welcome all family members and encourage them to participate in the program.

*The term *family* may include those adults, besides parents, with the responsibility of being involved in educating, nurturing, and advocating for the child.

I-2.4   To listen to families, acknowledge and build upon their strengths and competencies, and learn from families as we support them in their task of nurturing children.

I-2.5   To respect the dignity and preferences of each family and to make an effort to learn about its structure, culture, language, customs, and beliefs.

I-2.6   To acknowledge families' childrearing values and their right to make decisions for their children.

I-2.7   To share information about each child's education and development with families and to help them understand and appreciate the current knowledge base of the early childhood profession.

I-2.8   To help family members enhance their understanding of their children and support the continuing development of their skills as parents.

I-2.9   To participate in building support networks for families by providing them with opportunities to interact with program staff, other families, community resources, and professional services.

Principles

P-2.1   We shall not deny family members access to their child's classroom or program setting unless access is denied by court order or other legal restriction.

P-2.2   We shall inform families of program philosophy, policies, curriculum, assessment system, and personnel qualifications, and explain why we teach as we do—which should be in accordance with our ethical responsibilities to children (see Section I).

P-2.3   We shall inform families of and, when appropriate, involve them in policy decisions.

P-2.4   We shall involve the family in significant decisions affecting their child.

P-2.5   We shall make every effort to communicate effectively with all families in a language that they understand. We shall use community resources for translation and interpretation when we do not have sufficient resources in our own programs.

P-2.6   As families share information with us about their children and families, we shall consider this information to plan and implement the program.

P-2.7   We shall inform families about the nature and purpose of the program's child assessments and how data about their child will be used.

P-2.8   We shall treat child assessment information confidentially and share this information only when there is a legitimate need for it.

P-2.9   We shall inform the family of injuries and incidents involving their child, of risks such as exposures to communicable diseases that might result in infection, and of occurrences that might result in emotional stress.

P-2.10 Families shall be fully informed of any proposed research projects involving their children and shall have the opportunity to give or withhold consent without penalty. We shall not permit or participate in research that could in any way hinder the education, development, or well-being of children.

P-2.11 We shall not engage in or support exploitation of families. We shall not use our relationship with a family for private advantage or personal gain, or enter into relationships with family members that might impair our effectiveness working with their children.

P-2.12 We shall develop written policies for the protection of confidentiality and the disclosure of children's records. These policy documents shall be made available to all program personnel and families. Disclosure of children's records beyond family members, program personnel, and consultants having an obligation of confidentiality shall require familial consent (except in cases of abuse or neglect).

P-2.13 We shall maintain confidentiality and shall respect the family's right to privacy, refraining from disclosure of confidential information and intrusion into family life. However, when we have reason to believe that a child's welfare is at risk, it is permissible to share confidential information with agencies, as well as with individuals who have legal responsibility for intervening in the child's interest.

P-2.14 In cases where family members are in conflict with one another, we shall work openly, sharing our observations of the child, to help all parties involved make informed decisions. We shall refrain from becoming an advocate for one party.

P-2.15 We shall be familiar with and appropriately refer families to community resources and professional support services. After a referral has been made, we shall follow up to ensure that services have been appropriately provided.

❖ SECTION III: ETHICAL RESPONSIBILITIES TO COLLEAGUES

In a caring, cooperative workplace, human dignity is respected, professional satisfaction is promoted, and positive relationships are developed and sustained. Based upon our core values, our primary responsibility to colleagues is to establish and maintain settings and relationships that support productive work and meet professional needs. The same ideals that apply to children also apply as we interact with adults in the workplace.

A. Responsibilities to co-workers

Ideals

I-3A.1   To establish and maintain relationships of respect, trust, confidentiality, collaboration, and cooperation with co-workers.

I-3A.2   To share resources with co-workers, collaborating to ensure that the best possible early childhood care and education program is provided.

I-3A.3   To support co-workers in meeting their professional needs and in their professional development.

I-3A.4   To accord co-workers due recognition of professional achievement.

Principles

P-3A.1   We shall recognize the contributions of colleagues to our program and not participate in practices that diminish their reputations or impair their effectiveness in working with children and families.

P-3A.2   When we have concerns about the professional behavior of a co-worker, we shall first let that person know of our concern in a way that shows respect for personal dignity and for the diversity to be found among staff members, and then attempt to resolve the matter collegially and in a confidential manner.

P-3A.3   We shall exercise care in expressing views regarding the personal attributes or professional conduct of co-workers. Statements should be based on firsthand knowledge, not hearsay, and relevant to the interests of children and programs.

P-3A.4   We shall not participate in practices that discriminate against a co-worker because of sex, race, national origin, religious beliefs or other affiliations, age, marital status/family structure, disability, or sexual orientation.

B. Responsibilities to employers

Ideals

I-3B.1   To assist the program in providing the highest quality of service.

I-3B.2   To do nothing that diminishes the reputation of the program in which we work unless it is violating laws and regulations designed to protect children or is violating the provisions of this Code.

Principles

P-3B.1   We shall follow all program policies. When we do not agree with program policies, we shall attempt to effect change through constructive action within the organization.

P-3B.2   We shall speak or act on behalf of an organization only when authorized. We shall take care to acknowledge when we are speaking for the organization and when we are expressing a personal judgment.

P-3B.3   We shall not violate laws or regulations designed to protect children and shall take appropriate action consistent with this Code when aware of such violations.

P-3B.4   If we have concerns about a colleague's behavior, and children's well-being is not at risk, we may address the concern with that individual. If children are at risk or the situation does not improve after it has been brought to the colleague's attention, we shall report the colleague's unethical or incompetent behavior to an appropriate authority.

P-3B.5   When we have a concern about circumstances or conditions that impact the quality of care and education within the program, we shall inform the program's administration or, when necessary, other appropriate authorities.

C. Responsibilities to employees

Ideals

I-3C.1   To promote safe and healthy working conditions and policies that foster mutual respect, cooperation, collaboration, competence, well-being, confidentiality, and self-esteem in staff members.

I-3C.2   To create and maintain a climate of trust and candor that will enable staff to speak and act in the best interests of children, families, and the field of early childhood care and education.

I-3C.3   To strive to secure adequate and equitable compensation (salary and benefits) for those who work with or on behalf of young children.

I-3C.4   To encourage and support continual development of employees in becoming more skilled and knowledgeable practitioners.

Principles

P-3C.1   In decisions concerning children and programs, we shall draw upon the education, training, experience, and expertise of staff members.

P-3C.2   We shall provide staff members with safe and supportive working conditions that honor confidences and permit them to carry out their responsibilities through fair performance evaluation, written grievance procedures, constructive feedback, and opportunities for continuing professional development and advancement.

P-3C.3 We shall develop and maintain comprehensive written personnel policies that define program standards. These policies shall be given to new staff members and shall be available and easily accessible for review by all staff members.

P-3C.4 We shall inform employees whose performance does not meet program expectations of areas of concern and, when possible, assist in improving their performance.

P-3C.5 We shall conduct employee dismissals for just cause, in accordance with all applicable laws and regulations. We shall inform employees who are dismissed of the reasons for their termination. When a dismissal is for cause, justification must be based on evidence of inadequate or inappropriate behavior that is accurately documented, current, and available for the employee to review.

P-3C.6 In making evaluations and recommendations, we shall make judgments based on fact and relevant to the interests of children and programs.

P-3C.7 We shall make hiring, retention, termination, and promotion decisions based solely on a person's competence, record of accomplishment, ability to carry out the responsibilities of the position, and professional preparation specific to the developmental levels of children in his/her care.

P-3C.8 We shall not make hiring, retention, termination, and promotion decisions based on an individual's sex, race, national origin, religious beliefs or other affiliations, age, marital status/family structure, disability, or sexual orientation. We shall be familiar with and observe laws and regulations that pertain to employment discrimination. (Aspects of this principle do not apply to programs that have a lawful mandate to determine eligibility based on one or more of the criteria identified above.)

P-3C.9 We shall maintain confidentiality in dealing with issues related to an employee's job performance and shall respect an employee's right to privacy regarding personal issues.

❖ SECTION IV: ETHICAL RESPONSIBILITIES TO COMMUNITY AND SOCIETY

Early childhood programs operate within the context of their immediate community made up of families and other institutions concerned with children's welfare. Our responsibilities to the community are to provide programs that meet the diverse needs of families, to cooperate with agencies and professions that share the responsibility for children, to assist families in gaining access to those agencies and allied professionals, and to assist in the development of community programs that are needed but not currently available.

As individuals, we acknowledge our responsibility to provide the best possible programs of care and education for children and to conduct ourselves with honesty and integrity. Because of our specialized expertise in early childhood development and education and because the larger society shares responsibility for the welfare and protection of young children, we acknowledge a collective obligation to advocate for the best interests of children within early childhood programs and in the larger community and to serve as a voice for young children everywhere.

The ideals and principles in this section are presented to distinguish between those that pertain to the work of the individual early childhood educator and those that more typically are engaged in collectively on behalf of the best interests of children—with the understanding that individual early childhood educators have a shared responsibility for addressing the ideals and principles that are identified as "collective."

Ideal (Individual)

1-4.1   To provide the community with high-quality early childhood care and education programs and services.

Ideals (Collective)

I-4.2   To promote cooperation among professionals and agencies and interdisciplinary collaboration among professions concerned with addressing issues in the health, education, and well-being of young children, their families, and their early childhood educators.

I-4.3   To work through education, research, and advocacy toward an environmentally safe world in which all children receive health care, food, and shelter; are nurtured; and live free from violence in their home and their communities.

I-4.4   To work through education, research, and advocacy toward a society in which all young children have access to high-quality early care and education programs.

I-4.5   To work to ensure that appropriate assessment systems, which include multiple sources of information, are used for purposes that benefit children.

I-4.6   To promote knowledge and understanding of young children and their needs. To work toward greater societal acknowledgment of children's rights and greater social acceptance of responsibility for the well-being of all children.

I-4.7   To support policies and laws that promote the well-being of children and families, and to work to change those that impair their well-being. To participate in developing policies and laws that are needed, and to cooperate with other individuals and groups in these efforts.

I-4.8   To further the professional development of the field of early childhood care and education and to strengthen its commitment to realizing its core values as reflected in this Code.

Principles (Individual)

P-4.1   We shall communicate openly and truthfully about the nature and extent of services that we provide.

P-4.2   We shall apply for, accept, and work in positions for which we are personally well-suited and professionally qualified. We shall not offer services that we do not have the competence, qualifications, or resources to provide.

P-4.3   We shall carefully check references and shall not hire or recommend for employment any person whose competence, qualifications, or character makes him or her unsuited for the position.

P-4.4   We shall be objective and accurate in reporting the knowledge upon which we base our program practices.

P-4.5   We shall be knowledgeable about the appropriate use of assessment strategies and instruments and interpret results accurately to families.

P-4.6   We shall be familiar with laws and regulations that serve to protect the children in our programs and be vigilant in ensuring that these laws and regulations are followed.

P-4.7   When we become aware of a practice or situation that endangers the health, safety, or well-being of children, we have an ethical responsibility to protect children or inform parents and/or others who can.

P-4.8   We shall not participate in practices that are in violation of laws and regulations that protect the children in our programs.

P-4.9   When we have evidence that an early childhood program is violating laws or regulations protecting children, we shall report the violation to appropriate authorities who can be expected to remedy the situation.

P-4.10 When a program violates or requires its employees to violate this Code, it is permissible, after fair assessment of the evidence, to disclose the identity of that program.

Principles (Collective)

P-4.11 When policies are enacted for purposes that do not benefit children, we have a collective responsibility to work to change these practices.

P-4.12 When we have evidence that an agency that provides services intended to ensure children's well-being is failing to meet its obligations, we acknowledge a collective ethical responsibility to report the problem to appropriate authorities or to the public. We shall be vigilant in our follow-up until the situation is resolved.

P-4.13 When a child protection agency fails to provide adequate protection for abused or neglected children, we acknowledge a collective ethical responsibility to work toward the improvement of these services.

GLOSSARY OF TERMS RELATED TO ETHICS

Code of Ethics. Defines the core values of the field and provides guidance for what professionals should do when they encounter conflicting obligations or responsibilities in their work.

Values. Qualities or principles that individuals believe to be desirable or worthwhile and that they prize for themselves, for others, and for the world in which they live.

Core Values. Commitments held by a profession that are consciously and knowingly embraced by its practitioners because they make a contribution to society. There is a difference between personal values and the core values of a profession.

Morality. People's views of what is good, right, and proper; their beliefs about their obligations; and their ideas about how they should behave.

Ethics. The study of right and wrong, or duty and obligation, that involves critical reflection on morality and the ability to make choices between values and the examination of the moral dimensions of relationships.

Professional Ethics. The moral commitments of a profession that involve moral reflection that extends and enhances the personal morality practitioners bring to their work, that concern actions of right and wrong in the workplace, and that help individuals resolve moral dilemmas they encounter in their work.

Ethical Responsibilities. Behaviors that one must or must not engage in. Ethical responsibilities are clear-cut and are spelled out in the Code of Ethical Conduct (for example, early childhood educators should never share confidential information about a child or family with a person who has no legitimate need for knowing).

Ethical Dilemma. A moral conflict that involves determining appropriate conduct when an individual faces conflicting professional values and responsibilities.

SOURCES FOR GLOSSARY TERMS AND DEFINITIONS

Feeney, S., & N. Freeman. 1999. *Ethics and the early childhood educator: Using the NAEYC code.* Washington, DC: NAEYC.

Kidder, R.M. 1995. *How good people make tough choices: Resolving the dilemmas of ethical living.* New York: Fireside.

Kipnis, K. 1987. How to discuss professional ethics. *Young Children* 42(4): 26–30.

❖ STATEMENT OF COMMITMENT*

As an individual who works with young children, I commit myself to furthering the values of early childhood education as they are reflected in the ideals and principles of the NAEYC Code of Ethical Conduct. To the best of my ability I will

- Never harm children.
- Ensure that programs for young children are based on current knowledge and research of child development and early childhood education.
- Respect and support families in their task of nurturing children.
- Respect colleagues in early childhood care and education and support them in maintaining the NAEYC Code of Ethical Conduct.
- Serve as an advocate for children, their families and their teachers in community and society.
- Stay informed of and maintain high standards of professional conduct.
- Engage in an ongoing process of self-reflection, realizing that personal characteristics, biases, and beliefs have an impact on children and families.
- Be open to new ideas and be willing to learn from the suggestions of others.
- Continue to learn, grow and contribute as a professional.
- Honor the ideals and principles of the NAEYC Code of Ethical Conduct.

*This Statement of Commitment is not part of the Code but is a personal acknowledgment of the individual's willingness to embrace the distinctive values and moral obligations of the field of early childhood care and education. It is recognition of the moral obligations that lead to an individual becoming part of the profession.

Source: National Association for the Education of Young Children. 2005. *The Code of Ethical Conduct and Statement of Commitment.* Brochure. Washington, DC: Author. Available online at http://www.naeyc.org/org/about/positions/pdf/PSETHO5.pdf. Reprinted with permission of the National Association for the Education of Young Children.

NCATE Unit Standards
Standard 1: *Candidate Knowledge, Skills, and Professional Dispositions*

Candidates preparing to work in schools as teachers or other school professionals know and demonstrate the content knowledge, pedagogical content knowledge and skills, pedagogical and professional knowledge and skills, and professional dispositions necessary to help all students learn. Assessments indicate that candidates meet professional, state, and institutional standards.

❖ 1A. CONTENT KNOWLEDGE FOR TEACHER CANDIDATES

(Initial and Advanced Preparation of Teachers)

Unacceptable

Teacher candidates have inadequate knowledge of content that they plan to teach and are unable to give examples of important principles and concepts delineated in professional, state, and institutional standards. Fewer than 80 percent of the unit's program completers pass the content examinations in states that require examinations for licensure. Candidates in advanced programs for teachers do not have an in-depth knowledge of the content that they teach.

Acceptable

Teacher candidates know the content that they plan to teach and can explain important principles and concepts delineated in professional, state, and institutional standards. Eighty percent or more of the unit's program completers pass the content examinations in states that require examinations for licensure. Candidates in advanced programs for teachers have an in-depth knowledge of the content that they teach.

Target

Teacher candidates have in-depth knowledge of the content that they plan to teach as described in professional, state, and institutional standards. They demonstrate their knowledge through inquiry, critical analysis, and synthesis of the subject. All program completers pass the content examinations in states that require examinations for licensure. Candidates in advanced programs for teachers are recognized experts in the content that they teach.

❖ 1B. PEDAGOGICAL CONTENT KNOWLEDGE FOR TEACHER CANDIDATES

(Initial and Advanced Preparation of Teachers)

Unacceptable

Teacher candidates do not understand the relationship of content and content-specific pedagogy delineated in professional, state, and institutional standards in a way that helps them develop learning experiences that integrate technology and build on students' cultural backgrounds and knowledge of content so that students learn. Candidates in advanced programs for teachers have a limited understanding of the relationship between content and content-specific pedagogy; they are unable to explain the linkages between theory and practice. They are not able to select or use a broad range of instructional strategies that promote student learning.

Acceptable

Teacher candidates understand the relationship of content and content-specific pedagogy delineated in professional, state, and institutional standards. They have a broad knowledge of instructional strategies that draws upon content and pedagogical knowledge and skills delineated in professional, state, and institutional standards to help all students learn. They facilitate student learning of the content through presentation of the content in clear and meaningful ways and through the integration of technology. Candidates in advanced programs for teachers demonstrate an in-depth understanding of the content of their field and of the theories related to pedagogy and learning. They are able to select and use a broad range of instructional strategies and technologies that promote student learning and are able to clearly explain the choices they make in their practice.

Target

Teacher candidates reflect a thorough understanding of the relationship of content and content-specific pedagogy delineated in professional, state, and institutional standards. They have in-depth understanding of the content that they plan to teach and are able to provide multiple explanations and instructional strategies so that all students learn. They present the content to students in challenging, clear, and compelling ways, using real-world contexts and integrating technology appropriately. Candidates in advanced programs for teachers have expertise in pedagogical content knowledge and share their expertise through leadership and mentoring roles in their schools and communities. They understand and address student preconceptions that hinder learning. They are able to critique research and theories related to pedagogy and learning. They are able to select and develop instructional strategies and technologies, based on research and experience, that help all students learn.

❖ 1C. PROFESSIONAL AND PEDAGOGICAL KNOWLEDGE AND SKILLS FOR TEACHER CANDIDATES

(Initial and Advanced Preparation of Teachers)

Unacceptable

Teacher candidates have not mastered professional and pedagogical knowledge and skills delineated in professional, state, and institutional standards. They lack knowledge of school, family, and community contexts, and they are unable to develop learning experiences that draw on students' prior experience. They do not reflect on their work, nor do they use current research to inform their practice. They are unable to explain major schools of thought about schooling, teaching, and learning. Candidates in advanced programs for teachers do not reflect on their practice and cannot recognize their strengths and areas of needed improvement. They do not engage in professional development. They do not keep abreast of current research and policies on schooling, teaching, learning, and best practices. They are not engaged with the professional community to develop meaningful learning experiences.

Acceptable

Teacher candidates can apply the professional and pedagogical knowledge and skills delineated in professional, state, and institutional standards to facilitate learning. They consider the school, family, and community contexts in which they work and the prior experience of students to develop meaningful learning experiences. They reflect on their practice. They know major schools of thought about schooling, teaching, and learning. They are able to analyze educational research findings and incorporate new information into their practice as appropriate. Candidates in advanced programs for teachers reflect on their practice and are able to identify their strengths and areas of needed improvement. They engage in professional activities. They have a thorough understanding of the school, family, and community contexts in which they work, and they collaborate with the professional community to create meaningful learning experiences for all students. They are aware of current research and policies related to schooling, teaching, learning, and best practices. They are able to analyze educational research and policies and can explain the implications for their own practice and for the profession.

Target

Teacher candidates reflect a thorough understanding of professional and pedagogical knowledge and skills delineated in professional, state, and institutional standards. They develop meaningful learning experiences to facilitate learning for all students. They reflect on their practice and make necessary adjustments to enhance student learning. They know how students learn and how to make ideas accessible to them. They consider school, family, and community contexts in connecting concepts to students' prior experience and applying the ideas to real-world issues. Candidates in advanced programs for teachers develop expertise in certain aspects of professional and pedagogical knowledge and contribute to the dialogue based on their research and experiences. They take on leadership roles in the professional community and collaborate with colleagues to contribute to school improvement and renewal.

❖ 1D. STUDENT LEARNING FOR TEACHER CANDIDATES

(Initial and Advanced Preparation of Teachers)

Unacceptable

Teacher candidates cannot accurately assess student learning or develop learning experiences based on students' developmental levels or prior experience. Candidates in advanced programs for teachers have a limited understanding of the major concepts and theories related to assessing student learning. They do not use classroom performance data to make decisions about teaching strategies. They do not use community resources to support student learning.

Acceptable

Teacher candidates focus on student learning. Teacher candidates assess and analyze student learning, make appropriate adjustments to instruction, and monitor student progress. They are able to develop and implement meaningful learning experiences for students based on their developmental levels and prior experience. Candidates in advanced programs for teachers have a thorough understanding of the major concepts and theories related to assessing student learning and regularly apply these in their practice. They analyze student, classroom, and school performance data and make data-driven decisions about strategies for teaching and learning so that all students learn. They are aware of and utilize school and community resources that support student learning.

Target

Teacher candidates focus on student learning and study the effects of their work. They assess and analyze student learning, make appropriate adjustments to instruction, monitor student learning, and have a positive effect on learning for all students. Candidates in advanced programs for teachers have a thorough understanding of assessment. They analyze student, classroom, and school performance data and make data-driven decisions about strategies for teaching and learning so that all students learn. They collaborate with other professionals to identify and design strategies and interventions that support student learning.

❖ 1E. KNOWLEDGE AND SKILLS FOR OTHER SCHOOL PROFESSIONALS

(Initial and Advanced Preparation of Teachers)

Unacceptable

Candidates for other professional school roles have not mastered the knowledge that undergirds their fields and is delineated in professional, state, and institutional standards. They are not able to use data, research or technology. They do not understand the cultural contexts of the school(s) in which they provide professional services. Fewer than 80 percent of the unit's program completers pass the academic content examinations in states that require such examinations for licensure.

Acceptable

Candidates for other professional school roles have an adequate understanding of the knowledge expected in their fields and delineated in professional, state, and institutional standards. They know their students, families, and communities; use data and current research to inform their practices; use technology in their practices; and support student learning through their professional services. Eighty percent or more of the unit's program completers pass the academic content examinations in states that require such examinations for licensure.

Target

Candidates for other professional school roles have an in-depth understanding of knowledge in their fields as delineated in professional, state, and institutional standards and demonstrated through inquiry, critical analysis, and synthesis. They collect and analyze data related to their work, reflect on their practice, and use research and technology to support and improve student learning. All program completers pass the academic content examinations in states that require such examinations for licensure.

❖ 1F. STUDENT LEARNING FOR OTHER SCHOOL PROFESSIONALS

Unacceptable

Candidates for other professional school roles cannot facilitate student learning as they carry out their specialized roles in schools. They are unable to create positive environments for student learning appropriate to their responsibilities in schools. They do not have an understanding of the diversity and policy contexts within which they work.

Acceptable

Candidates for other professional school roles are able to create positive environments for student learning. They understand and build upon the developmental levels of students with whom they work; the diversity of students, families, and communities; and the policy contexts within which they work.

Target

Candidates for other professional school roles critique and are able to reflect on their work within the context of student learning. They establish educational environments that support student learning, collect and analyze data related to student learning, and apply strategies for improving student learning within their own jobs and schools.

❖ 1G. PROFESSIONAL DISPOSITIONS FOR ALL CANDIDATES

Unacceptable

Candidates are not familiar with professional dispositions delineated in professional, state, and institutional standards. Candidates do not demonstrate classroom behaviors that are consistent with the ideal of fairness and the belief that all students can learn. They do not model these professional dispositions in their work with students, families, colleagues, and communities.

Acceptable

Candidates are familiar with the professional dispositions delineated in professional, state, and institutional standards. Candidates demonstrate classroom behaviors that are consistent with the ideal of fairness and the belief that all students can learn. Their work with students, families, colleagues and communities reflects these professional dispositions.

Target

Candidates work with students, families, colleagues, and communities in ways that reflect the professional dispositions expected of professional educators as delineated in professional, state, and institutional standards. Candidates demonstrate classroom behaviors that create caring and supportive learning environments and encourage self-directed learning by all students. Candidates recognize when their own professional dispositions may need to be adjusted and are able to develop plans to do so.

Supporting Explanation

The knowledge, skills, and professional dispositions outlined in this standard are based on current research in teaching and learning and on best practices in professional education. Each element reflects an important component of the knowledge, skills, and professional dispositions that educators need to develop in order to help all students learn. The knowledge, skills, and professional dispositions in this standard should be reflected in the unit's conceptual framework and assessed as part of the unit's assessment system. The data from the assessment system should be used to demonstrate candidate learning of the knowledge, skills, and professional dispositions stated herein.

#

Teachers must have sufficient knowledge of content to help all students meet standards for P–12 education. The guiding principle of the teaching profession is that student learning is the goal of teaching. NCATE's Standard 1 reinforces the importance of this goal by requiring that teacher candidates know their content or subject matter, can teach effectively, and can help all students learn. All school professionals are expected to carry out their work in ways that are supportive of student learning.

#

Educator licensure standards adopted by most states require that educators demonstrate knowledge, skills, and professional dispositions that enable them to address the needs of all learners. Therefore, candidates preparing to teach or work as other professional educators in P–12 schools are expected to demonstrate the candidate learning proficiencies identified in the unit's conceptual framework, in the standards of national professional organizations which should be aligned with standards for P–12 students, and in state licensing standards.

#

To help institutions better prepare teacher candidates to meet state licensing requirements, NCATE has aligned its unit and program standards with the principles of the Interstate New Teacher Assessment and Support Consortium (INTASC). First and foremost, NCATE and INTASC expect teacher candidates to know the content of their disciplines, including their central concepts, tools of inquiry, and structures.

#

Teacher candidates are expected to meet professional standards for the subjects that they plan to teach as these have been defined in standards for students in P–12 schools and standards for the preparation of teachers. Candidates are expected to meet professional standards of other national accrediting organizations (e.g., the National Association of Schools of Music and the National Association of Schools of Art and Design) or NCATE's professional standards for teachers of early childhood education; elementary education; middle-level education; special education; gifted education; environmental education; and secondary education (including English/language arts, mathematics, science, social studies, computer science, technology education, health, physical education, foreign languages, and English as a second language).

#

As part of the program review process, institutions must submit candidate assessments, scoring guides, performance data, and other program documents that respond to professional standards for national and/or state review. The program review process is an important component of NCATE accreditation. Information from the program review process should be used to address the elements in Standard 1 on content knowledge, professional and pedagogical knowledge and skills, pedagogical content knowledge, and student learning.

#

NCATE expects teacher candidates to demonstrate knowledge, skills, and professional dispositions to provide learning opportunities supporting students' intellectual, social, and personal development. Teacher candidates are able to create instructional opportunities adapted to diverse learners. They encourage students' development of critical thinking, problem solving, and performance skills. They are able to create learning environments encouraging positive social interaction, active engagement in learning, and self-motivation. Teacher candidates foster active inquiry, collaboration, and supportive interaction in the classroom. They plan instruction based upon knowledge of content, students, families, the community, and curriculum goals. Teacher candidates evaluate students' academic achievement as well as their social and physical development and use the results to maximize students' motivation and learning. They are able to reflect on and continually evaluate the effects of choices and actions on others and actively seek out opportunities to grow professionally. They also are able to foster relationships with school colleagues, parents and families, and agencies in the larger community to support students' learning and well-being.

#

Candidates preparing to work in schools as teachers or other school professionals need a sound professional knowledge base to understand learning and the context of schools, families, and communities. They understand and are able to apply knowledge related to the social, historical, and philosophical foundations of education, professional ethics, law, and policy. They know the ways children and adolescents learn and develop, including their cognitive and affective development and the relationship of these to learning. They understand language acquisition; cultural influences on learning; exceptionalities; diversity of student populations, families, and communities; and inclusion and equity in classrooms and schools. They are able to appropriately and effectively integrate technology and information literacy in instruction to support student learning. They understand the importance of using research in teaching and other professional roles and know the roles and responsibilities of the education profession.

#

Candidates for all professional education roles develop and model professional dispositions that are expected of educators. The unit includes as professional dispositions the ideal of fairness and the belief that all students can learn. Based on its mission, the unit may determine additional professional dispositions it wants candidates to develop. The unit articulates professional dispositions as part of its conceptual framework. The unit systematically assesses the development of appropriate professional dispositions by candidates. Professional dispositions are not assessed directly; instead the unit assesses dispositions based on observable behavior in educational settings.

#

Candidates for all professional education roles are expected to demonstrate the ability to affect student learning. Teachers and teacher candidates have student learning as the focus of their work. They are able to develop and administer appropriate assessments and to use assessments as formative and summative tools. They are able to create meaningful learning experiences by judging prior student knowledge, planning and implementing lessons, assessing student learning, reflecting on student learning, and making adjustments to their teaching to improve learning. Other school professionals are able to create and maintain positive environments, as appropriate to their professional responsibilities, which support student learning in educational settings.

#

Throughout the program, teacher candidates develop the knowledge bases for analyzing student learning and practice by collecting data and assessing student learning through their work with students. Student learning should be demonstrated directly by all teacher candidates during clinical practice.

#

Experienced teachers in graduate programs build upon and extend their knowledge and experiences to improve their own teaching and student learning in classrooms. They further develop their knowledge, skills, and professional dispositions to meet the propositions of the National Board for Professional Teaching Standards (NBPTS) for the advanced certification of teachers. These candidates demonstrate their commitment to students, skills to manage and monitor student learning, capacity to think systematically about their practice, ability to learn from experience, and involvement as members of learning communities.

#

Candidates preparing to work in schools in professional roles other than teaching demonstrate the knowledge, skills, and professional dispositions necessary to meet professional, state, and institutional standards reflected in the unit's conceptual framework. Candidates in programs for other school professionals should meet professional standards designed for programs preparing:

- educational technology specialists
- instructional technology specialists
- reading specialists/literacy coaches
- school leaders, including principals, curriculum and instruction specialists, and superintendents
- school library media specialists
- school psychologists
- special education administrators, educational diagnosticians, and special education technology specialists

- technology facilitators
- technology leaders
- other school professionals

Candidates in these graduate programs develop the ability to apply research and research methods. They also develop knowledge of learning, the social and cultural context in which learning takes place, and practices that support learning in their professional roles. Candidates might assess the school environment by collecting and analyzing data on student learning as it relates to their professional roles and developing positive environments supportive of student learning. Institutions must submit program documentation, including candidate assessments, scoring guides, and performance data that responds to professional standards for national and/or state review prior to and during the on-site visit.

#

This standard includes expectations for the knowledge, skills, and professional dispositions of candidates in initial teacher preparation and advanced level programs. Initial teacher preparation programs include all programs that prepare individuals for their first license in teaching. These programs can be offered at the undergraduate or graduate levels. They include five-year programs, master's programs, and postbaccalaureate programs that prepare individuals for their first license in teaching.

#

Advanced programs include programs for licensed teachers continuing their education as well as programs for other school professionals. Advanced programs include programs for teachers who are preparing at the graduate level for a second license in a field different from the field in which they have their first license; programs for teachers who are seeking a master's degree in the field in which they teach; and programs not tied to licensure, such as programs in curriculum and instruction. In addition, advanced programs include programs for other school professionals. Examples of these are programs in school counseling, school psychology, educational administration, and reading specialization. All advanced level programs are taught at the graduate level. In instances where there is uncertainty about the program level, institutions should seek assistance from NCATE's website or contact the NCATE office for clarification.

Source: From NCATE Unit Standards. Standard 1: Candidate Knowledge, Skill, and Dispositions. 2007. Washington, DC: NCATE. Available online at *http://www.ncate.org/pubs/public/unitStandardsRubrics.asp?ch=4.* Reprinted with permission of the National Council for Accreditation of Teacher Education. All rights reserved.

References

AARP. (2007). *Pennsylvania. A state fact sheet for grandparents and other relatives raising children.* Retrieved January 4, 2009, from *http://www.aarp.org/grandparents*

Adams, N. G., Shea, C. M., Liston, D. D., & Deever, B. (1998). *Learning to teach: A critical approach to field experiences.* Mahwah, NJ: Erlbaum.

Airasian, P. W. (2001). *Classroom assessment concepts and applications* (4th ed.). Boston: McGraw-Hill.

Airasian, P. W. (2005). *Classroom assessment: Concepts and applications* (5th ed.). Boston: McGraw-Hill.

Alberto, P. A., & Troutman, A. C. (2003). *Applied behavior analysis for teachers.* Upper Saddle River, NJ: Merrill/Prentice Hall.

Alger, H. A. (1984). Transitions: Alternatives to manipulative management techniques. *Young Children, 39*(5), 16–26.

Allen, M. & Staley, L. (2007). Helping children cope when a loved one is on military deployment. *Young Children, 62*(1), 82–86.

American Association of State Colleges and Universities. (2005). *The facts and fictions about teacher shortages.* Retrieved January 10, 2009, from *http://www.aascu.org/policy-matters/pdf/v2n5.pdf*

Anderson, N. A. (1998). Providing feedback to preservice teachers of reading in the field. *Reading Research and Instruction, 37,* 123–136.

Anderson, N. A., & Radencich, M. C. (2001). The value of feedback in an early field experience: Peer, teacher, and supervisor coaching. *Action in Teacher Education, 23*(3), 66–74.

Armentrout, W. D. (1927). *The conduct of student teaching in teachers colleges.* Greeley: Colorado State Teachers College.

Atova, B. (2007). Communications is key when children face parents' deployment. *Military Family News.* Retrieved January 18, 2009, from *http://www.army.mil/-news/2007/08/15/4432-communication-is-key-when-children-face-parents-deployment*

Baptiste, N., & Reyes, L. (2008). *Understanding ethics in early care and education* (2nd ed.). Upper Saddle River, NJ: Merrill/Prentice Hall.

Barnett, W. S., & Camilli, G. (2002). Conpensatory preschool education, cognitive development and "race." In J. M. Fish (Ed.), *Race and intelligence: Separating science from myth* (pp. 369–406). Mahwah, NJ: Erlbaum.

Barnett, W. S., & Hustedt, J. T. (2003). Preschool: The most important grade. *Educational Leadership, 60*(7), 54–57.

Bartholomew, B. (2008). Sustaining the fire. *Educational Leadership, 65*(6), 55–60.

Beaty, J. J. (2002). *Observing development of the young child* (5th ed.). Upper Saddle River, NJ: Merrill/Prentice Hall.

Beaty, J. J. (2004). *Skills for preschool teachers* (7th ed.). Upper Saddle River, NJ: Merrill/Prentice Hall.

Belson, S. I. (2003). *Technology for exceptional learners.* Boston: Houghton Mifflin.

Bender, W. N. (2002). *Differentiating instruction for students with learning disabilities: Best teaching practices for general and special educators.* Thousand Oaks, CA: Corwin Press.

Benesh, B., Arbuckle, M., Robbins, P., & D'Arcangelo, M. (1998). *Facilitator's guide: The brain and learning.* Alexandria, VA: Association for Supervision and Curriculum Development.

Bergan, J. R., (1977). *Behavioral consultation.* Upper Saddle River, NJ: Merrill/Prentice Hall.

Berk, L. E. (1976). How well do classroom practices reflect teacher goals? *Young Children, 32*(1), 64–81.

Berk, L. E. (1994). Vygotsky's theory: The importance of make-believe play. *Young Children, 50*(1), 30–39.

Berk, L. E. (2002). *Infants and childhood* (4th ed). Boston: Allyn & Bacon.

Betz, C. (1994). Beyond time-out: Tips from a teacher. *Young Children, 49*(3), 10–14.

Bey, T. M., & Holmes, C. T. (1992). *Mentoring: Contemporary principles.* Reston, VA: Association of Teacher Educators.

Birchak, B., Connor, C., Crawford, K. M., Kahn, L. H., Kaser, S., & Short, K. (1998). *Teacher study groups: Building community through dialogue and reflection.* Urbana, IL: National Council of Teachers of English.

Birckmayer, J., Cohen, J., Jensen, I. D., & Variano, D. A. (2005). Supporting grandparents who raise grandchildren. *Young Children, 60*(3), 100–104.

Blair, T. R., & Jones, D. L. (1998). *Preparing for student teaching in a pluralistic classroom.* Needham Heights, MA: Allyn & Bacon.

Blue, T. W., Boothby, P. R., O'Grady, R. J., Toro, J. A., & Tyminski, C. R. (1999, winter). Good things take time (unless you get a little help from your friends). *AILCTE Views and News, 10*(4).

Boreen, J., Johnson, M. K., Niday, D., & Potts, J. (2000). *Mentoring beginning teachers: Guiding, reflecting, coaching.* York, ME: Stenhouse.

Bornstein, M. H., Haynes, O. M., Pascual, L., Painter, K. M., & Galperin, C. (1999). Play in two societies: Persuasiveness of process, specificity of structure. *Child Development, 70,* 317–331.

Bowers, C. A., & Flinders, D. J. (1990). *Responsive teaching: An ecological approach to classroom practices of language, culture, and thought.* New York: Teachers College Press.

Bowman, B. T. (2006). Standards at the heart of educational equity. *Young Children, 61*(5), 42–48.

Bowman, B. T., Donovan, M. S., & Burns, M. S. (Eds.). (2001). *Eager to learn: Educating our preschoolers.* Washington, DC: National Academy Press.

Branscombe, N. A., Castle, K., Dorsey, A. G., Surbeck, E., & Taylor, J. B. (2003). *Early childhood curriculum: A constructivist perspective.* Boston: Houghton Mifflin.

Brazelton, T. B., & Sparrow, J. D. (2001). *Touchpoints three to six.* Cambridge, MA: Perseus.

Bredekamp, S. (Ed.). (1987). *Developmentally appropriate practice in early childhood programs serving children from birth through age 8.* Washington, DC: National Association for the Education of Young Children.

Bredekamp, S., & Copple, C. (Eds.). (1997). *Developmentally appropriate practice in early childhood programs* (rev. ed.). Washington, DC: National Association for the Education of Young Children.

Bredekamp, S., & Willer, B. (1993). Professionalizing the field of early childhood education: Pros and cons. *Young Children, 48*(3), 82–84.

Breslin, D. (2005). Children's capacity to develop resiliency: How to nurture it. *Young Children, 60*(1), 47–52.

Brewer, J. (2001). *Introduction to early childhood education preschool through primary grades* (4th ed.). Boston: Allyn & Bacon.

Brill, N. I., & Levine, J. (2002). *Working with people* (7th ed.). Boston: Allyn & Bacon.

Brookfield, S. D. (1990). *The skillful teacher.* San Francisco: Jossey-Bass.

Brophy, J. (1988). Educating teachers about managing classrooms and students. *Teaching and Teacher Education, 4*(1), 1–18.

Brophy-Herb, H. E., Kostelnik, M. J., & Stein, L. C. (2001). A developmental approach to teaching about ethics using the NAEYC Code of Ethical Conduct. *Young Children, 56*(1), 80–84.

Bruneau-Balderrama, O. (1997). Inclusion: Making it work for teachers, too. *The Clearing House, 70*(6), 328–330.

Bruno, H. E. (2007). Problem solving to prevent power struggles. *Young Children, 62*(5), 26–33.

Buttery, T. J., & Weller, L. D. (1988). Group clinical supervision: A paradigm for preservice instructional enhancement. *Action in Teacher Education, 10,* 61–73.

Campbell, B. (2008). *Handbook of differentiated instruction using the multiple intelligences: Lesson plans and more.* Boston: Allyn & Bacon.

Canter, L. (1976). *Assertive discipline: A take-charge approach for today's educator.* Seal Beach, CA: Canter & Associates.

Canter, L., & Canter, M. (1992). *Lee Canter's assertive discipline: Positive behavior management for today's classroom.* Santa Monica, CA: Lee Canter & Associates.

Carter, C. W. (1998). The use of journals to promote reflection. *The Journal of the Association of Teacher Educators, 19*(4), 39–42.

Caruso, J., & Fawcett, M. T. (1986). *Supervision in early childhood education.* New York: Teachers College Press.

Catron, C. E., & Allen, J. (2003). *Early childhood curriculum* (3rd ed.). Upper Saddle River, NJ: Merrill/Prentice Hall.

Charles, C. M. (1996). *Building classroom discipline.* White Plains, NY: Longman.

Charles, C. M. (2002). *Essential elements of effective discipline.* Boston: Allyn & Bacon.

Charlesworth, R. (1998). Developmentally appropriate practice is for everyone. *Childhood Education, 74*(5): 274–283.

Charlesworth, R. (2004). *Understanding child development* (4th ed.). Albany, NY: Thomson Delmar Learning.

Chattin-McNichols, J. (1992). *The Montessori controversy.* Albany, NY: Thomson Delmar Learning.

Children's Defense Fund. (2002, June). *The state of children in America's union: A 2002 action guide to leave no child behind (PDP: 2268K).* Washington, DC: Author.

Children's Defense Fund. (2007). *2007 annual report: Planning for success in the future.* Washington, DC: Author.

Chisholm, J. S. (1989). Biology, culture, and the development of temperament: A Navajo example. In J. K. Nugent, B. M. Lester, & T. B. Brazelton (Eds.), *Biology, culture, and development* (pp. 341–364). Norwood, NJ: Ablex.

Choate, J. S. (Ed.). (2003). *Successful inclusive teaching. Proven ways to detect and correct special needs* (4th ed.). Boston: Allyn & Bacon.

Clay, J. W. (2004). Creating safe, just places to learn for children of lesbian and gay parents: The NAYEC Code of Ethics in action. *Young Children, 59*(6), 34–38.

Clements, D. H., & Sarama, J. (2003). Young children and technology: What does research say? *Young Children, 58*(6), 34–40.

Clewett, A. S. (1988). Guidance and discipline: Teaching young children appropriate behavior. *Young Children, 43*(3), 26–31.

Cole, A. L., & Knowles, J. G. (2000). *Researching teaching: Exploring teacher development through reflexive inquiry.* Boston: Allyn & Bacon.

Cook, R. E., Klein, M. D., & Tessier, A. (2008). *Adapting early childhood curricula for children with special needs* (7th ed.). Upper Saddle River, NJ: Merrill/Prentice Hall.

Couchenour, D., & Chrisman, K. (2008). *Families, schools, and communities* (3rd ed.). Clifton Park, NY: Thomson Delmar Learning.

Covey, S. R. (1992). *Principle-centered leadership.* New York: Fireside.

Crosser, S. (2005). *What do we know about early childhood education?* Clifton Park, NY: Thomson Delmar Learning.

Cruickshank, D. R., Jenkins, D. B., & Metcalf, K. K. (2003). *The act of teaching* (3rd ed.). Boston: McGraw-Hill.

Culhane, D. P., Khadduri, J., Cortes, A., Buron, L., & Poulin, S. (2008). *The 2007 annual homelessness assessment report to Congress.* Retrieved January 18, 2009, from *http://work_bepress.com/dennis_culhane/79*

Cutler, K. M., Gilkerson, D. Parrott, S., & Browne, M. T. (2003). Developing math games based on children's literature. *Young Children, 58*(1), 22–27.

D'Arcangelo, M. (2000). The scientist in the crib: A conversation with Andrew Meltzoff. *Educational Leadership, 58*(3): 8–13.

Daniels, D. H., Beaumont, L. J., & Doolin, C. A. (2002). *Understanding children: An interview and observation guide for educators.* Boston: McGraw-Hill.

Danielson, C. (1996). *Enhancing professional practice: A framework for teaching.* Alexandria, VA: Association for Supervision and Curriculum Development.

Davis, M. D., Kilgo, J. L., & Garnel-McCormick, M. (1998). *Young children with special needs: A developmentally appropriate approach.* Boston: Allyn & Bacon.

DeBord, K., Hestenes, L. L., Moore, R. C., Cosco, N., & McGinnis, J. R. (2002). Paying attention to the outdoor environment is as important as preparing the indoor environment. *Young Children, 57*(3), 32–34.

Derman-Sparks, L. (1999). Markers of multicultural/antibias education. *Young Children, 54*(5), 43.

Derman-Sparks, L., & Phillips, C. B. (1997). *Teaching/learning antiracism: A developmental approach.* New York: Teachers College Press.

Dewey, J. (1933). *How we think.* Chicago: Henry Regnery.

Dewey, J. (1959). The child and the curriculum. In M. Dworkin (Ed.), *Dewey on education.* New York: Teachers College Press. (Original work published 1902)

Dichtelmiller, M. L. (2004). Experiences from the field. New insights into infant/toddler assessment. *Young Children, 59*(1), 30–33.

Dickinson, D. K., & Tabors, P. O. (2002). Fostering language and literacy in classrooms and homes. *Young Children, 57*(2), 10–18.

Dieker, L. A., & Barnett, C. A. (1996). Effective co-teaching. *Teaching Exceptional Children, 29*(1), 5–7.

Dietz, M. E. (1995). Using portfolios as a framework for professional development. *Journal of Staff Development, 16*(2), 40–43.

Diller, J. V., & Moule, J. (2005). *Cultural competence: A primer for educators.* Belmont, CA: Thomson Wadsworth.

Dodge, D. T., & Colker, L. J. (2000). *The creative curriculum* (3rd ed.). Washington, DC: Teaching Strategies.

Doucette-Dudman, D., & LaCure, J. R. (1996). *Raising our children's children.* Minneapolis: Fairview Press.

Dreikers, R., & Cassel, P. (1972). *Discipline without tears.* New York: Hawthorne Books.

Drew, W. F., Christie, J., Johnson, J. E., Meckley, A. M., & Nell, M. L. (2008). Constructive play: A value-added strategy for meeting early learning standards. *Young Children, 63*(4), 38–44.

Driscoll, A., & Nagel, N. G. (2005). *Early childhood education, birth–8: The world of children, families, and educators* (3rd ed.). Boston: Allyn & Bacon.

Ducette, J. P., Sewell, T. E., & Shapiro, J. P. (1996). Diversity in education: Problems and possibilities. In F. B. Murray (Ed.), *The teacher educator's handbook* (pp. 323–380). San Franciso: Jossey-Bass.

Dufour, R. (2002). The learning centered principal. *Educational Leadership, 59*(8), 12–15.

Duke, D. L. (1987). Environmental influences. In M. J. Dunkin (Ed.), *The international encyclopedia of teaching and teacher education* (pp. 548–553). New York: Pergamon.

Eaton, D. E. (2002). Family child care accreditation and professional development. *Young Children, 57*(1), 23.

Egan, G. (2002). *The skilled helper* (7th ed.). Pacific Grove, CA: Brooks/Cole.

Eggan, P. D., & Kauchak, D. P. (2006). *Strategies and models for teachers: Teaching content and thinking skills* (5th ed.). Boston: Allyn & Bacon.

Eisner, E. W. (2002). The kind of schools we need. *Phi Delta Kappan, 83*(8), 576–583.

Elkind, D. (2001). *The hurried child* (3rd ed.). Cambridge, MA: Perseus.

Erikson, F. (2001). Culture in society and in educational practices. In J. A. Banks & C. A. Banks (Eds.), *Multicultural education: Issues and perspectives* (4th ed., pp. 31–58). New York: Wiley.

Executive summary. (2002). Early-childhood education and care: Quality counts. *Education Week, 21*(7), 8–9.

Faber, A., & Mazlish, E. (1982). *How to talk so kids will listen and listen so kids will talk.* New York: Avon.

Family Equality Council. (2007). *LGBT parenting.* Retrieved January 5, 2008, from *http://www.familyequality.org/*

Feeney, S., Christensen, D., & Moravcik, E. (2001). *Who am I in the lives of children?* (6th ed.). Columbus, OH: Merrill/Prentice Hall.

Feitler, F., & Tokar, E. (1992). Getting a handle on teacher stress: How bad is the problem? *Educational Leadership, 49*(6), 456–458.

Fernald, A. (1993). Approval and disapproval: Infant responsiveness to vocal affect in familiar and unfamiliar languages. *Child Development, 64,* 657–674.

Field, T. M., & Widmayer. S.M. (1981). Mother-infant interactions among lower SES black, Cuban, Puerto Rican, and South American immigrants. In T. M. Field, A. M. Sostek, P. Vietze, & P. H. Leiderman (Eds.), *Culture and early interactions* (pp. 41–60). Hillsdale, NJ: Erlbaum.

Fields, M. V., & Boesser, C. (2002). *Constructive guidance and discipline* (3rd ed.). Upper Saddle River, NJ: Merrill/Prentice Hall.

Filler, J., & Xu, Y. (2006). Including children with disabilities in early childhood education programs. Individualizing developmentally appropriate practices. *Childhood Education, 83*(2), 92–98.

Fischer, M. A., & Gillespie, C. W. (2003). Computers and young children's development. *Young Children, 58*(4), 85–91.

Fischer, P. (2002). Wow! Kindergarten/first-grade inquiry. *Primary Voices K-6, 10*(3), 9–16.

Flicker, E. S., & Hoffman, J. A. (2002). Developmental discipline in the early childhood classroom. *Young Children, 57*(5), 82–89.

Freeman, N. K. (2000). Professional ethics: A cornerstone of teachers' preservice curriculum. *Action in Teacher Education, 23*(3), 12–18.

Freidus, H. (1996). Mentoring portfolio development. In N. Lyons (Ed.), *With portfolio in hand: Validating the new teacher professionalism* (pp. 51–68). New York: Teachers College Press.

French, K., & Cain, H. M. (2006). Including a young child with spina bifida. *Young Children, 61*(3), 78–84.

Frieman, B. B. (2001). *What teachers need to know about children at risk.* Boston: McGraw-Hill.

Friend, M., & Bursuck, W. D. (2009). *Including students with special needs: A practical guide for classroom teachers* (5th ed.). Upper Saddle River, NJ: Merrill/Prentice Hall.

Fromberg, D. P. (1997). The professional and social status of the early childhood educator. In J. P. Isenberg & M. R. Jalongo (Eds.), *Major trends and issues in early childhood education* (pp. 188–204). New York: Teachers College Press.

Fuller, F. F., & Brown, O. H. (1975). Becoming a teacher. In K. Ryan (Ed.), *Teacher education (Seventy-fourth yearbook of the National Society for the Study of Education,* pp. 25–52). Chicago: University of Chicago Press.

Fuller, M. L. (2001). Multicultural concerns and classroom management. In C. A. Grant & M. L. Gomez (Eds.), *Campus and classroom. Making schooling multicultural* (2nd ed., pp. 109–134). Upper Saddle River, NJ: Merrill/Prentice Hall.

Gardner, H. (1999). *Intelligence reframed: Multiple intelligences for the 21st century.* New York: Basic Books.

Gartrell, D. (1995). Misbehavior or mistaken behavior? *Young Children, 50*(5), 27–34.

Gartrell, D. (2002). Replacing time-out. Part two—using guidance to maintain an encouraging classroom. *Young Children, 57*(2), 36–43.

Gartrell, D. (2006a). Guidance matters. *Young Children, 61*(2), 88–89.

Gartrell, D. (2006b). Guidance matters. *Young Children, 61*(6), 54–55.

Gellman, E. S. (1992–1993). The use of portfolios in assessing teacher competence: Measurement issues. *Action in Teacher Education, 14*(4), 39–44.

Gesell, A., Ilg, F., Ames, L. B., & Rodell, J. (1974). *Infant and child in the culture of today* (rev. ed.). New York: Harper & Row.

Gestwicki, C. (1999). *Developmentally appropriate practice* (2nd ed.) Boston: Delmar Publishers.

Gillespie, C. W., & Chick, A. (2001). Fussbusters: Using peers to mediate conflict resolution in a Head Start classroom. *Childhood Education, 77,* 192–195.

Glasser, W. A. (1965). *Reality therapy.* New York: Harper-Collins.

Glasser, W. A. (1969). *Schools without failure.* New York: HarperCollins.

Glasser, W. A. (1986). *Control theory in the classroom.* New York: HarperCollins.

Glasser, W. A. (1988). *Choice theory in the classroom.* New York: HarperCollins.

Glasser, W. A. (1998). Choice theory: *A new psychology of personal freedom.* New York: HarperCollins.

Glickman, C. (1981). *Developmental supervision: Alternative practices for helping teachers improve instruction.* Alexandria, VA: Association for Supervision and Curriculum Development.

Goethals, M. S., & Howard, R. A. (2000). *Student teaching: A process approach to reflective practice.* Upper Saddle River, NJ: Merrill/Prentice Hall.

Goldstein, S., & Brooks, R. B. (Eds.). (2005). *Handbook of resilience in children.* New York: Kluwer Academic/Plenum.

Gonzalez-Mena, J. (2002). *The child in the family and the community* (3rd ed.). Upper Saddle river, NJ: Merrill/Prentice Hall.

Gonzalez-Mena, J. (2007). *50 early childhood strategies for working and communicating with diverse families.* Upper Saddle River, NJ: Prentice Hall.

Gordon, T. (1974). *Teacher effectiveness training.* New York: Wyden.

Governor's Commission on Early Learning. (2000). *Early learning birth to age five.* Seattle, WA: Author.

Grant, C. A., & Gomez, M. L. (2001). *Campus and classroom* (2nd ed.). Upper Saddle River, NJ: Merrill/Prentice Hall.

Grant, D., & Haynes, D. (1995). A developmental framework for cultural competence training with children. *Social Work in Education, 17,* 171–182.

Gray, E. C. (2006). Children's use of language and pictures in classroom inquiry. *Language Arts, 83*(3), 227–237.

Greenberg, P. (Ed.). (1999). Using NAEYC's code of ethics to negotiate professional problems. *Young Children, 54*(6), 56–57.

Grieco, E. M., & Cassidy, R. C. (2001). *Overview of race and Hispanic origin, 2000.* Washington, DC: U.S. Department of Commerce, Economics and Statistics Administration, U.S. Census Bureau.

Guyton, E., & McIntyre, D. J. (1990). Student teaching and school experiences. In W. R. Houston (Ed.), *Handbook of research on teacher education* (pp. 514–534). New York: Macmillan.

Hallahan, D. P., & Kauffman, J. M. (2006). *Exceptional learners* (10th ed.). Boston: Allyn & Bacon.

Hamner, T. J., & Turner, P. H. (1996). *Parenting in contemporary society* (3rd ed.). Boston: Allyn & Bacon.

Hanson, M. J., & Lynch, E. W. (2004). *Understanding families: Approaches to diversity, disability, and risk.* Baltimore: Paul H. Brookes.

Hatch, D. D. (1993). Early encounters: Coaching in teacher education. In R. H. Anderson, K. J. Snyder, & J. M. Bahner (Eds.), *Clinical supervision: Coaching for higher performance* (pp. 169–182). Lancaster, PA: Technomic.

Haughland, S. W. (1999). What role should technology play in young children's learning? *Young Children, 54*(6), 6–31.

Haughland, S. W., & Wright, J. L. (1997). *Young children and technology: A world of discovery.* Boston: Allyn & Bacon.

Hearron, P. F., & Hildebrand, V. (2009). *Guiding young children* (8th ed.). Upper Saddle River, NJ: Merrill/Prentice Hall.

Heath, M. S. (2004). *Electronic portfolios: A guide to professional development and assessment.* Columbus, OH: Linworth.

Hendrick, J. (2003). *Total learning: Developmental curriculum for the young child* (6th ed.). Upper Saddle River, NJ: Merrill/Prentice Hall.

Henniger, M. L. (2002). *Teaching young children: An introduction* (2nd ed.). Upper Saddle River, NJ: Merrill/Prentice Hall.

Henry, M. A., Beasley, W. W., & Brighton, K. L. (2002). *Supervising student teachers the professional way* (6th ed.). Terre Haute, IN: Sycamore Press.

Hesse, P., & Lane, F. (2003). Media literacy starts young: An integrated curriculum approach. *Young Children, 58*(6), 20–26.

Hill, B. C., & Ruptic, C. (1994). *Practical aspects of authentic assessment: Putting the pieces together.* Norwood, MA: Christopher-Gordon.

Hilliard, A. (1999). Toward better teacher education: A conversation with Asa Hilliard. *Educational Leadership, 56*(8), 58–62.

Hodgkinson, H. (2002). Demographics and teacher education. *Journal of Teacher Education, 53*(2), 102–105.

Hole, S., & McEntee, G. H. (1999). Reflection is at the heart of practice. *Educational Leadership, 56*(8), 34–37.

Hollins, E. R. (1995). Revealing the deep meaning of culture in school learning: Framing a new paradigm for teacher preparation. *Action in Teacher Education, 27*(1), 70–79.

Honig, A. S. (1996). *Behavior guidance for infants and toddlers.* Little Rock, AR: Southern Early Childhood Association.

Hudson, P., Miller, S., Salzberg, C., & Morgan, R. (1994). The role of peer coaching in teacher education programs. *Teacher Education and Special Education, 17,* 224–235.

Humphryes, J. (1998). The developmental appropriateness of high-quality Montessori programs. *Young Children, 53*(4), 4–16.

Hunt, R. (1999). Making positive multicultural early childhood education happen. *Young Children, 54*(5), 39–42.

Hyson, M. (2002). Three perspectives on early childhood assessment. *Young Children, 57*(1), 62–64.

Jackson, B. R. (1997). Creating a climate for healing in a violent society. *Young Children, 52*(7), 68–70.

Jarolimek, J., Foster, C. D., Sr., & Kellough, R. D. (2005). *Teaching and learning in the elementary school* (8th ed.). Upper Saddle River, NJ: Merrill/Prentice Hall.

Jones, J. (2004). Framing the assessment discussion. *Young Children, 59*(1), 14–18.

Jones, M. W. (2008). Inquiry-based science lessons. Unpublished manuscript.

Jones, V., & Jones, L. (2004). *Comprehensive classroom management* (7th ed.). Boston: Allyn & Bacon.

Kaczmarek, L. A. (2006). *Supporting families of children with disabilities in inclusive programs: A team approach. Beyond the Journal–Young Children* on the Web. Retrieved January 19, 2009, from *http://journal.naeyc.org/btj/200601*

Kagan, S. L., & Scott-Little, C. (2004). Early learning standards: Changing the parlance and practice of early childhood education. *Phi Delta Kappan, 85*(5), 388–396.

Kaiser, B., & Rasminsky, J.S. (2007). *Challenging behavior in young children* (2nd ed.). Boston: Allyn & Bacon.

Kampwirth, T. J. (2003). *Collaborative consultation in the schools: Effective practices for students with learning and behavior problems* (2nd ed.). Upper Saddle River, NJ: Merrill/Prentice Hall.

Katz, L. G. (1994). *The project approach.* Champaign, IL: ERIC Clearinghouse on Elementary and Early Childhood Education.

Kendall, J. S. (2003). Setting standards in early childhood education. *Educational Leadership, 60*(7), 64–68.

Kersey, K. C., & Malley, C. R. (2005). Helping children develop resiliency. Providing supportive relationships. *Young Children, 60*(1), 53–58.

KIDS COUNT Data Center. (2006). *Children in single-parent families, by race: Percent: 2006.* Baltimore: Annie E. Casey Foundation.

KIDS COUNT Data Center. (2007). *Children under age 6 in poverty: Percent: 2007.* Baltimore: Annie E. Casey Foundation.

Kilbane, C., & McNergney, R. (1999). Digital teaching portfolios build, display talent. *AACTE Briefs, 20*(13), 6.

Knowles, J. G., & Cole, A. L. (1996). Developing practice through field experiences. In F. B. Murray (Ed.), *The teacher educator's handbook* (pp. 648–688). San Francisco: Jossey-Bass.

Kohn, A. (1996). *Beyond discipline: From compliance to community.* Alexandria, VA: Association for Supervision and Curriculum Development.

Koplow, L. (2007). Why homeless children can't sit still. In L. Koplow (Ed.), *Unsmiling faces: How preschools can heal* (2nd ed., pp. 215–225). New York: Teachers College Press.

Kostelnik, M. J., Onaga, E., Rohde, B., & Whiren, A. (2002). *Children with special needs: Lessons for early childhood professionals.* New York: Teachers College Press.

Kostelnik, M. J., Soderman, A. K., & Whiren, A. P. (2007). *Developmentally appropriate curriculum* (4th ed.). Upper Saddle River, NJ: Merrill/Prentice Hall.

Kratcoski, A. M., & Katz, K. B. (1998). Conversing with young language learners in the classroom. *Young Children, 53*(3), 30–33.

Krathwohl, D. R., Bloom, B. S., & Masia, B. B. (1956). *Taxonomy of educational goals: Handbook II: Affective domain.* New York: David McKay.

Krogh, S. (1995). *The integrated early childhood curriculum* (2nd ed.). New York: McGraw-Hill.

Kyle, P. B., & Rogien, L. R. (2004). *Opportunities and options in classroom management.* Boston: Allyn & Bacon.

Lally, J. R., & Mangione, P. (2006). The uniqueness of infancy demands a responsive approach to care. *Young Children, 61*(4), 14–20.

Lerner, J. W., Lowenthal, B., & Egan, R. (1998). *Preschool children with special needs.* Boston: Allyn & Bacon.

Levin, D. E. (2003). When the world is a dangerous place. *Educational Leadership, 60*(7), 72–75.

Litman, M., Anderson, C., Andrican, L., Buria, B., Christy, C., Koski, B., et al. (1999). Curriculum comes from the child! A Head Start family child care program. *Young Children, 54*(3), 4–9.

Lyons, N. (1999). How portfolios can shape emerging practice. *Educational Leadership, 56*(8), 63–65.

Machado, J. M., & Botnarescue, H. M. (2001). *Student teaching early childhood practicum guide* (4th ed.). Albany, NY: Thomson Delmar Learning.

Madsen, C. H., & Madsen, C. R. (1974). *Teaching discipline: Behavior principles towards a positive approach.* Boston: Allyn & Bacon.

Male, M. (2003). *Technology for inclusion.* Boston: Allyn & Bacon.

Mandlawitz, M. (2007). *What every teacher should know about IDEA 2004 laws and regulations.* Boston: Allyn & Bacon.

Marion, M. (2003). *Guidance of young children* (6th ed.). Upper Saddle River, NJ: Merrill/Prentice Hall.

Marion, M. (2007). *Guidance of young children* (7th ed.). Upper Saddle River, NJ: Merrill/Prentice Hall.

Marshall, P. L. (2002). *Cultural diversity in our schools.* Belmont, CA: Wadsworth/Thomson Learning.

Martin, G., & Pear, J. (1999). *Behavior modification: What it is and how to do it* (6th ed.). Upper Saddle River, NJ: Merrill/Prentice Hall.

Martin, J. N., & Nakayama, T. K. (2000). *Intercultural communication in contexts* (2nd ed.). Mountain View, CA: Mayfield.

Martin, J. N., & Nakayama, T. K. (2005). *Experiencing intercultural communication: An introduction* (2nd ed.). Boston: McGraw-Hill.

Martin, L. A., Chiodo, J. J., & Chang, L. H. (2001). First year teachers: Looking back after three years. *Action in Teacher Education, 23*(1), 55–63.

Maxwell, K. L., & Clifford, R. M. (2004). School readiness assessment. *Young Children, 59*(1), 42–46.

Mayberry, R. I. (1994). The importance of childhood to language acquisition: Evidence from American Sign Language. In J. C. Goodman & H. C. Nusbaum (Eds.), *The development of speech perception: The transition from speech sounds to spoken words* (pp. 57–90). Cambridge, MA: MIT Press.

McAllister, P. (2003, April). *The praxis series: Meeting the "highly qualified teacher" challenge.* Testimony presented before the New Hampshire Senate Education Committee, Concord, NH. Available from Educational Testing Service. (2004). *Where we stand on teacher quality: An issue paper from ETS.* Retrieved January 19, 2009, from *http://www.ets.org/Media/News_and_Media/position*

McCarty, T. L., Lynch, R. H., Wallace, S., & Benally, A. (1991). Classroom inquiry and Navajo learning styles: A call for reassessment. *Anthropology and Education Quarterly, 22,* 42–59.

McClurg, L. G. (1998). Building an ethical community in the classroom: Community meeting. *Young Children, 53*(2), 30–38.

McEwan, E. K. (2001). *10 traits of highly effective teachers.* Thousand Oaks, CA: Corwin Press.

McIntyre, D. J., & Byrd, D. M. (1998). Supervision in teacher education. In G. R. Firth & E. F. Pajak (Eds.), *Handbook of research on school supervision* (pp. 409–427). New York: Macmillan.

McMullen, M. B. (1999). Achieving best practices in infant and toddler care and education. *Young Children, 54*(4), 69–76.

McMullen, M. B., & Dixon, S. (2006). Building on common ground: Unifying practice with infant/toddler specialists through a mindful, relationship-based approach. *Young Children, 61*(4), 46–52.

Miller, D. F. (2007). *Positive child guidance.* Clifton Park, NY: Thomson Delmar Learning.

Miller, P. C., & Endo, H. (2004). Understanding and meeting the needs of ESL students. *Phi Delta Kappan, 85*(10), 786–791.

Mindes, G. (2003). *Assessing young children* (2nd ed.). Upper Saddle River, NJ: Merrill/Prentice Hall.

Moll, L. C. (1986). Writing as communication: Creating strategic learning environments for students. *Theory into Practice, 25*(2), 102–108.

Montessori, M. (1967). *The absorbent mind* (C. A. Claremont, Trans.). New York: Holt, Rinehart, & Winston.

Morris, J. E., & Morris, G. W. (1980). Stress in student teaching. *Action in Teacher Education, 2*(4), 57–62.

Morrison, G. S. (2000). *Fundamentals of early childhood education* (2nd ed.). Upper Saddle River, NJ: Merrill/Prentice Hall.

Morrison, T. (1998). Home. In W. Lubiano (Ed.), *The house that race built* (pp. 3–12). New York: Vintage Books.

Mulligan, S. A. (2003). Assistive technology: Suggesting the participation of children with disabilities. *Young Children, 58*(6), 50–53.

Murphy, K. L., DePasquale, R., & McNamara, E. (2003). Meaningful connections: Using technology in primary classrooms. *Young Children, 58*(6), 12–18.

NAEYC (National Association for the Education of Young Children). (1998). *Helping children learn self-control: A guide to discipline.* Washington, DC: Author.

NAEYC. (2001a). *Financing the early childhood education system.* Policy brief. Washington, DC: Author.

NAEYC. (2001b). *NAEYC standards for early childhood professional preparation.* Washington, DC: Author.

NAEYC. (2005a). *The code of ethical conduct and statement of commitment.* Brochure. Washington, DC: Author.

NAEYC. (2005b). *NAEYC early childhood program standards and accreditation criteria.* Retrieved January 5, 2009, from *http://www.naeyc.org/accreditation/standard*

NAEYC. (2005c). *Screening and assessment of young English-language learners: Supplement to the NAEYC and NAECS/SDE joint position statement on early childhood curriculum, assessment, and program evaluation.* Retrieved January 5, 2009, from *http://www.naeyc.org/*

NAEYC & NAECS/SDE (National Association of Early Childhood Specialists in State Department of Education). (2002). *Early learning standards: Creating the conditions for success.* Retrieved January 10, 2009, from *http://naecs.crc.uiuc.edu/position/creating_conditions.htm*

NAEYC & NAECS/SDE. (2003). *Early childhood curriculum, assessment, and program evaluation.* Joint position statement. Washington, DC: Author.

NASDTEC (National Association of State Directors of Teacher Education and Certification). 2002. *The NASDTEC interstate contract, 2002–2005.* Mashpoe, MA: Author.

National Association for Famild Child Care. (2009). *NAFCC marketing toolkit.* Salt Lake City, UT: Author. Retrieved January 10, 2009, from *http://www.nafcc.org/documents/NAFCC_Marketing_Toolkit.pdf*

National Center on Family Homelessness (NCFH). (2008). *The characteristics and needs of families experiencing homelessness.* Retrieved January 16, 2009, from *http://www.familyhomelessness.org/resources.factsheets.php*

National Child Traumatic Stress Network, (2008). *Traumatic grief in military children: Information for families.* Los Angeles, CA, and Durham, NC: National Center for Child Traumatic Stress.

National Coalition for the Homeless. (2008). *Education of homeless children and youth* (NCH Fact Sheet #12). Washington, DC: Author. Retrieved January 5, 2009, from *http://www.nationalhomeless.org*

National Law Center on Homelessness & Poverty (2007). *Educating homeless children and youth: The guide to their rights.* Washington, DC: Author. Retrieved January 5, 2009, from *http://www.nlchp.org*

NCATE (National Council for Accreditation of Teacher Education). (2007). *NCATE unit standards.* Retrieved January 5, 2009, from *http://www.ncate.org/public/unitStandardsRubrics.asp?ch=4*

NCCIC (National Child Care Information Center). (2007). *Selected state early learning guidelines on the Web.* Retrieved January 5, 2009, from *http://www.nccic.org/pubs/goodstart/elgwebsites.html*

Nelson, J., Erwin, C., & Duffy, R. (1998a). *Positive discipline for preschoolers* (2nd ed.). Roseville, CA: Prima.

Nelson, J., Erwin, C., & Duffy, R. (1998b). *Positive discipline: The first three years.* Roseville, CA: Prima.

Newcomer, P. (2003). *Understanding and teaching emotionally disturbed children and adolescents.* Austin, TX: Pro-ed.

Nicholson, S., & Shipstead, S. G. (2002). *Through the looking glass: Observations in the early childhood classroom* (3rd ed.). Upper Saddle River, NJ: Merrill/ Prentice Hall.

O'Hair, D., Friedrich, G. W., Wiemann, J. M., & Wiemann, M. O. (1995). *Competent communication.* New York: St. Martin's Press.

Olsen, G., & Fuller, M. L. (1998). Home-school relations: *Working successfully with parents and families.* Boston: Allyn & Bacon.

Olsen, G., & Fuller, M. L. (2003). *Home-school relations: Working successfully with parents and families* (2nd ed.). Boston: Allyn & Bacon.

Olsen, G., & Fuller, M. L. (2008). *Home-school relations: Working successfully with parents and families* (3rd ed.). Boston: Allyn & Bacon.

Olson, L. (2002). Starting early. *Education Week, 21*(17), 10–14, 16–22.

Opong-Brown, P. (2008). Families prepare to help children cope during military deployments. *The Military Family Network.* Retrieved January 5, 2009, from *http://www.emilitary.org/article.phop?aid=13170*

Ornstein, A. C., & Lasley, T. J. (2000). *Strategies for effective teaching.* Boston: McGraw-Hill.

Ovando, C. J. (2001). Language diversity and education. In J. A. Banks & C. A. Banks (Eds.), *Multicultural education: Issues and perspectives* (4th ed., pp. 268–292). New York: Wiley.

Painter, B. (2001). Using teaching portfolios. *Educational Leadership, 58*(5), 31–34.

Palmer, J. A. (1995). Environmental thinking in the early years: Understanding and misunderstanding of concepts related to waste management. *Environmental Education Research, 1*(1), 35–45.

Parette, H., & Petch-Hogan, B. (2000). Approaching families: Facilitating culturally/linguistically diverse family involvement. *Teaching Exceptional Children, 33*(2), 4–10.

Pataray-Ching, J., & Roberson, M. (2002). Misconceptions about a curriculum-as-inquiry framework. *Language Arts, 79*(6), 498–505.

PDE/DPW (Pennsylvania Department of Education/ Department of Public Works). (2007). *Pre-kindergarten: Pennsylvania learning standards for early childhood.* Retrieved January 5, 2009, from *http:// www.pde.state.pa.us/early_childhood/lib/early_ childhood/Pre-K_Standards_2007.pdf*

PDE/OCDL (Pennsylvania Department of Education/ Office of Child Development and Early Learning). (2008). *Pennsylvania pre-K counts for a brighter future: Mid-year report 2007–2008.* Retrieved January 18, 2009, from *http://ww.pakeys.org/pre-k-counts. aspx#report*

Peace Learning Center. 1997. *Building peace for a healthy community.* Columbus, IN: Author. Retrieved January 5, 2009, from *http://www.peacelearningcenter.org*

Pelletier, C. M. (2004). *Strategies for successful student teaching* (2nd ed.). Boston: Allyn & Bacon.

Perkins-Gough, D. (2002). Teacher quality. *Educational Leadership, 60*(1), 85–86.

Petersen, E. A. (1996). *A practical guide to early childhood planning, methods, and materials.* Boston: Allyn & Bacon.

Piaget, J. (1963). *The psychology of intelligence.* Totowa, NJ: Littlefield Adams. (Original work published in French in 1947).

Piaget, J. (1971). *The construction of reality in the child.* New York: Ballantine.

Pickett, A. L. (1999). *Strengthening and supporting teacher/provider-paraprofessional teams: Guidelines for paraeducator roles, supervision, and preparation.* New York: City University of New York.

Piland, D. E., & Anglin, J. M. (1993). It is only a stage they are going through: The development of student teachers. *Action in Teacher Education, 15*(3), 19–26.

Porter, L. (1999). *Young children's behavior.* Philadelphia: MacLennan & Petty Pty Limited.

Pugach, M. C., & Johnson, L. J. (1995). *Collaborative practitioners, collaborative schools.* Denver, CO: Love.

Rauch, K., & Whittaker, C. R. (1999). Observation and feedback during student teaching: Learning from peers. *Action in Teacher Education, 21*(3), 67–78.

Raver, C. C., & Zigler, E. F. (2004). Another step back? Assessing readiness in Head Start. *Young Children, 59*(1), 58–63.

Richards, D. D., & Siegler, R. S. (1986). Children's understandings of the attributes of life. *Journal of Experimental Child Psychology, 42*, 1–22.

Richert, A. E. (1992). Voice and power in teaching and learning to teach. In L. Valli (Ed.), *Reflective teacher education: Cases and critiques* (pp. 198–211). Albany: SUNY Press.

Robinson, L. (2003). Technology as a scaffold for emergent literacy: Interactive storybooks for toddlers. *Young Children, 58*(6), 42–48.

Rodgers, D., & Dunn, M. (2000). Communication, collaboration, and complexity: Personal theory building in context. *Journal of Early Childhood Teachers Education, 21*(2), 273–280.

Roe, B. D., & Ross, E. P. (2002). *Student teaching and field experiences handbook* (5th ed.). Upper Saddle River, NJ: Merrill/Prentice Hall.

Rosenberg, M. S., O'Shea, L., & O'Shea, D. (1998). *Student teacher to master teacher.* Upper Saddle River, NJ: Merrill/Prentice Hall.

Rousseau, J. J. (1969). *Emile* (B. Foxley, Trans.). New York: Dutton. (Original work published in 1762).

Ryan, J., & Kuhs, T. (1993). Assessment of preservice teachers and the use of portfolios. *Theory Into Practice, 32,* 75–81.

Sadker, D., & Sadker, M. (1994). *Failing at fairness: How our schools cheat girls.* New York: Simon & Schuster.

Salend, S. J. (2005). *Creating inclusive classrooms: Effective and reflective practices for all students* (5th ed.). Upper Saddle River, NJ: Merrill/Prentice Hall.

Salvia, J., & Ysseldyke, J. (2004). *Assessment in special and inclusive education* (9th ed.). Boston: Houghton Mifflin.

Sandholtz, J., Ringstaff, C., & Dwyer, D. (1997). *Teaching with technology: Creating student-centered classrooms.* New York: Teachers College Press.

Santrock, J. W. (2003). *Children* (7th ed.). Columbus, OH: McGraw-Hill.

Scarborough, A. A., Spiker, D., Mallik, S., Hebbeler, K. M., Bailey, D. B., & Simeonsson, R. J. (2004). A national look at children and families entering early intervention. *Exceptional Children, 70*(4), 469–483.

Schiller, P., & Willis, C. A. (2008). Using brain-based teaching strategies to create supportive early childhood environments that address learning standards. *Young Children, 63*(4), 52–55.

Schirrmacher, R. (2002). Art and creative development for young children (4th ed.). Albany, NY: Delmar.

Schoenfeldt, M. K., & Salsbury, D. E. (2009). *Lesson planning: A research-based model for k-12 classrooms.* Upper Saddle River, NJ: Merrill/Prentice Hall.

Schon, D. A. (1983). *The reflective practitioner: How professionals think in action.* San Francisco: Jossey-Bass.

Schwebel, A. I., Schwebel, B. L., Schwebel, C. R., & Schwebel, M. (1996). *The student teacher's handbook* (3rd ed.). Mahwah, NJ: Erlbaum.

Seplocha, H. (2004). Conferencing with families. *Young Children, 59*(5), 96–99.

Serdyukov, P., & Ryan, M. (2008). *Writing effective lesson plans: The 5-star approach.* Boston: Allyn & Bacon.

Shepard, L., Kagan, S. L., & Wurtz, E. (Eds.). (1998). *Principles and recommendations for early childhood assessments.* Washington, DC: National Education Goals Panel. Retrieved January 18, 2009, from *http://govinfo.library.unt.edu/negp/reports/prinrec.pdf*

Shore, R. (1997). *Rethinking the brain: New insights into early development.* New York: Families and Work Institute.

Shulman, L. (1998). Teacher portfolios. In N. Lyons (Ed.), *With portfolio in hand: Validating the new teacher professionalism.* New York: Teachers College Press.

Slavin, R. E. (2000). *Educational psychology* (6th ed.). Boston: Allyn & Bacon.

Slavin, R. E. (2003). *Educational psychology* (7th ed.). Boston: Allyn & Bacon.

Smith, D. J., & Sanche, R. P. (1993). Interns' personally expressed concerns: A need to extend the Fuller model. *Action in Teacher Education, 15*(3), 36–41.

Smith, P. L., Harris, C. M., Sammons, L., Waters, J., Jordan, D., Martin, D., et al. (2001). Using multimedia portfolios to assess preservice teacher and P-12 student learning. *Action in Teacher Education, 22*(4), 28–36.

Soundy, C. S., & Stout, N. L. (2002). Fostering the emotional and language needs of young learners. *Young Children, 57*(2), 21–24.

Spencer, L. (2004). *Creating an electronic portfolio.* Retrieved January 18, 2009, from *http://cte.jhu/.edu/techacademy/fellows/Spencer/webquest/lasindex.html*

Spina Bifida Association. 2007. *Latex in the home and community.* Retrieved January 18, 2009, from *http://www.spinabifidaassociation.org/site/c.liKWL7PLLrF/b.2700271/k.1779/Latex_Natural_Rubber_Allergy_in_Spina_Bifida.htm*

Stodolsky, S. (1985). Teacher evaluation: The limits of looking. *Educational Research, 13*(9), 11–18.

Styles, D. (2001). *Class meetings: Building leadership, problem-solving and decision-making skills in the respectful classroom.* Markham, ON: Pembroke.

Sudzina, M., Giebelhaus, C., & Coolican, M. (1997, Winter). Mentor or tormentor: The role of the cooperating teacher in student teacher success or failure. *Action in Teacher Education, 18*(4), 23–35.

Sullo, R. A. (2007). *Activating the desire to learn.* Alexandria, VA: Association for Supervision and Curriculum Development.

Thomas, C. C., Correa, V. I., & Morsink, C. V. (2001). *Interactive teaming* (3rd ed.). Upper Saddle River, NJ: Merrill/Prentice Hall.

Toro, J. A., & Newell, E. A. (2001, August). *Professional portfolios*. Paper presented at the annual meeting of the Association of Teacher Educators, Portland, OR.

TransAct Communications, Inc. (2003). *Why TransAct?* Retrieved January 18, 2009, from *http://www.transact.com/*

Trawick-Smith, J. (2003). *Early childhood development: A multicultural perspective* (3rd ed.). Upper Saddle River, NJ: Merrill/Prentice Hall.

Turner, S. B. (2000). Caretaking of children's souls. Teaching the deep song. *Young Children, 55*(1), 31–33.

U.S. Department of Labor Bureau of Labor Statistics. 2007. *Occupational employment and wages*. Retrieved January 5, 2009, from *http://bls.gov/oes/current/oes252011.htm*

U.S. Federal Register, January 23, 2008. Volume 23, #15. 2008. *Health and Human Services poverty guidelines*. Retrieved January 5, 2009, from *http://www.aspe.hhs.gov/poverty/08poverty.shtml*

Valdez, A. (1999). *Learning in living color.* Boston: Allyn & Bacon.

Valli, L. (1992). Beginning teacher problems: Areas for teacher education improvement. *Action in Teacher Education, 14*(1), 18–25.

Vaughn, S., & Bos, C. S. (2009). *Strategies for teaching students with learning and behavior problems* (7th ed.). Upper Saddle River, NJ: Pearson.

Venn, J. J. (2004). *Assessing students with special needs* (3rd ed.). Upper Saddle River, NJ: Merrill/Prentice Hall.

Vygotsky, L. S. (1978). *Mind in society: The development of higher psychological processes.* Cambridge, MA: Harvard University Press.

Warner, L., & Sower, J. C (2005). *Educating young children from preschool through primary grades.* Boston: Allyn & Bacon.

Watson, L., & Swim, T. (2008). *Infants and toddlers, curriculum and teaching* (6th ed.). Clifton Park, NY: Thomson Delmar Learning.

Weaver, R. H. (2002). The roots of quality care. *Young Children, 57*(1), 16–22.

Weinstein, C. S., Woolfolk, A. E., Dittmeier, L., & Shanker, U. (1994). Protector or prison guard? Using metaphors and media to explore student teachers' thinking about classroom management. *Action in Teacher Education, 16*(1), 41–54.

West, J. F., & Cannon, G, S. (1988). Essential collaborative consultation competencies for regular and special educators. *Journal of Learning Disabilities, 21*(1), 56–63, 28.

Westling, D. L., & Fox, L. (2000). *Teaching students with severe disabilities* (2nd ed.). Upper Saddle River, NJ: Prentice Hall.

Wheeler, P. H. (1996). Using portfolios to assess teacher performance. In K. Burke (Ed.), *Professional portfolios: A collection of articles* (pp. 75–94). Arlington Heights, IL: IRI/Skylight Training and Publishing.

Whitebook, M., Sakai, L., Gerber, E., & Howes, C. (2001). *Then and now: Changes in childcare staffing, 1994–2000.* Washington, DC: Center for the Childcare Workforce.

Whitehead, A. N. (1929). *The aims of education.* New York: Mentor.

Whitehead, L. C., & Ginsberg, S. I. (1999). Creating a family-like atmosphere in childcare settings: All the more difficult in large childcare centers. *Young Children, 54*(2), 4–10.

Williams, F. (1989). *The new communications.* Belmont, CA: Wadsworth.

Wilson, R. A. (2000). Developmentally appropriate interpretation with preschool children. In M. A. Jensen & M. A. Hannibal (Eds.), *Issues, advocacy, and leadership in early education* (2nd ed., pp. 166–169). Boston: Allyn & Bacon.

Wink, J., & Puney, L. G. (2002). *A vision of Vygotsky.* Boston: Allyn & Bacon.

Wolf, K. (1996). Developing an effective teaching portfolio. *Educational Leadership, 53*(6), 34–37.

Wolf, K., Whinery, B., & Hagerty, P. (1995). Teaching portfolios and portfolio conversations for teacher educators and teachers. *Action in Teacher Education, 17*(1), 30–39.

Wolfe, P., & Brandt, R. (1998). What do we know from brain research? *Educational Leadership, 56*(3), 8–13.

Wong, Fillmiere, L. (1992). When learning a second language means losing the first. *Early Childhood Research Quarterly, 6*(3), 323–346.

Woolley, J. D. (1997). Thinking about fantasy: Are children fundamentally different thinkers and believers from adults? *Child Development, 68,* 991–1011.

Workman, S., & Anziano, M. (1993). Curriculum webs: Weaving connections from children to teachers. *Young Children, 48*(2), 4–9.

Worsley, M., Beneke, S., & Helm, J. H. (2003). The pizza project: Planning and integrating math standards in project work. *Young Children, 58*(1), 44–50.

Wortham, S. C. (2002). *Early childhood curriculum* (3rd ed.). Upper Saddle River, NJ: Merrill/Prentice Hall.

Wright, K., & Stegelin, D. A. (2003). *Building school and community partnerships through parent involvement* (2nd ed.). Upper Saddle River, NJ: Merrill/Prentice Hall.

Yoo, S. (2001). Using portfolios to reflect on practice. *Educational Leadership, 58*(8), 78–81.

Zachary, L. J. (2000). *The mentor's guide.* San Francisco: Jossey-Bass.

Zeichner, K. M., & Liston, D. P. (1996). *Reflective teaching: An introduction.* Mahwah, NJ: Erlbaum.

Zubizarreta, J. (1994). Teaching portfolios and the beginning teacher. *Phi Delta Kappan, 76,* 323–326.